REWRITING REVOLUTION

REWRITING REVOLUTION

Women, Sexuality, and Memory in North Korean Fiction

Immanuel Kim

University of Hawai'i Press
Honolulu

Paperback edition 2022

Printed in the United States of America

Library of Congress Cataloging-in-Publication Data
Names: Kim, Immanuel, author.
Title: Rewriting revolution : women, sexuality, and memory in North Korean fiction / Immanuel Kim.
Description: Honolulu: University of Hawaiʻi Press, [2018] | Includes bibliographical references and index.
Identifiers: LCCN 2017022265 | ISBN 9780824872632 (cloth alk. paper)
Subjects: LCSH: Korean fiction—Korea (North)—20th century—History and criticism. | Women in literature. | Families in literature.
Classification: LCC PL957.5.W65 K55 2018 | DDC 895.7/099287—dc23
LC record available at https://lccn.loc.gov/2017022265

ISBN: 9780824892418 (paperback)

University of Hawaiʻi Press books are printed on acid-free paper and meet the guidelines for permanence and durability of the Council on Library Resources.

Cover: Two lovers walking along the streets in Pyongyang, 2011 (Photo courtesy of Korea Economic Institute of America; art by Hans Gindlesberger and Soyeon Jung.)

Contents

Acknowledgments

I still remember the day I met Professor Kim Chae-yong at Caffé Pascucci inside Seoul Station. I was ecstatic to begin my research on North Korean literature under his supervision. The long and arduous process of reading countless works of North Korean fiction began the very next day at the Information Center on North Korea on the fifth floor of the National Library in Seoul. After several months, Professor Kim and I met again at Caffé Pascucci. But this time, I was distraught at the seemingly hopeless journey that I had set myself on. Professor Kim offered me the greatest encouragement: "You have to be patient with North Korean literature." This succinct yet profound advice provided me the strength to endure past the ostensible political propaganda and read the humanity in the texts. I want to express my gratitude to Professor Kim for opening the world of North Korean literature to me and helping me understand that dynamic literary culture.

I owe special thanks to Kelly Jeong and Annmaria Shimabuku, who have given me excellent feedback and constructive criticism during the various stages of writing my chapters. John Kim, Namhee Lee, Dennis Lee, and other friends at UCLA supported me through the initial stages of my research. Ming Ming Liu took the time to help me shape my analyses of North Korean literature. I also want to thank Perry Link for offering invaluable advice on how to approach communist literature and for comparing Chinese literature with North Korean fiction. But none can compare to the generosity of Henk Maier, who read my chapters meticulously and pushed me to complete my manuscript.

My research would not have been possible without the funding I received from the Academy of Korean Studies Grant and the Korea Foundation Fellowship. Beyond financial support, these two grants provided me with the opportunity to meet new people and forge lifelong relationships. I want to thank the two librarians at the Information Center on North Korea, Mrs. Chŏng Hŭi-suk and Ms. Sin Ŭn-jŏng, for treating me kindly during the period of over a year that I spent in Korea and for helping me to find necessary information every day during that time. I also deeply value the friendships of Koen de Ceuster, Andrei

Lankov, Tatiana Gabbroussenko, Suzy Kim, Dima Mironenko, Janice Kim, Sarah Eunkyung Chee, Brother Anthony, North Korean defector Choi Jin-hee, Philo Kim of the Institute for Peace and Unification Studies at Seoul National University, and Min-Kyung Yoon. The discussions we shared had a great impact on the way I perceive North Korea and Korean Studies today. I want to thank the faculty at Yonsei University, Seoul National University, and Sogang University for giving me an opportunity to speak at their colloquia. I cannot thank Jacco Zwetsloot enough for the lasting friendship we have maintained since the day we first met at a talk I gave at Yonsei University.

The field of North Korean Studies is small, but it is made up of a powerful group of scholars. Some of us call ourselves the Canberra Group, which consists of Charles Armstrong, Ruth Barraclough, Dafna Zur, Cheehyung Harrison Kim, Dima Mironenko, Ted Hughes, and myself. I am grateful to the members of this group for their assistance with my book and other projects. In addition to this group, I extend my gratitude to Marsha Haufler, George Kallander, Stephen Epstein, Rüdiger Frank, and Heonik Kwon, scholars who work on North Korea and have helped me over the years.

My colleagues at Binghamton University have been one of my strongest support groups, and I feel privileged to be a part of the Department of Asian and Asian American Studies there. John Cheng has edited my chapters at various stages of writing the book. Robert Ku has been a great source of encouragement, along with Yoonkyung Lee, Sonja Kim, Sundai Cho, and Michael Pettid.

I want to thank Jun Yoo for invaluable advice on publishing my book and for introducing me to the University of Hawaiʻi Press. The decision to publish with this press was perhaps one of the best moves I have made in my professional career thus far. I thank the two anonymous readers who recommended the publication of this book and provided critical suggestions for improving the quality of the content. This could not have been done without the full support of my editor, Pamela Kelley. She has guided me through this process in the most efficient and effective manner, transforming what began as a mere possibility of publication into a reality. Her belief in my manuscript lifted my spirits at a time when I was undergoing some difficulty, and I am truly grateful for her kindness.

I will never forget the emotional and spiritual support I have received from my parents, Chul Young Kim and Sonya Kim; my brother Sam; my wife's parents, Hwang Hong Shik and Bae Jong Soon; my sisters-in-law, Hwang Yoo-kyung and Hwang Eun-kyung; my brother-in-law Kim Nam-suk; and my nieces and nephews, Myung-kil, Bum-jun, Min-kyung, and Min-jun. Above all, I want to thank my best friend and awesome wife, Angela Kim, and my son, Nathan, who have seen the best and worst sides of me during the process of writing my manuscript. Angela was with me before this project took shape, and, for the past fourteen years of our marriage, she has been my greatest comrade, who always comforted me with a spirit of positivity. It would be an understatement and a cliché to say that I could not have done this without her, but it is true. I love the two of you more than anything else.

Finally, I am forever indebted to the North Korean author Paek Nam-nyong, who committed his time and energy to helping me understand his world and his practice when I visited Pyongyang in 2015. Paek's novel *Friend* is the driving force behind this book, and so, when I met him in Pyongyang, I was star-struck. The three days I spent with him were a most insightful and eye-opening experience. If it were not for his novel, I probably would not be the scholar I am today, and I would have been unable to revise my initial perceptions of North Korean literature. I humbly dedicate this book to Paek Nam-nyong, wishing him health and happiness for many years to come.

Korean terms have been transliterated according to the McCune-Reischauer system of romanization, except for names and words that have become common usage such as Pyongyang, Kim Il Sung, and Juche. I have kept the last names of both North and South Korean authors first, as is customary in Korea unless they have their own romanized names. All translations are mine unless otherwise indicated.

This work was supported by Core University Program for Korean Studies through the Ministry of Education of Republic of Korea and Korean Studies Promotion Service of the Academy of Korean Studies (AKS-2011-BAA-2013).

Introduction

Changing North Korean Literature

"Change" is a term little associated with the Democratic People's Republic of Korea (DPRK), which is often referred to in Western media as a land where time stands still. Recent social changes in North Korea—exemplified by the possession of cell phones—have not significantly altered Western views of the "rogue" nation that is perceived to be depriving its citizens of their basic human rights, expanding its nuclear weapons program at the expense of its faltering economy, and generally refusing to abide by international political norms. One of the few vestiges of the Cold War that exist today, its demilitarization zone (DMZ) still intact and frighteningly real, North Korea is viewed as belligerent and oppressive, and impervious to the changes happening around the world. One of my primary purposes in writing this book is to challenge the existing discourse on the country and help promote a mutual exchange of cultures and ideas that have been so long separated by the ideological trenches of the Cold War.

Foreign diplomacy during the George W. Bush era limited the possibilities of open dialogue with North Korea, now enshrined as a member of Bush's "axis of evil." Any activity by the North, even a basically innocuous annual military parade, was seen as both bewildering spectacle and potential threat to the international community. The North Korean people were also subjected to skepticism and ridicule. Images of North Koreans mourning for the loss of Kim Jong Il in 2011 were interpreted in the Western media as staged performances, reinforcing the West's preconceptions of the citizens' lack of agency and real emotions. In short, the West has constructed such an adverse and reductive discourse about North Korea's political system, its people, and its cultural products that anyone and anything from North Korea is viewed as state propaganda.

In 2006, Words Without Borders published a collection of stories from countries branded as the "axis of evil," a number of which were from North Korea.[1] The editor of this collection notes:

> This book was born in conscientious objection to the use of "axis of evil" rhetoric and to the OFAC's [Office of Foreign Assets Control] apparent

> fear of "free trade" in ideas and literature. . . . Rather, we aim simply to stimulate international conversation through literature, with all its complexity and nuanced insights into the ideas, beliefs, daily lives and articles of reference of people in other cultures, who are thinking and writing in languages other than English.
>
> In the case of North Korea, our initial expectation of finding "samizdat"[2] literature turned out to be naïve; all that we could find was in fact propaganda literature. In North Korea, it seems there are not only things that must not be said, but every work must in the end praise the Great Leader or it never sees the light of day.[3]

Despite intentions of exposing North Korean literature to an international readership in order to demystify the negative reputation of the nation, the editor uses binary metaphors to describe the lives of writers and the literature of North Korea: light/dark, public/private, propaganda literature/dissident literature, as if binaries are implicit in writing, reading, and understanding North Korean literature. In fact, the expectation of finding *samizdat* literature in North Korea already frames the binary perception, which then leads to the irresponsible and groundless conclusion that "every work must in the end praise the Great Leader or it never sees the light of day."

But perhaps no claim by a foreigner has been more reckless than that of Adam Johnson, who won the Pulitzer Prize for Fiction in 2013 for his novel *The Orphan Master's Son,* which was intent on revealing the harrowing nature of North Korean life. After his visit to North Korea in 2007, he concluded: "This truly totalitarian narrative is difficult for us to conceive in America. But remember that North Korea is a nation without literary art. If we define art to mean revealing of the truth and speaking to the human condition, there has been no art whatsoever since the nation's founding. . . . Imagine a world in which no writer has written a literary novel in sixty years. Imagine a place where not a single person has read a book that is truly about the character at its center."[4]

A single visit to North Korea does not make one an expert in seventy-some-odd years of history and particularly in the literature and arts of that country. Perhaps most excessive is the casual imperialistic and condescending tone that Johnson voices as if he were touring a society full of staged puppets. For Johnson to say that North Korea is a nation without literary art is not only derogatory but is evidence of Eurocentric views on literature and lack of understanding of the significant changes that have occurred in the nation's literary culture since its establishment. Johnson's article perpetuates the demonization of North Korea for his American readers, a self-serving and security-oriented discourse that is circulated without critical assessment.

Unfortunately, this conception is symptomatic not only of those who know very little about North Korean literary culture but also of scholars in the field of East Asian and Korean Studies. In *Communism in Korea,* Robert A. Scalapino and Chong-Sik Lee assert that the "cultural life of North Korea (outside of the realms of science, technology and purely folk art) is a great desert of unalleviated mediocrity and monotony."[5] In his "Engineers of the Human Soul," Marshall Pihl claims that North Korean writers "diminished the excitement of literature for the popular reader and contributed to the precipitous decrease in public demand for literature immediately after liberation."[6] And Tatiana Gabroussenko contends in her book *Soldiers on the Cultural Front* that North Korean literature exhibits exceptional uniformity, unchallenged by any diversity.[7] South Korean scholar Kim Chong-hoe, in his essay "Ek'o'ui munhak" (Echo Literature), says, "At the moment, North Korean literature obsessively repeats the Party's guidelines, which I call 'echo literature,' rather than containing a creative voice."[8] According to Kim, North Korean literature that strays from the Party line has yet to be seen, and North Korea has not yet produced any literary works worth reading or analyzing.

Kim Chong-hoe fails to perceive two ironies in his reductive reading of North Korean literature as "echo literature." First, his criticism that North Korean literature merely echoes the Party's instructions mirrors his own "echoing" of South Korea's National Security Laws in his case against North Korean literature. Second, he does not fully realize the implications of his own metaphor. That is, the virtue of an echo is that it is not the same and will never be the same as that which produced it. To continue with Kim's metaphor, an echo always detaches itself from its producer, disseminating into unaccountable spaces and in unpredictable directions. Kim Chong-hoe's criticism of North Korean literature, in fact, supports the inexhaustible readings and interpretations that the notion of literature conditions.

Without having read a single piece of literary work published in North Korea, bowing to authoritative voices of scholars such as Kim who have rejected North Korean literature for overt politicization and banality, the general public approaches the literary culture with a systematic and ideological bias. In other words, scholars outside of the DPRK who fault the country's literary culture for generating a singular political meaning, deeming it unworthy to be read and studied, are themselves propagating a singular understanding of North Korean literature as a propaganda machine that endlessly reproduces a monochromatic product wholly lacking in creativity and imagination. While these scholars wait for *samizdat* literature to emerge from the thickets of ideological fiction (as if *samizdat* literature would bring truth to the North Korean literary system), they underestimate and overlook the dynamic interplay between the individual and the state that challenges, questions, and disrupts the monolithic meaning of the texts.

I do not deny the North Korean state's attempt at a teleological narrative with a dominant meaning, for this is my point of departure. North Korea acknowledges its project of threading a narrative with a single core meaning. Kim Jong Il calls this central theme the "seed" (*chongja*), which he describes in his treatise *On the Art of the Cinema* published in 1974. According to Kim Jong Il, the "seed" is the "guiding criterion which provides the principles for the organization of content and the unification of all formal elements of the work in conformity with the content."[9] For Kim, the seed theory does not only pertain to filmic content but also to literary content and other artworks. According to Alzo David-West, the value of this "seed" is found in its political didacticism, which "teaches people that the workers and everyone else must continuously revolutionize themselves at all times."[10] Following the seed theory, then, North Korean literature prescribes the way individuals in the narrative ought to speak, think, and behave according to state directives, which reinforce and privilege the singular discourse of the state.

The Fifteenth Plenary Meeting of the Fourth Central Party Committee of the Workers' Party on April 15, 1967, provided a demonstrable act of singularizing meaning in North Korean cultural products and political discourse. At the meeting, three ideological pillars were established as the core principles of the DPRK: first, the Juche ideology became the official state philosophy; second, the anti-Japanese revolutionary struggle was inscribed as the origin of the nation's history; and, third, the "monolithic system" (*yu'il ch'egye*) was to consider Kim Il Sung as the one and only leader of the DPRK. This historic meeting changed the social and cultural structure of writing literature, in that the narrative form and content were supposed to conform in praising the leader, the Party, the collective, and the state. Incorporating Kim Il Sung's philosophy, or Kimilsungism, into the narrative as the core value of meaning and worth in the lives of individuals became the normative and hegemonic writing practice from the early 1970s to present day.

One of the primary purposes behind rewriting the history of Kim Il Sung and his family (particularly his mother) was to legitimize and authenticate his leadership amid rival political factions that had existed since the formative years of the nation from 1945. From Kim Il Sung's point of view, the destruction of all factions except his own group of veteran guerrillas was a necessary precondition for gaining unlimited personal power.[11] The key posts in the Party were occupied by Kim's close battle comrades, all of them Manchurian veterans.[12] In order for Kim Il Sung to solidify his political power, he needed his loyal guerrillas' undying political, military, and moral support.

Kim Il Sung did not tolerate other political factions in the Party. He took any opportunity he could to eliminate antagonistic members. Purges of political leaders, cadres, intelligentsia, and academicians took place during the late 1950s and into the early 1960s in order to secure Kim's tenuous political power. At the Fifteenth Plenary Meeting in 1967, Kim Il Sung cemented permanent power within the Party. He implemented his Juche ideology and monolithic system as the official principles of the DPRK and declared his anti-Japanese guerrilla faction as the founder of the DPRK. Although Kim Il Sung had emphasized his anti-Japanese struggle in Party forums during the formative years of the nation, it was not until 1967 that such revolutionary history became the only legitimate history and the official state discourse in every DPRK media form throughout the entire country.[13] What had once been known only to a number of writers and guerrilla members now became a mandatory national discourse less concerned with revolutionizing the country with the dogmatic tenets of Marxism-Leninism and more concerned with institutionalizing Kim Il Sung's anti-Japanese struggle as the starting point of all political, economic, social, cultural, and historical measures in the DPRK.

Kim Jong Il's proclamation of the seed theory and Kimilsungism followed by the monolithic policy in the early 1970s could not have been a more contentious turning point in North Korean literary history. Unity and loyalty to the Great Leader were to be the basis of the writer's behavior and attitude as a whole. The monolithic policy heralded a different idealism of the modern state for North Korea, one that essentially called on its writers to overlook the tenets of socialist realism and articulate a monolithic political order. Hope for a perfected socialist world was not completely eradicated from political and literary discourses but justified by the superimposition of Kimilsungism.

Since the pivotal Fifteenth Plenary Meeting in 1967, a new language, a unitary language, was to be used in every aspect of the North Korean culture: fiction, songs, poetry, newspapers, journals, television and radio programs, artworks, and so on. This new language supposedly eliminated voices that posed threats to or undermined the wholesome and unified society of the DPRK. As much as purging opposing factions was necessary for Kim Il Sung to centralize his partisan group, the need to centralize and normalize a monolithic discourse was equally, if not more, important for controlling and disciplining the masses during this transition period. Thus, "during the early 1970s, North Koreans were made to memorize the works of Kim Il Sung (including public speeches, committee reports, and so on) by heart, word-for-word. . . . All public self-criticism sessions . . . were required to be opened with correct and exact quotations from Kim Il Sung's published works."[14]

The state's insistence on a singular method of reading and understanding its own literature was an attempt at enforcing and normalizing the regime of the "Same," a term I have appropriated from Western philosophical discourse for the singular political discourse of Kimilsungism that privileges the male-dominated social order and represses sexual difference in women. After the implementation of the monolithic system, North Korean literature had to project a teleological vision that integrated disparate individuals into the language of the Same. As a result, men are to be read as the inheritors of the nation and women as the supporters of the men; the patriarchal order continues to dominate political and cultural norms; and sexual difference is never fully addressed, but instead gendered identities are cemented in social practices. Every North Korean text is supposed to construct the unwavering identity of Kimilsungist revolutionaries and to ensure the seamless and indestructible totality of prescribed meaning for readers to interpret with absolute certainty.

In this book, my major concern is to expose the limits of political discourse that is designed solely to transform individuals in fiction to become Kimilsungist revolutionaries. I will argue that literary expression, in its varied attempts to link the imaginary to the real, is so capacious that it consumes even the ideological rigors dictated by the political state and inherently contains the warring forces of signification within the text itself.[15] My deconstructive reading of North Korean literature does not devalue or consider the Party-prescribed reading practices as meaningless in their cultural context, but rather is intended to resist the unequivocal domination of the singular mode of signifying over the possibilities of multiple readings.

Logocentrism and phallocentrism are the discourses of the Same in North Korean literature that provide the "seed" that has dominated the entire enterprise of the literary culture. For poststructuralist thinkers like Derrida, the regime of the Same has governed Western metaphysics by differentiating binary opposites as that which provide meaning to society, politics, and culture. For example, concepts such as man and woman are not simply natural terms, but they also have implications through other metaphors deeply rooted in political, ideological, and social thought such as man as the public sphere (reason, truth, and rational) and woman as the private domain (emotional, subconscious, and irrational). Deconstruction exposes the ways in which a binary of two distinct concepts is actually a single privileged term and its dependent, accidental, and derivative other.[16] The problem with binary opposites, for Derrida, is when the privileged concept dominates the other, thereby creating hierarchical relationships in politics, cultural practices, and social institutions.

Derrida's deconstructive method is not an attempt to overturn the hierarchicized binaries; rather, by recognizing that binary oppositions were culturally constructed within a structure of logocentric thought, it explains the reasons for their existence. For Derrida, the starting point that explains the identity or structure of the Same is no longer perceived as a stable entity that validates the uncontestable origin of meaning, the rationality of thought, and the absolute self-identity of truth. Rather, such a structure had to originate from differences—from what it is not. This means that logocentrism was always destabilized by its own limits and fault lines, and that it never had a stable ground on which to determine its identity. In "Structure, Sign, and Play," Derrida refers to these fault lines as the concept of play: "The concept of centered structure is in fact the concept of a play based on fundamental ground."[17] For Derrida, meaning is always already deferred or decentered within an endless chain of differences and signifiers. Derrida uses language as evidence that the origin of a word can never be determined and the intended meaning will never be resolutely decidable. This is because the *undecidability* of language preceded and therefore made possible the production of any of the determinate meanings that then had to be "decided" in order for meaning to unfold in any particular reading.[18]

Thus, from my perspective, the act of writing fiction in the North Korean context conditions the possibility of exposing ambiguities in the texts that debilitate the intended meaning of the state's hegemonic reading practices. North Korean literature did not begin uniformly out of Kimilsungism but was from its origin teeming with incongruities and heterogeneity. Irony, instability of political meaning, undecidability of concepts, and play have always been at work within the supposedly impervious political discourse in North Korean literature. Although North Korean literary works are products of a tightly controlled political environment, it is reductive to assume that every work of fiction is simply and only the materialization of direct state orders. This book will demonstrate that the relationship between Party expectations, the Writers' Union, writers themselves, literary critics, editors, censors, publishers, and readers formulates an intricate nexus of multiple intersections that carefully navigate within, through, and around the parameters of a monolithic political order. In particular, the state-prescribed teleological grand narrative that has attempted to totalize and stabilize the aesthetics of a revolutionary character through his or her political commitments to the leader, the Party, the nation, and the collective faced new literary frontiers in the portrayal of women, the nuclear family, and the state in literary works of the 1980s.

Portrayal of the family or the domestic space inevitably leads to the "woman question" that challenges the patriarchal state, posing difference within the regime of the Same. Each family member in North Korean literature has a higher calling for public and national service, but each must also negotiate his or her relationship to immediate family and the family-state. Though, in the end of these family-oriented narratives, family members all acquiesce in their loyalty to the state, the process through which this conclusion comes about and the development of characters provide a more dynamic and real insight into the complexity of human lives. Or, to put it in another way, the domestic space (and more particularly the role of women) has the potential to reeducate, rethink, and react to the prevailing discourse of how a member of society must behave. The "woman question" I pose in this book is not an attempt to find social equality for women in the DPRK but to disrupt the patriarchal social order by showing that the self-identity of the state was always haunted by the undecidability of the presence of women. That is, in order for the state to become a male-dominated society, it had to dispel and exorcise women, who stood as the other to men.

The family unit is not the antithesis of the state but is rather the immanent component that always puts the state into question by challenging the prescribed patriarchal political structure and by posing competing idealities of a different kind of family. This book highlights a noticeable shift in North Korean fiction that has provided women with agency and given them voices that empower them to question, resist, and potentially reconstruct the epistemological constraints of state-prescribed gendered norms. These women in fiction project and envision the variegated and, at times, conflicting dimensions of the society to which they are subordinated. Women in fiction are not simply passive characters that are thrown into their fictitious society with the assurance of discovering the path to ideological enlightenment within the prescriptions of a patriarchal state, but rather they define and redefine the male-dominated social realities around them. A number of North Korean fictional works of the 1980s opened up possibilities for generating new forms of narrative content that resisted defining women according to social norms. Such nuanced and problematic portrayals of the contention between women, the family, and the patriarchal state have contributed to what I consider to be the golden age of North Korean fiction.

The 1980s was not a decade of prolific publication of fiction in the DPRK. If golden age refers to sheer quantity, then the 1970s would be considered the most productive, as the Party and the Writers' Union pushed authors to publish works at an expedited pace in accordance with national campaigns. Instead, the 1980s was a period of new promises and hope in the literary world for both writers and readers in the DPRK, which for nearly two decades had been producing flat, infallible, and thus impersonal heroes and heroines. South Korean literary scholar Kim Chae-yong categorizes the literary works produced in the 1980s into three types: first, works dealing with the growing problem of the younger generation's desire to move to the city as opposed to remaining in the countryside; second, those addressing the older generation's transformation into recalcitrant and authoritative managers, unwilling to change with the times; and, third, fresh discussions about the woman question and the social, cultural, and political injustices women experienced despite the Party's abolishing of gender inequality.[19] Kim Chae-yong shows that the shifting momentum in fiction is representative of the social problems in the 1980s.

Unique to North Korean fiction of the 1980s is the projection of changing family values, sexual inequalities, and gender norms. For the first time in the history of North Korean literature, women's sexual desire, marital disillusionment and sexual discontentment between husband and wife, and divorce were explored. Also in the 1980s, past discussions on women's identity as laboring subjects in the public and private domain and issues with nurturing children resurfaced. Although women in North Korean society did not openly engage or were not given a platform to debate these issues in a public forum, as in the Soviet Union or in East Central Europe, raising concerns in the North Korean literary context was a way to address North Korean women's economic dependency on men and to envision different family values.

Serious efforts to revisit feminist and family issues in North Korean literature did not happen coincidentally in the 1980s but rather were a culmination of political, social, economic, historical, and legal issues that had been oppressing North Korean women in the patriarchal state since the Korean War. Overtly masculine state policies and national campaigns had attempted to deflect feminist voices in the DPRK since the nation's formative years by granting women equal access to the political domain. Although it had appeared as though the state had succeeded, there was never any restructuring of the male-dominated social order to recognize women's sexual difference. North Korean literature of the 1980s presents the agency of women, which had been subsumed in the political framework of traditional gendered identities. Writers of this period reframed women not only as supporting members of the state agenda but also as individuals, who can project alternative visions to improve social conditions.

The literary works of fiction that I analyze in this book highlight the new perspective on addressing tensions between women, the nuclear family, and the state. Paek Nam-nyong's *Pŏt* (Friend, 1988), Ri Hwa's *Sogŭm kkot* (Salt Deposits,

1984), Ch'oe Sang-sun's *Saebyŏk pyŏl* (Morning Star, 1987), Kim Mun-ch'ang's *T'anbu* (Miners, 1986), Kim Kyo-sŏp's *Saenghwalui ŏndŏk* (Heights of Life, 1984), and Ri Hŭi-nam's *Yŏdŏl sigan* (Eight Hours, 1986) are some of the exemplary novels that developed the qualities of modern female subjectivity and projected the changing family values of the 1980s. Of the novels listed here, I find Paek Nam-nyong's *Friend* to epitomize the transformation of North Korea's literary culture—in theme, writing practices, and reception.

The form and content of Paek's novel deviate from the usual narratives in North Korean fiction, but, more important, the novel delineates unabashedly the agency of women against the strictures of the patriarchal social system. South Korean specialists on North Korean literature such as Kim Chae-yong, O Ch'ang-un, and Ko In-hwan have hailed Paek Nam-nyong's *Friend* as representative of an optimistic outlook for literature in North Korea.[20] South Korean writer Hwang Sŏk-yŏng, who visited North Korea in 1989, mentions Paek's *Friend* as an eye-opening novel that challenged the way South Koreans had been educated to perceive the North.[21] Paek's novel has not only made an impact in South Korea, but it has also caught the eye of Korean literature scholar Patrick Maurus, who translated the novel into French and published it through Actes Sud Press in 2011.

Despite media representations of the DPRK as a hermit country, Paek Nam-nyong's *Friend* and other North Korean literature have had a transnational impact in the field of Korean Studies. The late 1980s and early 1990s were a dynamic period for democratization in South Korea and consequently for North Korean literature to gain visibility among scholars, students, and the public. The end of the South Korean dictatorship and the success of the student and the wider public democratization, or *minjung*, movement changed the political and social climate. Protestors shouted for freedom (*chaju*), democracy (*minju*), and unification (*t'ongil*) in the face of the existing political discourse of anticommunism and anti–North Koreanism.[22] According to Namhee Lee, "by the late 1980s, the *minjung* movement at large was under the spell of *chuch'e sasang* [North Korea's Juche ideology]."[23]

The period when the "northern wind" of North Korea's Juche ideology swept through university campuses, influencing the *minjung* movement for years to come,[24] was an ambivalent one for many of the participants in the democratization movement in South Korea. On the one hand, student protestors demanded political change and democratization, but, on the other hand, the majority did not anticipate an influx of pro–North Koreanism. In other words, fighting for democracy and sympathizing with North Korea are mutually exclusive, however often the South Korean government had conflated the two. This is because, as

Sunyoung Park says, the decades of the Cold War, which in Korea continues to this day, had severely damaged the reputation and perceived viability of any form of leftist culture on the peninsula.[25]

During these tumultuous times, a new movement emerged called "On Correctly Understanding North Korea" (Pukhan Paro Algi Undong), a hallmark event in the heavily anticommunist and anti-North Korean political climate. For the first time, academicians took North Korean literature seriously, following the increasing popularity of North Korea among university students, reading groups, and lectures.[26] The enthusiastic reception of North Korean novels opened up new possibilities for understanding North Korea, creating an optimistic outlook among scholars, students, and the public. Although much of North Korean literature is archived in the Ministry of Unification and in the Information Center on North Korea, which is now on the fifth floor of the National Library, public access in the late 1980s was still difficult. Many of the scholars interested in North Korean literature visited the Ministry of Unification in the late 1980s and were exposed (some for the first time) to a vast collection that had been restricted and banned to the public during the Park Chung Hee and Chun Doo Hwan regimes. North Korean literature then made its way out of the archives and into the hands of publishing houses and onto bookstore shelves for the public. However, police and representatives of the National Security Agency barged into bookstores near university campuses and confiscated pro-North Korean books. They also closed down the Taedong, Paektu, Him, and Sallimt'ŏ publishing companies, along with others that had printed North Korean novels, and arrested their affiliates.[27]

It has been an uphill battle for scholars to make North Korean literature public in South Korea, despite citizens' desire to know more about the country. The On Correctly Understanding North Korea movement began to wane in the 1990s after the fall of the Berlin Wall and the collapse of the Soviet Union. The South Korean public—who had been intrigued by North Korea's socialist structure—began to lose interest when socialism turned out to be a futile economic program. While some of the scholars from this group remained devoted to the task of continuing reading groups and lectures, others saw a dead end as public and academic interest drastically decreased.

However, a small group of scholars in English-speaking communities around the world ignited a new-found interest in North Korean literature. Brian Myers pioneered in the opening of this field with his analysis of the life and works of Korean Artist Proletariat Federation member Han Sŏr-ya. Tatiana Gabroussenko has been unearthing the dynamic relationship between the Soviet Union and North Korea and its influences on North Korean literature. Her most recent publication, *Soldiers on the Cultural Front* (2010), peers into the early history of North Korean literature and literary policy. Additionally, her examination of "rural fiction"[28] has been insightful in understanding another important aspect of North Korean political and social life during the Arduous March (*konan'ui haenggun*). Stephen Epstein reflects on short stories at the cusp of the new millennium and the way in which the new era has affected the relations among writers, the state, and the reader.[29] Sonia Ryang's rethinking of the notion of self-discipline in Foucauldian terms in 1980s novels has offered yet another layer to the understanding of reading practices in North Korea. Her most recent publication, *Reading North Korea: An Ethnological Inquiry* (2012), focuses on the way in which the connection between the people and the Great Leader has been secured and found meaningful in narratives of the 1970s and 1980s that deal with love, war, and the self.[30] Alzo David-West's reading of the literary ideas proposed by Kim Il Sung and Kim Jong Il refashions presuppositions and "fatalistic" readings of scholars in the past and opens up new possibilities for reading North Korean literature within the strictures of what he calls "intentional fallacies."[31] Hence, my effort to open up the field of North Korean literature is not a step into uncharted territory, but it is an attempt at a new reading of the topics of women, sexuality, family, and memory that have been silenced, elided, and neglected for so long in North Korean fiction.

My aim is not to denigrate the institution of the Writers' Union, North Korean literary culture, writers, or the Party. Furthermore, my project is not to find in texts opposing voices or "hidden messages" critical of the Great Leader. Instead, my method of reading North Korean literature seeks to disclose the internal slippages, inconsistencies, irony, fault lines, and fissures that already shake and disrupt the seemingly stable structure of the political discourse through the discussion of women. The diverse representations of women and the family in literature are indicative of the affirmative and positive changes that occurred in the 1980s and the possibility for further changes that can take the DPRK into hopeful and unforeseeable directions. These changes may not appear drastic enough to point to the *perestroika* that occurred in the Soviet Union, but they are clear indications that the DPRK is not a stagnant country with a regressing literary culture.

I cannot stress enough that North Korean writers (most of whom are still alive today) have no control over how their texts are going to be read, as meaning loses its navigation in the hands of the reader. Roland Barthes' "Death of the Author" is relevant in the North Korean context in many ways, as literature must depart from the interpretive tyranny of the writer and his or her singular meaning. It is, therefore, imperative to note that I am not suggesting any authorial intent in my analyses of literary texts. I am sure the authors discussed in this book are fervent and devout advocates of the Party and of the Great Leader, and they have no explicit inclination whatsoever to deviate from the Party's directives. The authors have done their job as dutiful and devoted engineers of the North Korean soul, and I do not (nor should the DPRK) hold these writers responsible for any of my (or anyone else's) interpretations of their texts. Nor is my purpose in bringing North Korean literature to a more visible ground based on rationalizing or justifying the authoritarian politics of the DPRK. Rather, it is to celebrate fictional individuals who express human emotions and reveal ethical dilemmas within their delimited sociopolitical living conditions.

Chapter 1 begins by providing the historical context of forging a revolutionary family based on political discourse delineating the state-prescribed mother. Kim Il Sung's progressive egalitarian system is premised on the fundamental role of women as patriots, who raise their children to become patriots and remain dutiful housewives to their husbands. The domestic space comprises the grounds for bearing patriotic and revolutionary citizens. In "On the Work of the Women's Union," Kim Il Sung informs the Women's Union of the practical objectives of their role as equal participants in building the nation-state of the DPRK. The entire speech instructs women about the country's famous patriotic generals and scholars who were taught by their respectable mothers. Kim says, "Mothers play a prominent role in the education of children,"[32] which lays emphasis on the function of women rather than on women's sexual difference.

The method used for displacing women from the male-dominated political discourse is to desexualize the women and turn them into mothers. The state has rewritten the historiographies of Kim Il Sung's mother, Kang Pan-sŏk, and his wife, Kim Chŏng-suk, as exemplars of motherhood by delineating their devotion to the revolutionary cause. The biographical accounts of these two women are not "historical" in that they trace the actual lives of Kang Pan-sŏk and Kim Chŏng-suk; rather, these women are discursively constructed to be historical so as to provide the DPRK with signification and political legitimacy during Kim Il Sung's rise to power. In short, the political discourse is not about the two women but about the iconography, a metonym of the teleological function of the state that reproduces revolutionary individuals.

Chapter 2, then, puts the notion of ardent revolutionaries into question as these individuals find themselves torn in the face of sexual desire. Although North Korean fiction is supposed to portray the teleological construction of desexualized Kimilsungist revolutionaries, the narratives actually erect sexualized discourses that produce competing desires for individuals. Rather than portraying the DPRK as a sexually repressive state, the descriptions of men and women in literature, film, and other forms of media generate sexual desire. In fact, many of the narratives are structured in "kiss and tell" form, where individuals commit a sexual act and confess it to an interlocutor. This chapter aims at divulging the discourse of affection and sexuality within the individual's profession of political love for the leader and the state, which is seen as two sets of discourses that disrupt the individual's reality in fiction. That is, the construction of a revolutionary character cannot be seen as a formulaic process that is predictable and static but rather is a negotiation between two competing desires that create a schizophrenic individual.

The language that is used to delineate a revolutionary subject proves to be unstable, revealing the irony and the limits of political discourse. In Chapter 3, the fault lines of the construction of individuals (particularly of women) are further exposed in terms of the "woman question(s)." The "woman question" revisits the institutional problems of repressed women in the patriarchal sociopolitical structure. At the same time, it is not a singular question that speaks for and answers the problems of every woman in North Korean fiction. Thus, "woman questions" in the plural form offer insight into the different class systems and family units in the DPRK and representations of disparate women from stratified social classes. Furthermore, to read "woman questions" as a verb, or as "woman who questions," highlights the agency of women and their suspicions of the political speech act that claims an individual's devotion to the leader and the state.

Ultimately, the "woman question(s)" puts the male-dominated state in crisis as the voices of women force the state to rethink irreducible sexual differences. The state-prescribed definition of a nuclear family is shaken up and loosened at the very foundations of gendered identities and pragmatic functions of women in society. Women in North Korean fiction resist the teleological, logocentric enclosure of their identity and subjectivity. Instead, their questions, doubts, and angst toward their husbands—who are a metonym for the state—keep the narratives suspended from ever reaching a "happy ending."

Chapter 4 raises the issue of divorce as an explicit contention between women and the patriarchal state. Women in fiction struggle to project their devotion to the state and also pursue individualistic goals that disrupt the totalizing narrative of the state from enclosing their sexual identities. They attempt to subvert the patriarchal social order and find ways to fulfill their own pleasurable desires. The real issue at hand, in this chapter, is not only the expression of women's subversive agency against their male counterparts but their agency to not participate in the patriarchal linguistic system, which has subjugated them in the patriarchal culture. The women refuse to answer the men, who are metaphors of the state, because if they answer, then they will be drawn back into the patriarchal system. Instead, they envision their own identities and create for themselves a space in which the state cannot transform them into the prescribed revolutionary subjects.

Whereas literature since the inception of the DPRK has promoted "family revolution" and women's active participation in society and politics, literature in the 1980s began to show much more irony in women's public and private spaces. If mothers were to take Kim Il Sung's statement that "mothers play a prominent role in the education of children" seriously, then mothers would have the agency to deprogram and reprogram their children into thinking outside the patriarchal state discourse. Recognizing the potential danger, the state needed to create a historiography that would control women (so that they could educate children according to state standards) and legitimize the political structure and unity of the male-dominated society.

The most effective way of consolidating ideological differences in North Korean society has been through collective memory of a singular history of the nation. Kim Il Sung had to be the sole proprietor of the founding of the nation. His anti-Japanese revolutionary exploits and his victory over the Americans during the Korean War were signatory events that legitimized his political power. History, in the DPRK, is not based on "facts" but on ritualized practices that perpetuate the discursive construction of the nation's identity and by extension the people's identity.

Chapter 5 analyzes the reconceptualization of the function of memory within the grand narrative of the nation. Memory questions the very agenda of seeking the "truth" (*chinsil*) of the nation's past as if the past were an attainable object of inquiry. The past is a lost referential and, therefore, requires conscious memorialization or reconstruction of events not to recover the past but to create the past. Reading memory in this way opens up a space within the common trope of memory in most North Korean novels that refers to the dignified and nostalgic past of Kim Il Sung's revolutionary history. The state's insistence on the "truth" of the nation's history comes undone when individuals recognize the discursive power to rewrite, reconstruct, and reimagine the past. This chapter will demonstrate that memory is a contestable liminality where the unity of the subject is irreconcilable and disjointed from the hinges of the nation's grand narrative.

CHAPTER ONE

Desexualizing Motherhood

The Lost Referential of Women

> Then Mother Kang Ban Sok made a deep bow, with her young son on her back. . . . She had made up her mind not to return until her homeland was free.
>
> *The Year 1932*

In the novel *The Year 1932* (1972), Kim Hyŏng-jik and Kang Pan-sŏk set off on the road to revolution with young Kim Il Sung on Kang's back. They head north of Mangyŏngdae—the birthplace of Kim Il Sung—to Manchuria to join forces with the national liberation activists. The road to revolution is not only going to be difficult, but it is going to lead to Kim Hyŏng-jik's death. The burden of leading the people to national liberation is then bequeathed to Kim Il Sung as a symbolic passing of the torch.

The novel describes neither Kim Hyŏng-jik's revolutionary activities against the Japanese colonialists nor his death. The novel is not about one revolutionary hero passing his legacy down to another; it is not about the relationship between a father and his son. In some respects, the novel is not even about the revolutionary exploits of Kim Il Sung, although he is the central figure. Instead, the novel is about the dissipation of the nuclear family and the forging of a revolutionary family. It is about the filial relationship between Kim Il Sung and his mother, Kang Pan-sŏk—the discursive construction of a state-desired motherhood.

The Year 1932 is premised on the historicized violence of Japanese colonialism in Korea and the notion that Kim Il Sung's guerrilla army had attained the correct political consciousness to achieve revolution on the Korean peninsula. A loose interpretation and application of Marx' dialectics of class conflict constitutes the narrative, in that the exploited and oppressed Koreans need to overthrow the Japanese colonialists. Unlike Marx' view, however, class struggle is not rooted in social relations of production but in nationalist identity whereby the individual recognizes his or her identity and subjectivity in the imagined collectivity of Kim Il Sung's revolutionary family.

According to *The Year 1932,* the driving force behind the actualization of Kim Il Sung's revolutionary family is the allegory of the mother, who urges her son to leave her and fulfill his political destiny. Kang Pan-sŏk is a pedagogical exemplar who advocates the dissipation of the nuclear family in order for individuals to realize their true identity in the state. She represents the intersection of domestic virtue and progressive consciousness. The North Korean state discourse first desexualizes the woman by transforming her into a mother figure in order to construct the revolutionary family and, second, delineates the mother as possessing the ability to transcend her maternal role by allowing her child to enter the state and find his true identity. According to official DPRK discourse, the mother is portrayed not as having lost her child but as having done her political duty, which elevates her to the immortal status of motherhood.

However, this chapter is less concerned with the modality of how the state discourse valorizes Kang Pan-sŏk and Kim Chŏng-suk (Kim Il Sung's wife) as representatives of divine motherhood and wifehood than with how the two iconic women have come to be considered real beings that are identifiable within a historical spatiality and temporality. The delineation of Kang Pan-sŏk and Kim Chŏng-suk in literature and other forms of cultural media precedes the actual personages. My point is not that the cultural products that portray the two women are historically inaccurate or that these two women did not exist at all. Instead, the cultural products are their own reality and representations of historicity in the continuation of their reproduction through the present day, which has no relation to a historical past or persons. The biographies of the two women are discursive constructions that historicize a specific spatiality and temporality of their lives in order to legitimize the origins of the nation.

The fictionalization of Kang Pan-sŏk and Kim Chŏng-suk—in which the revolutionary history is preserved by the ritualization of writing—reflects Jean Baudrillard's claim that "history is our lost referential, that is to say our myth."[1] The reproduction of this discourse creates what Baudrillard calls simulation, or the *hyperreal:* the product of an irradiating synthesis of combinatory models in a hyperspace without atmosphere.[2] Following the theoretical lines of poststructuralism, Baudrillard asserts that historical truth is a lost referential within a system of signifiers through which the world is constituted only by the self-referential signs. In the case of North Korea, the practice of writing such a narrative (re)produces the literary and hagiographical discourses of *a* Kang Pan-sŏk and *a* Kim Chŏng-suk rather than referring to the actual women and their actual lives. On one level, the hagiographies are about Kang Pan-sŏk and Kim Chŏng-suk; on another level, however, they are not about them at all. The historical reference to the names "Kang Pan-sŏk" and "Kim Chŏng-suk" are self-referential signifiers that only become "real" through the reproduction of cultural forms that inculcate meaning into them.

The value of their names is given to them by the state's discursive construction, which then creates an entirely new narrative that is legitimated and appropriated into the grand narrative of Kim Il Sung's revolutionary family-state in the mid-1960s. To look at it in a different way, Kang Pan-sŏk's and Kim Chŏng-suk's lives do not actually matter; what matters is how their lives have been delineated in literature to create the iconography of motherhood and wifehood for North Koreans to read, learn, and emulate. Kang Pan-sŏk did not give birth to the nation; the North Korean discourse gave birth to her in the mid-1960s. And it is this discourse alone that constitutes the real and generates the ritualization of discourses on motherhood thereafter.

The discourse of motherhood and wifehood was the result of centralizing the competing visions of various women's groups and others of the domestic role and political function of women in the early years of the DPRK. As women were (re)defining themselves in the social space, the state established a singular definition of motherhood for women by providing them with the names and historical contexts of Kang Pan-sŏk and Kim Chŏng-suk. The invention of the two iconographic women was given meaning and political significance to justify the male-centered discourse that curtailed women's struggle for sexual and gender equality. Hence, the desexualization of the mother/wife was a critical discursive strategy to prepare for the construction of fictional heroines in literature by the 1970s.

Defining the Woman and the Family

The discourse on the liberation of Korean women emerged in the 1920s with the advent of the New Woman (*sin yŏsŏng*) and the leftist organization known as the Korean Artist Proletariat Federation (1925–1935). New Woman advocates like Na Hye-sŏk, Kim Ir-yŏp, and Kim Myŏng-sun broke the centuries-old silence imposed on Korean women and began to express their personal thoughts and visions in fictional form, demonstrating to Korean women the possibility of imaginative writings as both a profession and a form of public engagement.[3] As Sunyoung Park says, "The New Women leaders of early feminism advocated women's individual autonomy without necessarily associating their cause with that of national interest."[4] The advocates of the New Woman supported women's rights to education, financial independence, and sexual freedom, all of which had an effect on social policies and public affairs. However, the popularity of the New Woman declined, as the idea was considered a Western import, and "traditional" and nationalistic views of women reemerged to counter the New Woman. Suzy Kim argues that the New Woman discourse gave way to the resurgence of the "wise mother good wife" as a way to mobilize women to become the rear guard in the imperial war effort in the 1940s.[5] The image of women was discursively constructed as mothers who embodied the nation and protected the home front during the war.

Meanwhile, socialist feminist writers such as Kang Kyŏng-ae were more attentive to class differences among women, addressing the material and economic dimensions of women's oppression and advocating class struggle and revolution as a way of achieving women's emancipation.[6] In this respect, scholars such as Ha Sang-il and Kumari Jayawardena have poignantly identified the lack of feminist thought in Kang Kyŏn-ae's works. Ha Sang-il claims that Kang prioritized class difference above feminism in her struggle to liberate Korea from Japanese colonialism.[7] Kumari Jayawardena observes that Kang wrote novels and short stories dealing especially with women's problems, but the standpoint implicit in her writings was not by any means feminist.[8] Her writings called on women to read more socialist books, newspapers, and journals in order to fight for liberation.[9] In her essay titled "The Path for Korean Women" (Chosŏnyŏsŏngŭi palbŭl kil), Kang accepts the masculine endeavor of achieving socialism in Korea as the path that Korean women ought to take as well. She reclaims the patriarchal family order when she suggests that a woman's liberation is to be educated on socialism in order to "support her husband." In short, the political discourse used to reshape the New Woman into a vision of motherhood during Japan's colonial war effort was inherently identical to the discourse socialist feminists used to construct motherhood/wifehood in the DPRK.

Contemporaneously, men and women of colonial Korea also entertained the fad of Red Love, a "new erotic sensibility" that socialists all over the world explored after the Russian Revolution as they experimented with the limits and possibilities of their own reorganized societies.[10] According to Ruth Barraclough, Hŏ Chŏng-suk was a prominent socialist woman who traveled to various countries advocating education and experiencing the world. She was also notorious for her sexual promiscuity, which would haunt her political standing in North Korea and taint her reputation in South Korea for years.[11] Barraclough says, "Hŏ Chŏng-suk is one of a number of communist women who played a part in the creation of North Korea . . . but lived to see the once feminist Women's League turned into an organization that could endorse an absolutist patriarchal state."[12]

The legacy of the short-lived New Woman, socialist feminist writers, and communist activists had an impact during the formation of the DPRK, as it shaped the parameters and the expectations for the role of the North Korean

Democratic Women's League (Pukjosŏn Minju Yŏsŏng Tongmaeng). Suzy Kim maps out the diverse formations of women's groups across the DPRK in the nation's formative years before they were centralized under the women's league. She notes that the women's league faced problems with local male officials regarding the Gender Equality Law, but there were also disagreements among women on the political role of the league.[13] In these early years, women participated in public forums on ways to reform their status and political engagement. However, Suzy Kim notes that in order to participate in political affairs women had to learn to speak and appropriate the masculine language of the state, which transformed women into mothers.[14] In "Gender in Oblivion," Sonia Ryang argues that the North Korean state has depicted the revolutionary female figure not as "woman" but as "mother" in order to legitimate her productive/reproductive role in society. For Ryang, the DPRK has never raised the "woman question" but instead has asserted the "mother question" or the "worker question."[15] It was imperative for the DPRK to create a discourse around the naturalness of women as mothers in order to justify the exploitation and subordination of women under its patriarchal sociopolitics.

The Women's League shifted away from resolving issues of sexual inequality in the DPRK and instead became a medium through which the state implemented its sexist political discourse of motherhood under the guise of gender equality and socialist revolution. In his speech "The Duty of Mothers in the Education of Children," Kim Il Sung stated, "In the past, there were not a few women who went about dressed to kill and wearing fancy hats. They remained isolated from the masses and greatly impeded the progress of Women's League work."[16] Kim was referring to North Korean women who had been influenced by the New Woman at the turn of the century. For Kim Il Sung, the New Woman in the past implanted misguided ideas (such as sexual liberation)[17] in the minds of Korean women and cared about fashion and university education rather than fighting for the revolutionary cause. Kim lauded the Women's League for eliminating these kinds of so-called liberal-minded women and replacing them with working women in factories and rural villages.[18] Kim Il Sung concluded his speech with his most salient point: "The important task facing the Women's Union is to make all women communist mothers."[19] Kim Il Sung's concept of motherhood desexualized women, deprived them of their sexual rights, and transformed them into a state product for educational use and ideological signification. Motherhood was no longer a relationship between mother and child but rather the ethical commitment of the woman to the state.

North Korean fiction in the 1960s and 1970s portrays the state-desired revolutionary family as one where the wife devotes herself to her husband's political life or contributes her labor and efforts to the collective alongside her husband. With the revision of the DPRK Constitution in 1972, the Party stressed the importance of reinforcing the stability of the family through revolutionary women. The language "family is the fundamental cell of society," which is familiar to many socialist countries, was incorporated into the DPRK Constitution as a way of legally binding the nuclear family to the state, blurring the dichotomy of private and public spheres and obliterating the "woman question" and women's agency from the political lexicon.

Characters in fiction not only carry out the duty to fortify their identity in the state, but they also raise political consciousness in the family and lead the family toward revolutionary victory. For example, both Rim Tong-su's short story "Tu sedae" (Two Generations, 1962) and Chŏng Hang-mu's short story "Anhae" (Wife, 1965) portray wives' supportive efforts in their husbands' political labor while holding the fort in the domestic space. This discursive strategy has been the dominant method of illustrating the revolutionary family and substantiating the "natural" functionality of women in the DPRK. The formulation reproduced itself not only in fiction but also in other disciplines such as history, medicine, and law. The wife, in this framework, is not supposed to be seen as lacking agency but to be displaying her agency to engage in the national cause within the confines of the home. Wives willfully, and at times militantly, participate in national affairs through their moral support and physical labor both in and out of the domestic space. Thus, husband and wife are too busy with their political life to engage in petty domestic quarrels or for the wife to question the state's systemic sexist apparatus.

The onus of revolutionizing the nuclear family was on the women. The state-sponsored feminist movement in the formative years of the DPRK did not liberate women from their unequal role in state politics. Rather than expose women's dual and unequal role in both the public and the private spheres, the literary discourse concerning women's role in society in the 1960s and 1970s rearticulated domestic labor as a service to the state. In his speech "The Duty of Mothers in the Education of Children" in 1961, Kim Il Sung states, "Mother has to bear the major responsibility for home education because it is she who gives birth to children and brings them up."[20] He emphasizes the mother's responsibility to bear the burden at home because of her biological, sexual difference from men. The error of this reasoning is that the conclusion does not follow the premise. The female body may possess the biological anatomy to reproduce, but there is nothing *natural* about raising the children, especially as the woman's sole responsibility for the state. Yet the social construction of the notion of "woman" has never been questioned in North Korea and is taken for granted.

The irony of all this is that North Korean political discourse asserts that one is not born but becomes a revolutionary.[21] Nearly every work of fiction in North Korea past and present, in one form or another, attempts to delineate the transformation of an ordinary character into an extraordinary, revolutionary hero or heroine. This is because the individual's commitment to the state has to be learned and realized; there is nothing *natural* about becoming a revolutionary. Meanwhile, the essentialist view of the relationship between man and woman has been immutable and has resulted in relegating women to their double and unequal role. Gender issues were largely marginalized, even dismissed, in North Korean literature for not encapsulating the ideological rigor needed to show a truly Kimilsungist hero, while struggling against the Japanese colonialists and battling against the Americans during the Korean War remained the staple form and content in narratives. The silence on feminist issues in North Korean official and literary discourse serves to prevent the possibility of disrupting the state's teleological agenda on constructing, controlling, and normalizing women. Hence, by inventing the discourse of Kang Pan-sŏk and by having her embody the intersection of traditional virtues of a mother and progressive revolutionary consciousness, the state justifies the legitimacy of Kim Il Sung's political power.

However, there is an obvious contradiction in the state discourse on revolutionary mothers. The state juxtaposes the "traditional" image of mothers from the Chosŏn period with the modern context of North Korea and refers to them as "revolutionary" workers of the nation. In *Illusive Utopia,* Suk-Young Kim analyzes this paradox through the sartorial transformation from traditional Korean dress to modern military uniform: "Military uniforms mark women's entry into social and economic structures, but at the same time, their feminine shapes were constant reminders of different positions between men and women in the public sphere; military skirts were adopted to mark women's auxiliary position in relation to their male comrades with a purpose of confining the parameters of women's role."[22]

Suk-Young Kim finds that the sartorial representations of femininity and masculinity are perpetuated and performed in state discourses, artworks, theater, film, magazines, and everyday life. For Kim, military uniforms do not offer a sense of gender equality but rather a reminder to the women that their bodies are state owned and an essential part of daily routine. Indeed, gender-specific identities are not eliminated or blurred through uniforms or artworks that represent the sartorial spectra; they are reinforced and reiterated as cultural decorum and social practice. The male-centered political society thus exercises its power through traditional Korean dresses, uniforms, and other articles of clothing that shape and configure women's bodies to satisfy the state's desire.

Dress codes and sartorial representations of femininity are examples of how North Korean women have been appropriated into the language of men and the semantics of social construction, and became a byproduct of the hegemonic regime of the Same. Women's entrance into the public space did not overturn the normativity of sexual difference, but it created yet another space through which the state discourse named the "woman" and regulated and exercised its powers through the woman and through the family. In *Bodies That Matter,* Judith Butler says that "sex" not only functions as a norm but is part of a regulatory practice that produces the bodies it governs.[23] For Butler, the regulatory practice of naming and codifying man and woman works within a set of normalizing discourses that already assumes the materialization and functions of such bodies. A serious discussion of sexual difference has been evaded in North Korean political and social discourses, and instead measures of women's performativity have been enforced more than ever, instructing women on what to do and what not to do in both the private and public spheres.

What is at stake, then, in North Korean fiction is questioning and challenging the epistemological limits of the patriarchal discourse that has normalized the performativity of sexuality for women. The grand narrative of North Korean fiction is a prescriptive *telos* that forcibly drags women to a universal state where happiness supposedly dwells. The narrative content, then, portrays the performances of women who have willfully and unquestionably complied with the state's vision, which includes their desexualization.

The renowned female North Korean author Ri Chŏng-suk recognized the lack and improper depiction of relationships between family members (particularly the women) in literature and urged her contemporary writers to address these concerns in their works. In the 1967 September issue of North Korea's leading literary journal, *Chosŏn munhak* (Korean Literature), Ri provided her thoughts on writers' duty to create fiction that deeply examines the dynamics of family members: "If one is to call himself or herself a communist writer, then it is not enough to love and understand society. The writer must also make the effort to instill the revolutionary pulse and fervency in the family. . . . Despite our writers' efforts at delineating revolutionary soldiers, our novels, for some reason, have been sparsely or incorrectly handling the protagonist's family members."[24]

Ri Chŏng-suk makes several points: first, political revolution begins in the family rather than in the public domain; second, the family has the capability of inspiring or conversely hindering the revolution, or, to put it in another way, the family has the ability to program or reprogram the individual to cooperate with the state; and, third, writers had not been creating literary works that focus attention on family members, particularly women. Ri understood the family to be a "revolutionary pulse," as she put it, that signifies its ability to sustain or terminate nation building. She argued that the reason for the lack of narratives on the family was writers' failure to recognize the family's individuated role and ontological connections with society. It was therefore imperative for Ri that writers produce literary works that represent the family above all else.

This is not to say that Ri Chŏng-suk desired a better portrayal of the family in order to illustrate that the family exists solely to serve the state. On the contrary, her concerns about the lack of portrayals of the family in fiction came in response to the oppression that women in North Korea had been facing in the 1960s. Ri recognized the absence of depictions of sexual and gender inequality in the domestic space as symptomatic of North Korea's sexist cultural practices that undermined the importance of women (via the family) in male-dominated politics. The family or the domestic space was still perceived as the domain where women labored and reproduced for the state. The double burden women bore at the workplace and at home was indicative of the state's deterministic views on the naturalness of the woman. Gender equality was written into the DPRK Constitution—giving political rights to women and emancipating the women from domestic burdens—but social, cultural, political, and discursive practices showed otherwise. That is, the state expected women to fulfill their "natural" responsibility of nurturing the family, adhering to the patriarch at home and at the workplace, and rearing the next generation of children. For Ri, a deeper reflection on the family entailed a serious reconsideration of gender equality and methods through which fiction could articulate a truly socialist community, as she wrote in her magnum opus *San saedŭl* (Mountain Birds, 1964).[25] Regrettably, Ri Chŏng-suk's voice was stifled by the overbearing patriarchal literary and political culture of her time.

The Party prescribes moral and political responsibility to individuals (particularly women) to regulate sexuality and fortify the male-dominated state through fiction. Men, women, and children, in fiction, do not explicitly enjoy or explore their sexuality or individuality in the privacy of their homes. Instead they prepare themselves to enter the state, wherein lies their true home. The DPRK discourse of the family as the "fundamental cell of society" desexualizes family members and turns them into utilitarian members of the nation so that the state can exercise its power over the people.

An old phrase had reentered the literary lexicon with a new significance: *family revolution*.[26] This phrase attempts to reconstruct the state-desired individual in North Korea through fiction. Fictional heroes and heroines of the mid-1960s exemplified a new type of revolutionary, one that was constructed contemporaneously with the heroic invention of Kim Il Sung and his family members during the anti-Japanese revolutionary struggle. North Korean writers in the 1960s and 1970s were not looking to past fiction or historical documents from the 1930s for inspiration; writers of this period were creating the inspiration for people to read. They were required to design the literary landscape for future writers to follow. Metaphorically speaking, these writers were drawing a map without the presence of the territory to be mapped—the map preceded the territory; it was the map that engendered the territory.[27] Every family needed to learn from Kim Il Sung's family through the state-orchestrated discursive project of inventing the cartographic historicity of the nation's leader and his family. His revolutionary consciousness indeed made him great; his success in liberating the Koreans from the yoke of the Japanese colonialists made him even greater.

The discourse of elevating Kim Il Sung and his family was a state-sponsored strategy of regulating and sterilizing the people of their sexual desires, implementing revolutionary love that transcends all carnal desires. Both intimate love between husband and wife and nurturing love between mother and child were supposed to support the sacred love for the revolution. North Korean women in the narratives of the 1960s and 1970s were not individuals with personal ambitions but rather emulations of Kim Il Sung's mother, Kang Pan-sŏk. Literature and other cultural products idolized Kim's revolutionary family as the model for every nuclear family. From the 1960s, discourses on Kang Pan-sŏk elevated her to the highest national position as the Mother of the DPRK for her sacrificial support of her husband, Kim Hyŏng-jik, and son, Kim Il Sung. Each member of Kim's family was extolled in every form of media not because each actually achieved something extraordinary for the revolution but because the (re)production of such discourses offered no alternatives to thinking beyond the existing ones. The significance of Kang Pan-sŏk's status in literary works as the Mother of the DPRK is located in the context of inventing revolutionary history and Kim Il Sung's cult of personality.

Sexually Sterilizing the Discourse of Motherhood

In her *Everyday Life in the North Korean Revolution, 1945–1950,* Suzy Kim traces the discursive reconstitution of the concepts of "woman" and "motherhood" in the formative years of establishing the DPRK. Kim argues that women as mothers became the ideal selfless public servant and the embodiment of the Korean nation; yet insofar as women's identities were tied to motherhood, they did not have the power to define themselves outside of this very framework.[28] North Korean women had struggled to liberate themselves from traditional concepts of motherhood only to be reinscribed in that concept under a different guise.

Mothers were extolled and elevated to the status of ideal citizens, taking center stage as revolutionary heroines of the DPRK.[29]

While I agree with Suzy Kim, I add to her argument the notion that the discursive gesture to reconstitute the image of mothers in North Korea was essentially a desexualizing process to repress both men's libido and the remnants of the Korean New Woman who had emerged in the early part of the twentieth century. Just as sexual freedom was seen as a threat in the Soviet Union under Stalin's dictatorship, and, therefore, sexual repression was an instrument through which the state controlled the people, the DPRK also appropriated measures to desexualize women from images of desire to functionality. The state used discursive strategies to elevate mothers as model citizens for everyone (men, women, and children alike) to emulate, while simultaneously restricting women from imagining themselves as anything other than mothers of the nation. By inscribing women into the discourse of motherhood, the state established the imaginary kinship of the family-state.

There is a distinct difference between the Great Family (*taegajŏng*) and the Great Revolutionary Family (*hyŏngmyŏngjŏk taegajŏng*) in the official state discourse. According to South Korean scholar No Kwi-nam, the discourse of the Great Family, which began in the early 1960s, constructed the modern North Korean subject around nationalism and loyalty to the state.[30] For instance, Kim Chae-gyu's short story "Hyŏngmyŏngga'ŭi chip" (The Home of a Revolutionary Family, 1959) portrays members of a peasant family who join Kim Il Sung's anti-Japanese struggle and sacrifice their lives for the revolution, asserting that love for the revolution supersedes the love shared among family members. The discourse that surrounds the Great Revolutionary Family, in contrast, claims that no civilian family could ever live up to the standards by which this particular family lived. The Great Revolutionary Family consisted of Kim Hyŏng-jik (father), Kang Pan-sŏk (mother), Kim Il Sung (both father and mother), Kim Chŏng-suk (mother), and Kim Jong Il (son).[31]

The official discourse of the Great Revolutionary Family is premised on a paradox. The state extols Kim Il Sung as a member of the "revolutionary lineage" (*hyŏngmyŏngjŏk kagye*), which establishes the kinship in his family. The state discourse calling Kim Il Sung's family the revolutionary lineage is intended to justify his political leadership through biological, genetic makeup in his DNA—Kim Il Sung had the revolution gene; he knew it all along, ever since he was a child. The literary portrayal of Kim Il Sung and his family contrasts with the Party's directives for transforming individuals into revolutionaries. The claim that Kim's family had the revolution gene in their DNA elevates its members to the sacred pantheon of demigods, while every other individual in fiction must live with the curse of imperfection.

Even in the early years of the nation-state, North Korean propaganda noted Kim Il Sung's "revolutionary lineage" as one of his qualification for leadership.[32] Advocates of Kim Il Sung used circular reasoning to prove Kim's political legitimacy. The logical fallacy is as follows: Kim Il Sung is a revolutionary leader because he comes from a family of revolutionaries; therefore, he is a revolutionary leader. North Koreans were expected to accept the truth of the premise and the conclusion without question. The premise already assumed that Kim Il Sung's father and mother were revolutionaries, which would then prove Kim's revolutionary proclivities. The proof of the conclusion was in the premise, and the proof of the premise was in the conclusion. The propaganda claimed that Kim Il Sung's revolutionary success was already running in the genetic makeup of the Great Revolutionary Family, which, therefore, would naturally be passed on to Kim Il Sung, Kim Jong Il, and now Kim Jong Un. Since no other families or individuals in the DPRK possessed the revolutionary genome, Kim Il Sung and his family members were the rightful heirs to the throne. North Korean literature and media needed to propagate this *truth* to the people.

Circular reasoning was a powerful and uncontended writing strategy that propagandists used in the DPRK to propagate the unquestionable veracity of the Great Leader's revolutionary history. This circular argument was primarily used in fiction, journal articles, newspapers, or biographies that were about Kim Il Sung and his family's revolutionary exploits. In other narratives or tales, characters develop into revolutionaries rather than being born that way, which reconfirms that no hero or protagonist in North Korean fiction can surmount the revolutionary feats of the Great Leader. Writers and artists were instructed to engineer narratives celebrating Kim Il Sung's anti-Japanese struggle and his revolutionary consciousness to perpetuate the circular reasoning rather than because such a historical past is a referential truth.

If we are to take the "revolutionary lineage" argument literally, then the logical appellation for each family member would be Kim Hyŏng-jik as the father, Kang Pan-sŏk as the mother, Kim Il Sung as the son, Kim Chŏng-suk as the daughter-in-law, and Kim Jong Il as the grandson. However, this is not the norm in North Korean literature. Kim Hyŏng-jik is not readily referred to as the Father of Korea and certainly not as the Grandfather of Korea. Likewise, Kim Il Sung is not referred to as the Son of Korea, although he is often referred to as the Sun of Korea. Kang Pan-sŏk is not the Mother of Korea because she gave birth to Kim Il Sung, but, at the same time, she did give birth to him. This would then put Kim Chŏng-suk in an incestuous relationship with Kim Il Sung because she, too, is designated as the Mother of Korea. Did Kim Chŏng-suk also give birth to Kim Il Sung? Of course not; that would be absurd. The revolutionary lineage is not referring to actual kinship but a symbolic system of signs that allegorizes each member as sacrosanct national emblem. Kang Pan-sŏk as the Mother of Korea has strong leverage in North Korean society only because the state constructed a discourse around motherhood to revere the allegory of motherhood rather than referring to the actual bodies of women. To put it in another way, mothers in North Korea were not revered for being mothers; they had to work on gaining the correct political consciousness to become the state-desired ideality of motherhood. The meaning of motherhood is given to the people as an imaginary ideality of state politics. This explains why Kang Pan-sŏk, Kim Chŏng-suk, Kim Il Sung (he is referred to as the parent, which embodies both father and mother), and Kim Jong Il are often delineated as mothers in state discourse.

Motherhood in North Korean literature does not have any "natural" connection with giving birth or nurturing; it is a metonym that describes absolute loyalty from individuals. Both Kang Pan-sŏk and Kim Chŏng-suk are Mothers of Korea because the state has already determined their political function in society and made their functionality possible through the discursive repetition of their performance. Their titles are not based on kinship or revolutionary lineage but on the myriad signifiers that constitute the meaning of motherhood. Kang Pan-sŏk did not create her image; it was made for her, in place of her, despite her. She was constructed with patriarchal linguistics, a state system of language that dictated and imposed meaning onto her. Kang Pan-sŏk in literature speaks the male discourse, endorses the patriarchal society, and represents motherhood that all North Koreans are supposed to emulate. "Kang Pan-sŏk," then, is not a woman in the literal sense but a discursive instrument through which the state secures its national identity and political legitimacy.

The concept of motherhood associated with Kang Pan-sŏk and Kim Chŏng-suk was elevated to a political status beyond the reach of any mortal. In the mid-1960s and early 1970s, the Great Revolutionary Family became officially a national emblem of ineffable magnitude and spirituality. Each member of the Great Revolutionary Family took a share of the national spotlight, appearing in school textbooks, songs, fiction, poetry, paintings, murals, and other cultural media. The idea was clear: the Great Revolutionary Family was the holy family of the DPRK that exceeded the capacity of cultural intelligibility and human understanding. Or, at least, that is what the official discourse says about Kim Il Sung's family.

The cult of Kang Pan-sŏk was created to personify the state image of motherhood, which comprised sexual virtue through monogamy and fidelity in addition to domestic and public services. Kang was not only monogamous and faithful to her husband, Kim Hyŏng-jik, but she was also monogamously wedded to the revolutionary ideals of Kim Il Sung and faithful to the building of the family-state. Tales about Kang Pan-sŏk claimed that she had her mind set undividedly on the revolutionary cause. Her personal desires never competed with the collective desire to liberate the country from the Japanese colonialists. The discursive image of Kang Pan-sŏk was constructed as such to serve as an exemplary mother figure in whom there are no faults or shortcomings.

In 1968, the Central Committee of the Korean Democratic Women's Union published *Mrs. Kang Pan-sŏk: Mother of the Great Leader of Korea*. This book provides a biographical account of Kang's revolutionary activities since her childhood. Like most biographies of legendary figures, this book highlights unparalleled feats of Kang Pan-sŏk. She married Kim Hyŏng-jik when she was seventeen years old and began her career as a revolutionary wife and mother. The story recounts the numerous days Kim Hyŏng-jik spent away from home, leaving Kang Pan-sŏk to do all the housework. The biographer wrote, "Mrs. Kang Pan-sŏk did not blame her husband for his lack of attention to household affairs, but, instead, felt very proud to be the wife of such a good husband fighting for the country and the nation."[33] The book does not offer details of what the neglected household affairs were, but they would include bringing home income for the welfare of the family, assisting with household chores, raising Kim Il Sung and his siblings, and tending to his wife's sexual and emotional needs. The elision of the details of Kang Pan-sŏk's intimate life is necessary so that her revolutionary ideals can be highlighted. The biography functions as a manual of the correct ideological method by which North Koreans ought to live. As the biographer says: "The wife must accompany [her husband] on that road. She must love not only her husband, but also her revolutionary comrades. This is all the more difficult for a woman and therefore more honorable and glorious. Kang Pan-sŏk took that path."[34] Whether she was really so proud of her husband and uncomplaining is not the issue at hand. Biographical accounts of Kang Pan-sŏk elevated her to an infallible and perfect national emblem, untarnished and unadulterated by potentially viral thoughts. The story of Kang penetrated into her domestic space and opened it up for public viewing and instruction.

Such biographical stories did not penetrate into the emotional state of the heroine, or, in this case, her sexual intimacy with her husband, Kim Hyŏng-jik. The discursive project in Kang's legendary tale was to sterilize her sexuality as a woman and delineate her as an instrumental persona for utilitarian purposes. Kang gave birth to Kim Il Sung—what more was there to say? Her body was the vessel that housed the savior of the DPRK, a tale analogous to the hagiography of Mother Mary.

Thus, the discourse of Kang's revolutionary assistance to her husband desexualizes her body and transforms her into the mother of the nation. Kang Pan-sŏk's biographer writes, "Her whole life was dedicated to the struggle against all that were old and for the creation of the new."[35] Of course, the idea of "her whole life" is hyperbolic rhetoric, referring to her faithful commitment to the formation of the family-state. And this trite rhetoric imagines the delineation of the ideal mother of the DPRK rather than Kang Pan-sŏk herself. If her whole life had been dedicated to the revolution, then she would not have had time for personal matters or pleasure. Her marriage to Kim Hyŏng-jik would have been for political reasons and not because she was arranged to marry him or because she was irresistibly attracted to him. If she had been attracted to him, it would have been because of his revolutionary consciousness. Her sexual relations with her husband must have been for procreation and not for recreation because there is no time for orgasms when the revolution is on the horizon.

In fact, the act of sex for personal pleasure or eroticism in fiction of this period falls in the category of the *unsaid*. This is not because sexual descriptions in fiction were met with consternation or vehement disapproval. The state never explicitly prohibited writers from describing sexual intercourse in narratives; this topic was literally *unsaid,* or not discussed in public state affairs. It was understood that such writing would be indecent and valueless to the trajectory of the revolutionary narrative. Kang Pan-sŏk's "whole life" describes everything other than her sexuality as a woman. This must remain silent, marginal, and invisible. The discursive strategy of "her whole life" totalizes and regulates the cult of Kang Pan-sŏk as a desexualized woman that is aligned with the present-day depiction of motherhood.

The iconography of the mother was constructed around the discourse of the patriarchal state, which relegated women to the status of service and function rather than that of a person. The state invaded the domestic space, desexualized the woman by transforming her into a mother, and then called on the mother to nurture her children for the public space. The transformation of women into mothers whose voice recited the prescribed desires of the state would be epitomized in the 1970s through the discursive construction of Kang Pan-sŏk in the novel *The Year 1932.*

Mother of the Nation in *The Year 1932*

One of Kim Jong Il's greatest literary accomplishments was creating and institutionalizing a subgroup of the Writers' Union called the 4.15 Munhak Ch'angjakdan (April 15 Literary Production Unit) in the mid-1960s. He commissioned this group to produce a novel that celebrated Kim Il Sung's revolutionary activities in time for his father's sixtieth birthday extravaganza in 1972. The Literary Production Unit (LPU) published a novel called *The Year 1932* under the heading Immortal History Series to honor the birth of the Great Leader and also the birth of the nation, despite the fact that most North Koreans knew that the DPRK was established in 1948. The novel was Kim Jong Il's gift to his father, but, more important, it marked the advent of an institutionalized system of writing for the April 15 LPU writers. *The Year 1932* not only retold the forging of Kim Il Sung's anti-Japanese guerrilla army, but it also highlighted the motherly role of Kang Pan-sŏk toward her revolutionary children, reconstructing the image of the state-desired mother.

When Kim Jong Il called on the April 15 LPU to novelize the exploits of Kim Il Sung in *The Year 1932,* the writers did not know how to approach this task. In 2007, on the fortieth anniversary of the establishment of the April 15 LPU, Kwon Chŏng-ung (the author of *The Year 1932*) wrote an article about his experiences with the group titled "Ch'ongsŏ *Pulmyŏlui Ryŏksa* chung changp'yŏn sosŏl *1932*-i naogikkaji" (Publishing the Immortal History Series, Particularly *The Year 1932*). Kwon confessed:

> One day in January of 1968, we began to write about the revolutionary work of the Great Leader for his sixtieth birthday celebration. . . . How are we to write this? We debated over and over again, and, in the end, we decided to ask Kim Jong Il for advice. After writing the plot of the novel, we showed it to him. . . . To write *The Year 1932,* I had to do research and explore the history before I could begin. I completed the novel in the summer of 1971 and gave it to the Dear General. He came back to me and asked me to change the dialogue between the son [Kim Il Sung] and his mother [Kang Pan-sŏk] because this was to be the central theme of the novel.[36]

For Kim Jong Il, descriptive passages alone were not enough to educate the readers in the correct imagery of motherhood. The mother needed to speak in order for her tone, words, and loving spirit to delineate the characteristics of state-prescribed motherhood. Kim Jong Il instructed Kwon Chŏng-ung to highlight the sentimental moment when Kim Il Sung tends to his dying mother while the battle against the Japanese is imminent. In the novel, Kang Pan-sŏk urges Kim Il Sung to join his guerrilla soldiers rather than to stay with her. This conversation between the Mother of the DPRK and the son became the template for the way in which all mothers in North Korean fiction ought to speak to their children and the way children ought to respond to the state's beckoning through the words of the mother.

In *The Year 1932,* Kim Il Sung is ethically torn between looking after his dying mother and leading his soldiers to national liberation. Kang Pan-sŏk says to Kim Il Sung, "You cannot make a revolution if you worry about your family."[37] Kim Il Sung heeds his mother's words and departs from her with a formal bow, a bow that represents respect, gratitude, blessing, and parting. It is a bittersweet farewell for the son, who realizes that the road to revolution requires such severance from personal desires. The emotional moment of leaving his nuclear family for his revolutionary family becomes the thematic center of the novel, and perhaps of all literary works of fiction in North Korea.

> He shut the door briskly, and turned around. There was not a sound in the room.
>
> Her son was setting out on a long journey, and she would have liked to accompany him for ten or twenty *ri* or more. But she controlled her desire and did not even venture out to see him off. . . . Comrade Kŭm Sŏng [Kim Il Sung] stood for a brief moment on the porch by the closed door and then started to walk not toward the field, but around his house.[38]

Here Kwon Chŏng-ung intensifies the sentimental moment between mother and son. He reveals the emotional struggle of both Kim Il Sung and his mother in the statement "There was not a sound in the room." Kim Il Sung resolutely shuts the door, gesturing his determination to walk the path toward revolution. His mother, too, resolves to send her son away. But the silence that pervades this moment indicates that both Kim Il Sung and his mother would have liked the other to stay a bit longer. As Kim Il Sung stands in front of the door, listening to what his mother is doing inside the room, his mother, too, is listening to what Kim Il Sung is doing outside. If he had heard his mother rustling around in her room and going about her daily business, it would have meant that she had accepted without ambivalence her son's destiny as a revolutionary. But the fact that she, too, is listening (perhaps for Kim's fading footsteps) reveals the mother's deeper concern for her son. She does not open the door to see her son off because she does not want her son to regret leaving his mother.

Kwon Chŏng-ung, then, dramatizes this moment by having Kim Il Sung circle the hut. Kwon shows that Kim is harboring tumultuous thoughts that are keeping him from leaving his mother. Kim Il Sung is juggling two strands of thought that are equally significant to him: his mother and the revolution. This passage reveals the human quality of Kim in his struggle against leaving his dying mother behind. On the one hand, he wants to be a filial son, but, on the other, he needs to save his people. The ethical dilemma is clearly and vividly delineated. But then the mother intercedes:

> "What are you doing here?" Mother's voice shook as she spoke. "I know what you are worrying about. You cannot free your country if you worry about trifles. If you want to make revolution, you have to go out and do it. Though if you want to live at home, you can. Make up your mind."[39]

At this point, the mother can no longer stand to have her son contemplating outside her room. She demands that her son leave for the revolution, but her voice quivers at her own utterance. Her words are stern, but there is an element of hesitancy in her words. She knows Kim Il Sung must go, but she also would like for him to stay a bit longer. Author Kwon Chŏng-ung shows the difficulty the mother faces in having to let go of her son. She resorts to scolding Kim as a method of hiding her maternal care, a demonstration of tough love for her indecisive son. The mother's role is to educate her son to prioritize national duties over filial responsibilities.

In *Mrs. Kang Pan-sŏk: Mother of the Great Leader of Korea,* the biographers acknowledge Kim Il Sung's filial piety to his mother and honor it in its own right, but they add, "To her more precious was the fatherland than her own life, and the revolution came before her dear son."[40] Kang Pan-sŏk's scolding is an invitation for Kim Il sung to suspend the Neo-Confucian directives of *hyo,* or filial duties, and supplant them with revolutionary consciousness. Ironically, Kim obeys his mother's instructions. This filial submissiveness reinforces the Neo-Confucian tenets in North Korean society and culture, and Kim Il Sung's ethical gesture elevates the image of the mother as the sacrosanct foundation of the DPRK.

The sentimental moment in *The Year 1932* is heightened when Kim Il Sung finally takes leave of his mother for good. He realizes that his mother is correct in saying that the revolution is what is most important. In order to contain his emotions, Kim walks away without looking back. He needs to keep his vision focused on what is ahead of him rather than on those he has just left behind. The gesture of looking back would be a sign of weakness, longing, and irresoluteness. But Kim Il Sung is also human. He cannot hold back his longing for his mother. Even though she has scolded him and shut the door on him, Kim needs to take one last glance at his mother. He slowly turns his head toward the rustic hut. To Kim's surprise and reassurance, he finds his mother outside her room, waving good-bye to her son.

It strains the mother's heart to send her courageous son away, but it would devastate her to think that her son would not achieve the revolution. She waves good-bye as a sign of motherly love. She had lost her husband and many other comrades to the fight against the Japanese colonialists, and so the premonition of also losing her son is visceral. Yet she understands that selfish, individualistic desires to protect her son by keeping him at home will not bring about the revolutionary victory. She has come to accept her son's destiny. She waves good-bye no longer as a mother but as a proud comrade. Kang Pan-sŏk transcends her individualism and achieves the sacred understanding of comrade-love (*tongji'ae*), which is the desexualized platonic love among revolutionary comrades.

The mother figure represents both the family and the nation; the two are not supposed to be bifurcated or distinct in North Korean culture. In the DPRK Constitution and in other literature, the family is identified as the "fundamental cell of society." The use of biomedical terminology to describe the family is political rhetoric of the state: the state is the life of the family as much as the family is the life of the state—they are essentially one and the same. In this sense, Charles Armstrong is correct in saying that North Korea never experimented with breaking up the family unit and that the political system of the DPRK would build on the structures and metaphors of the nuclear family throughout its existence.[41]

However, North Korean fiction reveals the deconstruction of the family for the sake of constructing the revolutionary family. In *The Year 1932,* the nuclear family of Kim Il Sung has already been broken and deconstructed by the absence of the father, Kim Hyŏng-jik. The father figure remains in the margins or outside the narrative as he is mentioned only a few times in the novel. One of the significant moments in *The Year 1932* is when the narrator says that "[Kim Hyŏng-jik] has taken the road never to return" to remind readers of the revolutionary passion the great nationalist possessed.[42] The road Kim Hyŏng-jik took was also in the direction of national liberation, but it was unsuccessful in getting there (as proven by his death) because it was not the path to revolution Kim Il Sung paved. The novel neither mourns the death of Kim Hyŏng-jik nor eulogizes his revolutionary activities. Kim Hyŏng-jik is nearly absent, forgotten, and erased from the relationship between Kim Il Sung and his mother.

The competing discourses between Kim Il Sung's revolutionary vision and those of other male national liberation activists, such as his father, shows an allegorical reconstitution of the Oedipus complex. At the age of five, young Kim Il Sung witnesses his mother intervening in the beating of his father by Japanese policemen.[43] He recalls how his mother washed his father's bruised body after his release from prison; he observed the way in which his mother nursed his dying father to no avail. The object of desire in this memory is not Kim Il Sung's dying father but his mother, who embodies providence and the hearth of the nation. The father represents the failure of the Korean national liberation movement in the March First Movement of 1919, which becomes the impetus for Kim Il Sung to take over his father's quest with his mother by his side. In the novel, Kang Pan-sŏk hands Kim Il Sung two pistols that his father left behind as a gift and as a reminder to succeed in liberating the nation in the place of his father. However, the victory is not to be achieved by the methods of Kim Il Sung's predecessors (i.e., his father) but through new means and with a completely different group of revolutionaries. The gift of the two pistols is both a reminder of his father's failed revolution and a symbol of Kim Il Sung's new path to revolution, to which his mother is wedded. Kim Il Sung's memory of his father is thus marginalized in *The Year 1932,* as this novel glorifies the construction of Kim Il Sung's revolutionary guerrilla army, who become the founding fathers of the DPRK.

In *North Korea: Beyond Charismatic Politics,* Heonik Kwon and Byung-Ho Chung retrace the "barrel-of-a-gun family genealogy" to critique the historiography of Kim Il Sung's revolutionary exploits, the political succession process of his son Kim Jong Il, and the military-first (*sŏn'gun*) politics that governs North Korea today. Kwon and Chung argue, "Kim Il Sung's revolutionary historical career has increasingly become more of a family genealogical history, departing from the singularly personalized charismatic history that had been prevalent in the previous decades and becoming increasingly a part of an extensive historical genealogical background for a continuously evolving, hereditary revolutionary political commitment."[44] In present-day North Korea, the legend of the gift of the pistols has been retold to justify the succession of three generations: Kim Hyŏng-jik to Kim Il Sung to Kim Jong Il. (We have yet to see whether the gift of the pistols has been bequeathed to Kim Jong Un now that Kim Jong Il has passed away.) In other words, the gift of the guns has been historicized in North Korean politics as a patrilineal genealogy of the Kim patriarchs, whereas the narrative in *The Year 1932* details the intimacy between Kim Il Sung and his mother.

Kim Jong Il advised author Kwon Chŏng-ung to center the theme of *The Year 1932* on the separation between Kim Il Sung and his mother, Kang Pan-sŏk, not only to intensify the sentimental value of the narrative but to underscore the value of sublating the nuclear family for the sake of the Kimilsungist revolutionary family. The discursive strategy in North Korean fiction suggests that individuals must prioritize the Great Family above one's nuclear family. The literary discourse asserts the Great Family as the completion of the individual's political identity and self-worth. Mothers in North Korean fiction provide the teleological path of self-completion for their children by pointing in the direction of the state. What greater example is there than Kang Pan-sŏk, who demonstrated the importance of the revolutionary family over the nuclear family? And what greater revolutionary is there than Kim Il Sung, who obeyed his mother?

The sublation of the nuclear family in fiction is considered a righteous, self-sacrificing decision as long as it is for the cause of the Kimilsungist revolution. The individuals in a nuclear family cannot and must not remain isolated from the public. Family life is political life in the DPRK; the two are ineluctably interwoven. The family is the training ground on which individuals experience political life, and the educator in the family is the mother. For example, in the self-proclaimed masterpiece of North Korean film and literature *Sea of Blood* (1982),[45] Mother (the nameless heroine of the novel) loses everything she possessed to the Japanese colonialists: her husband, her village, and her youngest son, Ul-lam. In the course of the novel, Mother comes to realize the importance of the Kimilsungist revolution and sends off her eldest son and daughter to the guerrilla force:

> The mother saw them off, waving to them, standing on that same height at the foot of Mount Salgu where she had once stood one early dawn, seeing off her eldest son, Wŏl-lam, on his way to the guerrillas. Today, along with her eldest son, her daughter Kap-sun was going with the guerrillas, and Yŏng-sil, who perhaps one day would become her daughter-in-law. Along with them, Tu-hyŏk, Ch'il-sŏng, and other village lads were leaving. The mother saw only dots in green uniforms, she could not distinguish faces. At last, the tears restrained for so long gushed to the surface together with happiness and blurred her vision. Through her tears, the mother saw a broad road stretching far into the future—the road to the revolution.[46]

The future of the Kimilsungist revolution is also prioritized over the nuclear family in *Sea of Blood*. Mother's tears sending off her children to the guerrillas are tears of joy rather than maternal tears of worry over her children. She has come to terms with the idea that the guerrilla force will provide her children with comfort, food, shelter, and victory. The dissolution of the nuclear family is not a necessary evil for Mother; it is simply necessary for the construction of the Kimilsungist state. There may have been unutterable pain in losing her husband and her youngest son to the Japanese, but there is no pain in losing Wŏl-lam and Kap-sun to the revolutionary state. She is proud that her children will contribute to the building of a new future but more so that she too has contributed to the nation. Heonik Kwon and Byung-Ho Chung put it this way: "*Sea of Blood* manifests this powerful aesthetic of revolutionary redemption and advocates for the transformation of a consanguine familial unity into a higher political familial solidarity centered on the partisan leader from whom the hope for virtuous rebirth emanates."[47] Mother transcends her maternal desires and offers her children as gifts to be incorporated into a new family, a revolutionary family that is created by Kim Il Sung.

In *Sea of Blood,* Mother stands by the road to see her children off just as Kang Pan-sŏk stands by the road to see Kim Il Sung off in *The Year 1932.* The difference is that Mother in *Sea of Blood* can no longer distinguish her children's faces as they continue to march ahead. It is not because her children are walking far into the distance but because all the guerrilla soldiers merge from "dots in green uniform" into one big green mob. This is a rather ideological description of revolutionary soldiers, who become faceless when they enter into the collective world, as I discuss in Chapter 5. Mother's revolutionary attitude in *Sea of Blood* is symmetrical to Kang Pan-sŏk's revolutionary fervor in *The Year 1932* when Kang says, "But what a lucky mother I am! I'm weeping because I'm so happy."[48] Kang Pan-sŏk realizes that if the revolution is to happen the nuclear family cannot and ought not remain within the confines of the private. People of the DPRK are supposed to learn from Kang Pan-sŏk and her dedication to the forging of the family-state prior to the Soviet occupation in the mid-1940s. The implications are clear-cut: the DPRK was always a family-state, and it was founded not through the aid of a foreign country or a foreign ideology but by Kim Il Sung and his indigenous and unparalleled ideology of Juche. These implications were not conceived in the actual past but invented in the 1970s and superimposed onto the imaginary past.

The formation of the anti-Japanese guerrilla without foreign aid is explicitly narrated in Sŏk Yun-gi's *Pom'ure* (Spring Thunder),[49] published in 1985 as part of the Immortal History Series thirteen years after the publication of *The Year 1932.* Similar to *The Year 1932,* this novel tells of the sacrifices revolutionaries made in order to forge a new family among themselves: "[The revolutionaries] had to offer to abandon their parents, siblings, children, and even lovers. Therefore, on this day, April 25, 1932, the revolutionaries, having abandoned their parents, siblings, wives, and children and with only the revolution in mind, stood on the road."[50] This novel makes a strong appeal to the function of the nuclear family as a laboring machine that produces and reproduces revolutionaries for the state. The title of the novel, *Spring Thunder,* refers to the metaphor of the thunderous clatter of rifles in the hands of the restless revolutionaries who have joined Kim Il Sung's guerrilla force and are prepared to drive the Japanese out of Korea.

The narrative of *The Year 1932* continues where *Spring Thunder* leaves off. The historically significant events of *The Year 1932* are the formation of the anti-Japanese guerrilla army, Kim Il Sung's departure from his mother, and the death of his mother. Kim's father, Kim Hyŏng-jik, has already been killed by the Japanese without having the opportunity to form an army. His mother, who had worked alongside her husband, will not live to see the day of Korea's liberation but witnesses the day of the soldiers' departure toward revolution. The novel purports that Kang Pan-sŏk has done everything in her power to assist Kim Il Sung in accomplishing the victorious task, therefore becoming a venerable mother.

As the centerpiece of the narrative, the conversation between mother and son delineates the iconographies of the nation's mother and the nation's leader. Kang Pan-sŏk's instructions for her son to leave and Kim Il Sung's march toward revolution encapsulate the state-desired behavioral responses, which were organized around comrade-love or camaraderie that justified and systematized the codes of conduct for men and women.

Kim Chŏng-suk: A Dual Role of Wifehood and Motherhood

State-sponsored feminism in the early days of the DPRK made progressive gestures to promote economic equality. The state allowed women to enter the workforce alongside men and granted voting rights to women. Socialized welfare programs such as daycare, collective cooking, and other means to relieve women of their household duties were implemented to promote gender equality. The DPRK, along with other communist countries, supposedly relieves women of the double burden of doing heavy household chores and laboring in the workforce by establishing childcare facilities committed to raising children in lieu of their mothers. Nurseries (*t'akaso*) take a child from the hands of the mother so that the mother can focus more on her job. Kindergarten, primary, middle, and high schools also take the child from the mother and serve as training grounds for students to learn about Kim Il Sung and his Juche theory.[51] Students join an organization called the Socialist Youth League, where they further develop their ideological consciousness for the state. The purpose of these socialized institutions and organizations is to provide a space in which children commit their lives to the construction of their political subjectivity. The way children are supposed to think, speak, and behave is developed in these rigorous education programs.

However, these state-run socialized programs are gendered. In fiction, female characters labor in the fields and in industry alongside their male counterparts. They also take on roles in raising or nurturing children such as that of teacher. Nearly every occupation that deals with service, such as secretaries, restaurant servers, or nurses, is portrayed by female characters. Conversely, anything that requires physical strength or scientific acumen is typically delegated to male characters. In relation to men, women remain depended on but taken for granted.[52] Although North Korean fiction is supposed to project a classless and gender-equal society, it has yet to question and challenge the dual roles women have in the public workplace and in the domestic space. This is because fiction reflects the state-projected image of motherhood, implicitly reinstating male-dominated social and cultural politics.

North Korean fiction perpetuated the representation of motherhood to substantiate the patriarchal hierarchy. The delineation of Kang Pan-sŏk was not intended to detail her life but to use her as an object of the male-dominated social politics where mothers were considered the ontological providers for the nation. In other words, their entire existence was predicated on providing for the state. While North Korean women worked and labored with the men in the fields and factories, the labor division was clearly demarcated and power relations were unbalanced. Depictions of women in asymmetrical power relations became the normative social and political practice in fiction, with women placed beneath men. Women had to work under men in the public workplace. Then, when they came home from work, they had to be mothers in the domestic space.

In North Korean discourse, the category of "sex" (*sŏngbyŏl*) is normative, already determined, and constructed by the patriarchal system. The efforts of North Korean women to fight for gender equality during the formative years of building the DPRK did not liberate women but instead reframed them as a social and political function that serves the male-dominated society. The Women's League, for example, required its voice to be approved by the counsel of men, who then decided on how the "woman question" could be used to edify the patriarchal system and benefit male interests. That is, according to Suzy Kim, "women's participation in the social, economic, and political arenas was fostered without fundamentally questioning the social differentiation between women and men."[53] The state allowed women to enter the public space, but they also needed to complete their duties in the domestic space without question.

A similar situation occurred in the Soviet Union when the state under Stalin reinscribed what it considered to be traditional values of the family and neglected to address sexual and gender inequality. Looking back to the 1980s, Olga Voronina criticizes the Soviet Union for not emancipating women and never resolving the "woman question," which had been considered one of class inequality and not gender. Voronina disengages political discourse from reality, arguing that the Soviet government, in spite of the progressive promises in the country's

Constitution, discriminated against women. She says, "Within the framework of a masculinist ideology, the family always serves as an instrument for suppressing a woman's individuality and subordinating her interests to the interests of all the other members of the family."[54] North Korea in fact brought problems of gender inequality into the North Korean social context by modeling itself after other communist countries such as the Soviet Union.

Women's role at home was never challenged: the state ostensibly relieved women from their household duties but still considered those duties to be inherently a feminine imperative. In *Nyŏsŏng munje haegyŏl kyŏnghŏm* (Resolving the Woman Question, 1990), Ri Kyŏng-hye historicizes the problems of women in Korea by examining the lives of women from the feudal period to the present-day DPRK. From the title alone, we might suspect that Ri's approach to resolving the problems of gender inequality is through state-sponsored feminism, which promotes women's participation in the public sphere alongside men, rather than an earnest attempt at implementing a feminist position.[55] The woman question as posed in Ri Kyŏng-hye's writings does not challenge the patriarchal state but, instead, adopts the male lexicon and uses it to self-inscribe women's identity within the established sexist order. Ri Kyŏng-hye articulates and valorizes the patriarchal discourse through a biographical account of Kim Il Sung's wife, Kim Chŏng-suk. Ri exalts the way in which Kim Chŏng-suk has helped women across the DPRK to become integrated into the patriarchal political order: "One day, before liberation, Comrade Kim Chŏng-suk went to a house located in the district of Sŏngyo in Pyongyang and met the wife of a manual laborer who had been struggling to make a living. The wife asked, 'I was told that our People are the best in the world. Are we wives also part of the People? Is it true that once we join the Women's League we have to speak well?' "[56]

The women in Ri Kyŏng-hye's narrative represent a long history of disenfranchised women in a male-dominated society. They are economically, socially, and politically heterogeneous. The only commonality that these women share is the Korean language and social and cultural oppression by the patriarchal political order. When the DPRK was established in 1948, these women found hope. The two questions that the wife asks in the fictionalized anecdote above demonstrate women's passage into the male-dominated political system. She is not challenging the chauvinistic state but rather asking to participate in it. The wife has only heard about the People (or Kimilsungist citizens) and inquires as to the method through which she can become integrated. "Are wives also part of the People?" is an innocent, pure, and simplistic (*sobakham*) question. To Kim Chŏng-suk, this is a silly question. Why, of course, the wives are part of the People. What else would they be in the DPRK? The wives are *naturally* part of the People; they have been *naturalized* as public and domestic servants without their consent. Through this question, the wives become a singular group of wives and mothers under the patriarchal state and no longer heterogeneous women.

According to *Resolving the Woman Question,* women did not enter the workforce because of the communist economic revolution but rather because of Kim Il Sung's visionary providence that places them in the public domain through the exemplification of his wife Kim Chŏng-suk. Kim Chŏng-suk was depicted as the exemplary wife of the DPRK who enlightened other women to accept the state-desired role of both wife and mother. Anecdotes constantly refer to the privileged life of Kim Chŏng-suk in supporting her husband, Kim Il Sung, and raising her son, Kim Jong Il. For Kim Chŏng-suk, the laborer's wife appears to ask a simple question, but this question is anything but simple.

The second question is equally, if not more, important to sustaining the patriarchal system: "Is it true that once we join the Women's League we have to speak well?" Here there is a sense of reluctance to join the political system as it is predicated on speaking the male discourse. In various articles in *Chosŏn yŏsŏng* (Korean Women) published in the late 1960s, women voiced their political opinions in support of the state. They called on the women of the DPRK to do well in their respective workplaces and at home, all with the intention of pleasing Kim Il Sung. None of these articles ever challenged the state or resisted the patriarchal political order. To speak well meant to recite the state-desired prescriptions of wifehood and motherhood. In Ri Kyŏng-hye's writing, women never had a chance to resist the encroaching political system; they were already coalesced as subjects and required to speak a language foreign to them. The state instructed women to appropriate the correct language to perform the state-desired femininity. This was because the state suspected a threat to the political order if women were to be neglected in state affairs. It was a deliberate act to bind women into one homogeneous group.

In *Resolving the Woman Question,* Ri Kyŏng-hye raises shamanism and superstition (*misin*), widespread in the DPRK, as a cultural problem that has affected women more than the political system. Ri gives credit to Kim Il Sung for liberating women from ignorance and illiteracy so that they realized the materiality of the world and ceased their dependence on ethereal phenomena.[57] North Korean women were targets of criticism up to the time Ri wrote her exposition for continuing to rely on shamanism and superstition in their daily practices. Ri says, "Even after liberation, women, who practice shamanism in their daily lives, continue to hinder the construction of the state."[58] Women were to cast away the outdated practices and learn the science of Juche ideology, which Kim Jong Il claimed to be the most scientific and rational of all ideologies.[59] The state needed to find a way to pull women away from their dependence on shamanism and incorporate them into the patriarchal system.

Ri Kyŏng-hye takes a lengthy yet interesting diversion in her argument that connects North Korean women with the problem of the persistence of shamanism in the DPRK. Ri Kyŏng-hye believes that women's dependence on superstition derives from a lack of correct political education. She praises Kim Il Sung for establishing local schools throughout the remote parts of the country for men and women to attend. But then she claims that the construction of schools in local areas and the collectivization of land were concurrent projects of the state. In other words, the collectivization of land in the mid-1940s served not only to eliminate oppressive landlords and give the land to the peasants and farmers but also to identify sites where villagers had been practicing shamanism. According to Ri Kyŏng-hye, part of the state's cartographic agenda to map every village was effectively to identify and eliminate shamans. Villagers would have to depend on Kim Il Sung rather than on shamans for spiritual answers. After this brief reinterpretation of the history of Kim Il Sung's collectivization of land, Ri Kyŏng-hye proceeds to how the Great Leader promoted gender equality in the DPRK.

The DPRK needed workers, and women were an unexploited labor force. The state found a way to draw women into the public sphere and call it social progress. The elimination of shamans and the erection of schools throughout the country provided women (and men) a new form of education. It was developed around reading the hagiographies of Kang Pan-sŏk and Kim Chŏng-suk, which was the primary method of introducing women to male politics and achieving the discursive construction of motherhood in the DPRK in order to control women in both the public and private spheres.

Olga Voronina astutely states, "The discussion is never about the participation of women in politics, but only about drawing them in."[60] The state's oppressive demands for women to acquire and emulate the male discourse are indeed an agenda to engineer a woman's soul without actually desiring her participation in politics. The woman question "Are wives also part of the People?" or, read another way, "Must wives be part of the People?" is effectively erased and silenced, ushering the modal discourse of motherhood into the male-centered lexicon. The state assures women that motherhood is the true form of liberation and happiness.[61]

The pursuit of sexual equality is never addressed in the state-sponsored feminism of the DPRK; instead, state feminist discourse continues to focus on socially normalized gender behavior and the duties women and men are designated to perform in the patriarchal state. The DPRK does not deny patriarchal governance but enforces its legitimacy through its cultural practice, placing the man as the head of the household / ruler of the nation and women as the subjugated. Women, then, are perpetually oppressed in nearly every aspect of the North Korean social system dominated by men, despite the socialized institutions that were established to support the "equality" of the sexes.

In this chapter, through the iconographies of Kang Pan-sŏk and Kim Chŏng-suk, I have examined the literary lexicon of a desexualized motherhood and wifehood devised to serve a specific teleological state agenda on women. In Ri Kyŏng-hye's *Resolving the Woman Question*, for example, the expectation for women to remain monogamously attached to the patriarchal state is never questioned or challenged. In the 1980s, despite the vociferous demands for women to emulate the state-prescribed ideal of motherhood and wifehood in the majority of works of fiction, a number of works resist the hegemonic discourse. In the next chapter, I will analyze how the language in fiction can disrupt (even if only for a moment) the development of politically conscious individuals as they struggle with sexual desire. Although the state desires a uniform interpretation and reading of fiction, the language of affection and sexuality becomes the site of contention and indeterminacy, thus decentering and displacing the state-desired singular meaning.

CHAPTER TWO

Kiss and Tell

Words That Come Undone

> Sŏk-ch'un was so driven by his impulses that he reached his hands out and grabbed Sun-hŭi's hands. She felt a little bashful, but she allowed him to hold her hands.
>
> *Paek Nam-nyong, Friend*

Jun-sang and Mi-ran looked forward to meeting each other at night just as the lights in Pyongyang went out. As North Korea faced problems during the Arduous March in the 1990s with generating and maintaining electricity throughout the country, streetlights and other lights in residential areas would be turned off at night, inviting the serenity of darkness to dwell until the next morning. The nation's lack of electricity helped lovers to meet at night in absolute darkness and avoid public scrutiny.[1] At times, they experienced close calls. One night, Jun-sang secretly visited Mi-ran at her home, where she had been alone. Her father unexpectedly returned home from work earlier than usual, and Jun-sang had to hide until it was safe for him to make an exit. "Later, Jun-sang and Mi-ran laughed for hours about these incidents. The truth was that they enjoyed deceiving their parents. The secrecy was not merely necessary, it was fun. It injected a frisson of the illicit and gave them a shared psychic space in a society where privacy didn't exist. It was a relatively safe way to rebel against the confines of their lives."[2]

In *Nothing to Envy*, Barbara Demick describes the quotidian life of North Koreans through interviews with defectors. She reveals ways in which one particular interviewee evaded the ominous gaze of the Party and her parents to gratify her sexual desires. Demick's narrative is more than the typical defector odyssey of a formerly enslaved North Korean who fought his way through the thickets of the totalitarian regime to find salvation on the shores of South Korean democracy. For Demick, the everyday life of a North Korean entails sexual life and erotic pleasures.

Although *Nothing to Envy* is not about sexual experiences of North Koreans, Demick's portrayal of Mi-ran's encounter with Jun-sang is playful with a hint of mischievousness. Mi-ran, who now lives in South Korea, feels safer now talking openly about her moonlight trysts, albeit still a little reserved and embarrassed, but her sexual secret with Jun-sang in North Korea provided a "shared psychic space" that was perhaps more playful than the sexual experience itself. Demick says that Mi-ran and Jun-sang's secrecy was a "safe way to rebel" against the strictures of the state in which they lived. It is not so much the actual encounter with Jun-sang that has a lasting impression on Mi-ran but the secret, the keeping of the secret, the speaking about the secret to a foreign journalist, and Demick's reconstruction of that secret. Demick demonstrates that for North Koreans sexual desire and sexual encounters can have playful effects of breaking the social rules that confine their lives.

In this chapter I explore two fundamental critiques of sexual desire in my reading of 1980s North Korean fiction. First, I take the Foucauldian approach that the law does not repress desire but rather generates it through socialized institutions and discursive instruments for regulating power. In the case of Jung-san and Mi-ran, their romantic rendezvous were more than deliberate resistance of social and political codes against sexuality. It may appear as though their expression of love was a daring gesture to engage secretive, private emotions hidden beneath the surface of the ascetic, public demeanor of the state-prescribed revolutionary. However, it is important to note that the North Korean state provided the conditions for them to gratify their sexual desires by conveniently shutting off the electrical power throughout the city. Rather than reducing Jung-san's and Mi-ran's sexual desire to libido in the Freudian sense, we must also see their tryst as the effect of circumstantial and institutional design. Additionally, Mi-ran's confession of sexual relations with Jung-san to a foreign journalist reveals sexuality as the object of the speaking subject. That is, desire is generated through the speaker and reproduced through Demick's writing.

My opposition to Freud's concept of repressed sexual drives is based on volume 1 of Foucault's *History of Sexuality*, where he says, "Rather than the uniform concern to hide sex, rather than a general prudishness of language, what distinguishes these last three centuries is the variety, the wide dispersion of devices that were invented for speaking about it, for having it be spoken about, for inducing it to speak of itself, for listening, recording, transcribing, and redistributing what is said about it."[3] Foucault is most concerned with the way in which sex is put into discourse and the effects or functioning power that discourse has had on, around, and within the body. I began this chapter with the anecdote of Mi-ran's relationship with Jung-san in order to elucidate how sexual desire in North Korean fictional works is not simply prohibited or repressed by the draconian state but rather may be disclosed and articulated to an interlocutor through discursive forms (e.g., confession, narration, medical reports, and personal letters) by which the social and cultural prohibition against open sexuality serves to produce and reproduce desire in various forms.

My second point of departure is what Cathy Popkin calls the "kiss and tell" storytelling strategy. Popkin's analysis of Anton Chekov's short story "The Kiss" is an assessment of Chekov's storytelling skill. Popkin says, "The prerequisite for the existence of narrative is contingent on the quality of the tale."[4] The questions that obsessed Chekov as a storyteller—Has something happened or not? Was it extraordinary or not? And is it worth telling or not?—also concern the modality of storytelling in North Korean fiction. In North Korean romantic plots, lovers commit their sexual act in private and openly confess the act to a third party without the slightest shame or regret. The lovers do not repress their sexual desires but carry them out in the "kiss and tell" narrative. According to Popkin, the expression "kiss and tell" links two indiscretions, two irrepressible desires, casting one oral function as the necessary complement of the other—as if without the indiscretion of the kiss there is nothing to tell.[5] This is because "kiss and tell" not only reports the kiss but also operates like one, connecting the erotic intimacy to the seductive design of storytelling.

In this chapter, I explore the "kiss and tell" modality of storytelling as speech acts that question the intentionality of the speaking subject in the larger context of reading and understanding North Korean literature. The intentions of the speaker's speech act always risk irony in the very linguistic performance that is supposed to attach the utterance to its speaker. For example, all state-produced North Korean literature is supposed to articulate the Party's directives and deliver a teleological message to readers. The intention of North Korean writers is supposed to be clear and direct, without ambiguity or uncertainty. However, North Korean literature as a speech act is always haunted by the possibility of misunderstanding, misinterpretation, and misreading because of the instability of the language that it uses to construct its narrative. Despite the state's attempt at purifying fiction from moral or political contamination, North Korean literature (and literature in general) is already contaminated by uncertainties that are present in the text, which then condition the possibility of having the text come undone.

The sexual encounters that I discuss in this chapter are not explicit or gratuitous descriptions of eroticism. I am neither claiming nor certifying that North Korean writers intentionally inscribed sexual activity into their texts. My reading of sexual activities in North Korean narratives is found in the very language, the very speech acts that the speaking subject uses to indicate his or her intentionality of being an ardent revolutionary. For me, the claim of loving the leader in these texts is a schizophrenic speech act that reveals the unstable and constantly changing self, constructed on multiple intersections of discourses, desires, and relations with others. My purpose is to demonstrate the instability and therefore the impossibility of the trajectory of North Korean fiction that decides once and for all the intention of the writer, the speaking subject in the narrative, and the text itself within the seemingly impervious totality of literary discourse.

The Eternal Love Triangle

Characters in North Korean fiction in the 1980s learn that the course of their true love for another person never did run smoothly and that the state's demand to live a political life and to love only Kim Il Sung interferes with the pursuit of happiness in personal pleasures. But this is not how the Party wants readers to interpret a story; it is supposed to be the other way around. The characters in North Korean fiction learn that the course of their true love for Kim Il Sung never did run smoothly and that obstacles and conflicts had divided their emotions for the leader. Other thoughts and feelings interfered with the character's pursuit of ideological perfection. In the end, the characters must learn to reconfirm their love for the state, the Party, and the Great Leader.

In *Reading North Korea*, Sonia Ryang explains the internal logic of how actual North Koreans feel and think about Kim Il Sung in literary narratives. As a man and a woman face each other with affection, their sense of true love is not complete until they realize that their love is grounded in their devotion to Kim Il Sung. The Party projects one's loyalty to Kim Il Sung as the only quality that makes marriage and raising a family worthwhile. Ryang calls this the "eternal triangle":

> North Korean love flows only in one direction: from the people to Kim, from a people who constantly strive to elevate their love for Kim to an increasingly higher and purer level, where Kim's a priori love for the people is taken for granted. Furthermore, the people's love for Kim Il Sung is to be identified through their ties with each other in their common journey of dedication and devotion toward him. Along the long journey taken to demonstrate their loyalty toward Kim, men and women find companions in each other. This is how North Korean love forms an eternal triangle.[6]

Romantic plots are common in North Korean fiction, as they reveal the emotional interactions between two revolutionaries and how their love for each other must be directed at the Great Leader. In Sonia Ryang's triangular model, a true revolutionary expresses his or her love for the construction of the Kimilsungist state—the prototypical end-all rhetoric of North Korean political discourse. All of the descriptions of ascetic revolutionaries in North Korean fiction focus on their actions overcoming obstacles that might hinder the achievement of revolution rather than on gratifying their personal desires. The male hero suspends or exorcises his sexual desire for the woman until he successfully accomplishes his task. Meanwhile, the woman not only waits for her lover to return to her, but she also observes his heroism. When the hero succeeds in his task, he wins his lover's hand in marriage, and together they honor Kim Il Sung. Sonia Ryang asserts that, even if one character has fallen madly in love with another, he or she learns throughout the narrative that the greatest pleasure is in pleasing the Great Leader. Man and woman, husband and wife appear to be desexualized, utilitarian subjects of the state. Yet this model is not entirely unique to North Korean fiction.

In *The Soviet Novel*, Katerina Clark claims that love is an "auxiliary ingredient" in the plot, in that the hero's love life is not valuable in itself; it serves only to aid him in fulfilling his tasks and attaining "consciousness."[7] Western observers of Soviet fiction have snidely called this kind of plot structure "boy-gets-tractor, boy-gets-girl," a reductive understanding of socialist realist narrative structures. The hero overcomes his crisis, is celebrated by the collective, and wins his lover's hand in marriage. The hero does not necessarily need to obtain "the girl" as long as he completes his public task, which is inextricably tied to his quest for "consciousness."[8] Oleg in *The Young Guard* and Gleb in *Cement* are examples of heroes who devote their energy to their political tasks rather than occupying their thoughts with bourgeois emotions of love. Clark adds that the puritanism of socialist realism prevents the woman from being an erotic object and that she becomes a spiritual companion and a means of adding to the new generation of the "family."[9] Clark admits that there are variants of love, sex, and eroticism in Soviet fiction in the 1930s. However, for Clark, all such impulses are expressions of spontaneous and individualistic willfulness that need to be mastered: the hero must attain an extrapersonal perspective.[10]

In *Revolution of the Heart*, Haiyan Lee describes a similar situation in China during the May Fourth era in the 1920s that theorized a hierarchical binary of revolution and love in literature and the struggle to construct a new heroic subject. Political ideologues, according to Lee, called for the postponement of love and the subordination of sexual relationships to the revolutionary agenda.[11] In the 1920s, Chinese youths voiced their ideas about love, marriage, and sex in magazines. They determined that love was a threat to the revolution because it disrupts and divides an individual's revolutionary passion. Lee says, "[Love] restricts one's attention to personal loss and gain, thereby causing one to lose sight of the larger enterprise."[12] Eroticism, sexuality, and romantic tales tapped into the personal—all too personal—and therefore seduced people away from revolution.

Lee refers to a new set of rhetoric that pervaded Chinese fiction, which she calls the "socialist grammar of emotion." The socialist grammar of emotion defines the collective sentiment by which love is to be exclusively aligned with a new universal category: class. "A socialist subject 'loves' another socialist subject for his or her class belonging, not for his or her moral qualities, intellectual prowess, economic standing, social status, sexual appeal."[13] Lee offers Ding Ling's short story "Du Wanxiang" as an example of a wife (Wanxiang) who overcomes her domestic problems and lack of spousal affection by finding her true socialist self among the working class. Wanxiang not only transforms her political consciousness through the collective but also changes her manner of speaking, which is now aligned with the correct socialist grammar. Wanxiang's externalized rhetoric coincides with her internal political emotions, proving her love for the collective supersedes all other forms of individualistic love.

Much as in May Fourth fiction, romantic love between young adults in North Korean literature must not occupy the central theme of the novel but may only supplement the revolution. The critical difference between Chinese and North Korean fiction is North Korea's supplanting of love for the revolution or class-consciousness with rhetoric expressing platonic love for Kim Il Sung. Romantic love must not interfere in this enterprise, and it certainly must not be obstructive to the characters' devotion to Kim Il Sung. Unlike Chinese critics of romantic tales, North Korean literary critics in both *Chosŏn munhak* (Korean Literature) and the *DPRK Almanac* from the 1970s and 1980s have never publicly approved of a short story, novella, or novel for its beautified romantic plot devoid of the protagonists' love for the Great Leader. Perhaps the fictional piece that has come closest to receiving the Party's recognition for its love content may be Nam Tae-hyŏn's novella *Ch'ŏngch'un songga* (Hymn of Youth, 1987), regarding which the critic in the *DPRK Almanac* said: "Many literary works were created this past year such as Nam Tae-hyŏn's *Ch'ŏngch'un songga*, which depicted our era's young adult intellectuals' heart, passion, conscience, and love."[14] "Heart" refers to the characters' platonic love for Kim Il Sung, and "love" refers to the romantic plot between two young intellectuals in the novella. Yet, even in the critic's list of the novel's aesthetic qualities, romantic love comes last, which may be indicative of the state's discursive attempts to subordinate such ephemeral passion to the more important revolutionary mindset that all North Korean fiction must possess and articulate. The Party's instructive measures enjoin youths to curtail sexual relationships that could lead them astray from their ethical responsibilities to the state.

In *Chosŏn ch'ŏngnyŏnŭi changjŏm* (The Virtue of Korean Youth, 1991), North Korean sociologists Ch'oe Chŏng-hyŏn and Kim Min-ae map out the behavior, spirit, duty, and attitude of the ideal North Korean youth. Their study valorizes the youth through the historiography of revolutionaries from the Japanese colonial period to the present day. In the preface to their book, Ch'oe and Kim write: "The youth of today are showing inherent qualities of noble virtue through their devotion and filial piety to the Party and the Great Leader, burning nationalism and collectivism, camaraderie and loyalty, organization and administration, diligence and simplicity, and noble behavioral ethics."[15] For Ch'oe and Kim, political consciousness—both the understanding of Kimilsungism and expressing platonic love for Kim Il Sung—is the monad of the individual that determines his or her subjectivity to the state and normalizes his or her behavior and speech acts in everyday life.

Ch'oe and Kim remind the youth that true and meaningful life derives only from the Party and the Great Leader's directives, eliminating the possibility of other discourses that could destabilize the subjectivity of the youth.[16] Overdetermination to acquire political consciousness is the rhetorical strategy to silence or efface other forms of thought and desires. The acquisition of the correct political discourse is understood to answer and resolve all existential crises and the ontological reality of North Koreans. Not adhering to the Great Leader's directives, then, results in self-destruction and worthlessness as a citizen of the DPRK. Ch'oe and Kim go so far as to argue that apart from these directives the youth will not find worth in their lives or hope in their futures. A North Korean individual's self-worth is determined by his or her undivided platonic love for the Great Leader, which also verifies the individual's monadic identity. Centering Kim Il Sung in one's unified identity is, according to Ch'oe and Kim, the correct perspective for youth in the DPRK to achieve.[17] A unified self is not a composite of disparate identities but the elimination of otherness within the predetermined self-identity. Becoming a Kimilsungist revolutionary, then, according to Ch'oe and Kim, is not simply acquiring a new set of linguistics and behaviors to add to the already existing self that predates the knowledge of Kimilsungism but rather realizing that the self was already inclined to be revolutionary at its very core and, therefore, requires a defensive strategy against wanton behavior and other detrimental elements. Ch'oe and Kim's choice of words to argue for the discourse of Kimilsungism excludes the possibility of otherness and navigates cautiously around ideas that might recognize the existence of otherness.

The kind of love mentioned in Ch'oe and Kim's book is camaraderie, or literally comrade-love (*tongji-ae*). According to the authors, true love can only occur when a man and a woman find themselves on the single path toward revolution.[18] Comrade-love requires individuals to prioritize Kim Il Sung, the Party, and the state above all other material objects or personal and private emotions. Ch'oe and Kim say, "Revolutionary comrade-love regards sociopolitical life as more important than physical life, and it is not derived from family ties or compassion but from sociopolitical and revolutionary ties."[19] What Ch'oe and Kim expect from youth is materialized in North Korean fiction, which exemplifies the correct method of expressing and verbalizing platonic love for Kim Il Sung and comrade-love among the people. Comrade-love is essentially the noblest and the most ideal love that is shared among fellow North Korean comrades, which means that, much like platonic love, comrade-love is by no means erotic or sexual. Comrades in fiction are not supposed to gaze at each other with perverse sexual thoughts or carnal desires; their minds are supposed to be set on higher goals for the state. Much as the state discourse transforms men and women into desexualized revolutionaries, as seen in Chapter 1, it also attempts to transform the discourse of erotic love into comrade-love.

Ch'oe and Kim differentiate familial bonds from revolutionary bonds in order to map out the metaphysical domain of the concept of love. On the most rudimentary level of love, Ch'oe and Kim argue, the family develops physical love, a bond between mother and child. This kind of love has its limits because the child will eventually outgrow his dependence on his mother and will need to leave the domestic space for the public space. As the child experiences life outside of domesticity, he learns that dwelling among his comrades is the highest kind of love. Thus, say Ch'oe and Kim, comrade-love is realized in the child's journey in the public world, which lies beyond the natural bond between family members. The child's realization of comrade-love is the revolutionary consciousness that prioritizes his political life over his family life. By prioritizing sociopolitical life above physical life, Ch'oe and Kim reiterate the Juche ideology of man as the center of the world and the requirement to conquer his natural surroundings.[20] Individuals must hone the power to dominate their sexual, natural urges. Ch'oe and Kim's intentions seem clear; they rearticulate Party directives that physical life of comrades is subordinate to the sociopolitical life of living for Kim Il Sung.

Not once do Ch'oe and Kim mention sexuality or eroticism in their book; they remain silent about the issue, or at least they try to. Unlike the explicit anti-sex slogans seen in the Soviet Union in the 1920s that said "Sex: Enemy of the Revolution,"[21] North Korean official discourse hardly (if ever) mentions sexuality or eroticism as one of the vices in the Kimilsungist revolution. Whereas bourgeois, revisionism, reactionaries, conservatism, capitalism, imperialism, and other negative classifications commonplace in communist discourse are mentioned readily in state media such as Kim Il Sung's and Kim Jong Il's speeches, films, and fiction, gratuitous sexual depictions are avoided. Ch'oe and Kim's explicit silence on sexual matters is their implicit way of diverting attention from the topic.

The irony is that the North Korean state can only survive when revolutionary individuals have sexual relations. Whether this relation is through marriage, premarital sex, extramarital affairs, or other forms of sexual encounter that enable procreation, the individual will have to learn to balance and negotiate his platonic, comrade-love with erotic love. In other words, what Ch'oe and Kim fail to mention in their book is that a community is dependent on the sexual activities of individuals rather than on the individuals' political consciousness in order to sustain the cycle of life. This seems rather obvious and too simplistic even for Ch'oe and Kim when they assert that comrade-love is the only form of love of which the youth of the present generation should be mindful.

Comrade-love and revolution are one in the same, according to the North Korean sociologist Kwak Yŏng-ch'an. In *Ch'amdwen samgwa ch'ŏngch'un* (True Life and Youth, 1986), Kwak says, "Love and revolution, revolution and love. These two must unite so that love can become true love and revolution can become true revolution."[22] Kwak Yŏng-ch'an reiterates the state discourse that a spouse or a lover is a fellow revolutionary comrade, who must be perceived as more than a sexually desirable individual. This kind of discourse makes matrimony completely utilitarian, to the extent that sexual intercourse would only be for the purpose of procreation and not for personal pleasure. Openly discussing revolution or one's love for the revolution is permissible and encouraged, but anything about one's private sexuality is excluded from public discourse as part of the unwritten and unspoken code of sexual behavior. North Korean propaganda stands on the frontline to safeguard state-sanctioned sexual morality by exemplifying images of model citizens, who are supposed to be seen as desexualized revolutionaries. These figures contain the passion for the revolution in their eyes and have their gaze set beyond the horizon to indicate the dawning of a new future.

The individual in fiction expresses his or her gratitude and love for Kim Il Sung, the Party, and the state in accordance with socially and politically constructed rhetoric. The timing is precise and calculated; the words are saccharine, packed with a sentimental tone. A male character typically reminisces about the revolutionary days when Kim Il Sung single-handedly drove out the Japanese imperialists, liberating Korea from the chains of colonialism. The thought alone is enough for any character to feel compelled to praise the Great Leader. A character may recall a time when Kim Il Sung visited him and complimented him. The leader's encouraging words are enough to fill the character's eyes with tears. In another instance, a character may misbehave and be reprimanded by a local leader. "Don't you know that your misbehavior pains our dear comrade Kim Il Sung?" is prototypical rhetoric that is used to correct a misguided character in fiction, reminding the character that the Great Leader is always watching him. The character, then, changes his attitude and recommits to living a life for only Kim Il Sung.

North Korean fiction serves as textbooks for readers to adopt new verbiage or what Haiyan Lee calls the socialist grammar of emotion. The copious fiction produced in North Korean monthly journals such as *Chosŏn munhak*[23] and *Chŏllima*[24] exemplifies the repeated training writers underwent to normalize the political discourse honoring Kim Il Sung. Starting from the late 1960s, fiction methodically systematized or engineered a plot structure that simplified the relationship between characters in favor of installing Kim Il Sung and his revolutionary activities as the moral impetus and the driving force behind each narrative. Characters work in various sectors of industry or risk their lives in their workplace for the sake of pleasing the Great Leader. For example, in Sŏ Chŏng-ho's short story "Padaka ch'ŏnyŏdŭl" (Young Women of the Sea, 1974),[25] fisherwomen nearly drown collecting kelp. When the manager scolds the women for endangering their lives, they respond, "We were only thinking about the ways to please our Dear Great Leader and to have our people eat well."

The greatest satisfaction for this type of character, particularly in 1970s fiction, derives from devotion to Kim Il Sung, even at the expense of risking one's own life. The desire to revolutionize the nation with the socialist creed that characters possessed in literary works in the 1960s changes to conflate personal pleasure with pleasing the Great Leader in the 1970s. Individualistic desires in North Korean fiction exist insofar as they ultimately correspond with the desire of the state. A phrase like "We were only thinking about the ways to please our Dear Great Leader" encapsulates a character's personal desire, an orgasmic excitement that individualizes a character's responsibilities to herself as a Kimilsungist revolutionary. Other characters in the narrative do not necessarily have to witness one's performance for the state; but, if others observe, watch, or gaze at the character's actions, it heightens the orgasmic intensity, knowing that his or her actions satisfies many.

No matter what the narrative is about or where it takes place, characters display a hyperbolic emotional euphoria when they express their commitment to the nation, Party, and Kim Il Sung. Tears of overwhelming joy that stream down faces of characters when Kim Il Sung stands before them are not gender specific in North Korean fiction but applicable to everyone in the DRK. Such emotional images project the desirable verbal and bodily behavior onto North Korean society, reinforcing an imagined and homogeneous collective of Kimilsungist revolutionaries.

North Korean fiction is designed to subordinate the hero or heroine's love for the opposite sex so that one's self-cultivating life in the Kim Il Sung–centric state can be fully actualized. Devotion to Kim Il Sung is a physical act, a mental determination, and an emotional justification to be loyal vanguards of the leader as comrades prepare to build a revolutionary nuclear family. Love that does not contribute to the edification of the people's political ideology is seen as tainted with bourgeois backward ideology and harmful for both individuals and the nation.[26] North Korean literature, then, functions as a moral and ethical map on which individuals in the narrative navigate through their relations with each other in order to pursue and arrive at their ultimate destination: pleasing the leader. However, the very discourse that is used to desexualize the relationship between man and woman in fiction may come undone as it actually produces sexually charged images of them and uncontrollably generates their reproduction.

Generating Desire from Linguistic Codes of Affection

According to Kim Jong Il, love, sex, or even a discussion on love has no place in the consciousness of the socialist hero. Kim Jong Il criticized a film called *Nyŏsŏng ttŭlaktto unjŏnsa* (A Woman Tractor Driver, 1970) for reflecting a bourgeois lifestyle of leisure in his speech "Let Us Create More Revolutionary Films Based on Socialist Life": "The kind of character which finds pleasure in gossip about unfaithful love and in trivial personal affairs does not suit the sound ideal and life of our contemporary young people. Not even the smallest element of bourgeois ideology, feudal-Confucian ideas, revisionism or any other unsound ideas has its place in revolutionary cinema."[27]

According to Kim Jong Il, heroes and heroines who engage in illicit affairs only arouse the desire to fulfill their sexual appetites. He equates explicit sexuality with unsound ideas not because sex (or talking about sex) is sinful in and of itself but because sex ought to be a public matter that the state can control and manage. Sexuality is not supposed to be explored by individuals in the privacy of their bedrooms but rather coded, regulated, and administered by the state's discourse. Kim Jong Il attaches antistate labels (bourgeois ideology, feudal Confucian ideas, revisionism, and so forth) on sex as a way of instilling guilt in the people and threatening them with juridical consequences. He refers "young people" to the state-prescribed virgins, who abstain from physical contact with the opposite sex along with remaining pure at heart.

The prescriptions and expectations for women in literature to remain virgins are coded in the North Korean cultural practice of dating and marriage. It is the responsibility of the woman to remain chaste for her future husband. Meanwhile, she is expected to fend off any sexual advances from men. Therefore, a promiscuous woman is not only culturally and socially disgraced but also morally burdened for failing to live up to the Party's expectations. Her licentious sexuality is both a physical and a symbolic breach of cultural and political integrity. The man is also responsible for remaining chaste before marriage, but the literary discourse on abstinence applies more to women than it does to men.

This is an obvious double standard that gives men the advantage of satisfying their desire to be the first to conquer a woman's body. Julia Kristeva says, "Only the man will be entitled to sexual pleasures. . . . The society protects itself from the *jouissance* that can drive it to madness or revolution: it keeps itself stable, permanent, eternal."[28] The discourse in North Korean fiction to keep women chaste and virginal is not for their safety and well-being but to give men the illusion of sexual potency and patriarchal authority. As Anke Bernau says in *Virgins: A Cultural History*, "The virginal body is never just—or perhaps is simply never—a real body, but rather always determined by cultural contexts and traditions."[29] Virginity, for Bernau, not only refers to sexually inexperienced women, but is a cultural, political, and sociological practice performed between gender identities in a patriarchal system through which Christian ideas and values from the Middle Ages have shaped modern Western society. Much of Bernau's exploration of virginity can be applied to North Korea's systematic discourse on the revolutionary heroine, whose subjectivity is constructed on her sexual abstinence and her religious devotion to the leader. The discourse that erects the image of Kim Il Sung simultaneously erects the discourse on the virginal heroines, who are not to be distracted from their revolutionary duties and adulterated by perverse thoughts on sexuality.

Discourse on virginity has had a significant impact on imagining the ideal North Korean woman. The overtly masculine literary culture in North Korea constructs and perpetuates (intentionally or unintentionally) socially desirable femaleness in narratives, which prescribes sexual attraction toward women who embody such femininity. Gendered discourse on virginity is not a prohibitive measure to deter men and women from having sex or to repress the desire for sex. It is, instead, a discursive system of power to control and monitor the ways in which men and women ought to behave and conduct themselves in both the private and public domains. North Korean fiction gave rise to modern sexuality (the state-desired femininity and masculinity) in its relation to the construction of gender (the state's assumptive definition of the woman and the man), particularly desire toward individuals of the opposite sex. In short, North Korea's discursive construction of the virgin woman normalizes the way men fantasize about women as sexual objects of domination rather than as revolutionary comrades.

Viewed according to today's Western standards of sexuality, most of the romantic plots in North Korean fiction can be characterized as puritanical and prudish, where the female characters are often bashful, coy, and coquettish toward the male characters. Hardly any public display of affection—holding hands, embracing, and kissing—occurs between a man and a woman in many of these literary works. North Korean men are depicted either as chivalrous gentlemen, who are conscientious about their behavior and etiquette around women, or as artless men, who fumble with their words in the presence of women. North Korean women often have their heads lowered and are reticent to speak their opinions freely and openly, which is thought to display their most feminine qualities. Some of these masculine and feminine characteristics and behaviors may change or be represented differently in fiction, as they are contingent on the social and historical contexts. Yet premarital sex, extramarital affairs, sexual promiscuity, prostitution, pornography, masturbation, homosexuality, and teenage pregnancies are all considered immoral and inappropriate acts embedded in the unspoken and unwritten cultural codes of the DPRK.

Desire for the other (whoever or whatever this other may be) is controlled and directed away from individualistic *jouissance*, and toward this end the North Korean state enforces repressive discourse on the people. Every cultural product and media form appears to abide by the state's regulations against sexuality—disseminating a singular version of a desexualized, homogeneous culture. However, it would be reductive to claim that North Korea is a backward or repressive state because sexuality is not as open and liberal as in contemporary Western countries. Dispersing and transferring power over the human body as a systematic unit of epistemic discourse and biopolitics in North Korean society has been instrumental in the state use of sexuality to proscribe women from the patriarchal political order since the formative years of the country's establishment and in Korea's long history as a Confucian-dominated society. If the difference is measured not by how much more Western countries proliferate sexuality than the DPRK but rather by how sexuality is coded, normalized, and administered in various class, ethnic, and religious groups, social institutions, bureaucracies, and cultural discourses, then more similarities than differences exist between Western and North Korean societies. Much like other cultures around the world,

North Korea constructs its sexual codes and regulates them judiciously in literary discourse, through medicalization, media representations, art, music, various forms of popular culture, and foreign influences, which affect the imaginations of gendered identities and sexualized bodies.

One of the lasting tales in Korean history that is reproduced in diverse media forms is the tale of Ch'un-hyang, which is a moral story of a chaste wife who is also the epitome of erotic beauty and sexuality, as she is the daughter of a *kisaeng*, or courtesan.[30] Although North Korea had made the legendary tale into a film production called *The Tale of Ch'un-hyang* (1980), South Korean filmmaker Sin Sang-ok came to North Korea and remade the tale of Ch'un-hyang as *Love, Love, My Love* (1984) with bolder expressions of sexual desire and concrete physical imagery.[31] Ch'un-hyang embodies and represents the intersections of state-prescribed wifehood, moral chastity, a national icon, and an object of erotic desire for the male gaze. Ch'un-hyang is not the only exception to prudish imaginations of women in North Korea. In Pyongyang, there is a district called Wŏl-hyang that is devoted to celebrating Kye Wŏl-hyang, the *kisaeng* who sacrificed her life by taking the life of a Japanese military officer during the invasion of Korea in 1593. She is recognized as one of the greatest national martyrs in North Korea, and the neighborhood erected a shrine for her with restaurants and souvenir shops for consumption by tourists and locals. Sexualized images of Kye Wŏl-hyang decorate the small neighborhood, objectifying the national heroine for male pleasure. And, finally, *Flower Girl* is yet another popular film in North Korea whose heroine embodies national pride and physical beauty. Hong Yŏng-hŭi, who played the main role of Kkot-bun, became a quintessential icon of purity, beauty, and sexuality. She appeared on magazine covers, the North Korean currency, posters, murals, and other media forms, all of which reproduced her "virginal" smiling face. As much as the film impacted North Korean cinematic history, Hong Yŏng-hŭi and her sensual smile became a national emblem of the desiring gaze.

In *Illusive Utopia*, Suk-Young Kim argues that sexuality and eroticism are perhaps most evident in North Korea's visual culture, which has attempted to "cleanse" itself of sexualizing expressions. She says, "But as ironic as it may sound, art endorsed and sponsored by the state is the only sphere where members of the society can explore the clandestine visual pleasure of the sexualized gaze, since any form of art expressing individual erotic desires does not openly exist for public consumption."[32] Indeed, it is ironic at first sight how the state creates its own inconsistencies and incongruities through the very political medium that is supposed to unify, homogenize, and desexualize the society. At the same time, it is not so much ironic as unavoidable that sexuality and erotic desires generate from North Korea's visual culture. The state has to come to realize that desire cannot be controlled and interpretations cannot be predetermined.

Inasmuch as North Korean visual culture evokes sexual desire, literature also explores the world of sexual imagination through the linguistic code of affection in dialogue, narrator's descriptions, and characters' psyches. In North Korean fiction, conversations between men and women are gendered and designed in a way that reveals a dominating patriarchal social order. Men typically speak to women in informal speech, while women speak to men in the honorific manner. Even between lovers, the man speaks more assertively and the woman responds passively. For example, in Kim Mun-ch'ang's *T'anbu* (Miners, 1986), Chin-ho and Mi-sun take a stroll together after Mi-sun has waited for Chin-ho to finish class at the Youth School. Below is their conversation and ensuing actions.

> "Comrade Mi-sun, I feel strange walking with you like this," Chin-ho said with a hint of excitement in his voice.
>
> Mi-sun did not know how to respond.
>
> "Would you allow me to explain?"
>
> "Please, do so," Mi-sun said quietly. She then gazed at Chin-ho.
>
> "What is the real reason for giving me these books?" he asked.
>
> "I explained to you earlier," she replied.
>
> "I just don't understand and believe what you've said," Chin-ho retorted.
>
> "When I went to my uncle's house and saw these books, the first person I thought of was you."
>
> Chin-ho stopped walking and faced Mi-sun. Under the moonlight, joy and excitement beamed from Chin-ho's eyes. Mi-sun recognized Chin-ho's joy and stood to receive him. Chin-ho feared that he was being too hasty and thought that there might be passersby watching them, so he picked up the books and proceeded to walk.[33]

My translation cannot display the manner in which Chin-ho and Mi-sun converse with each other in Korean because English does not have an honorific form. In nearly every dialogue between a man and a woman, husband and wife, or two heterosexual lovers, the women speak with the utmost respect to the men (in the honorific *yo* form), reinforcing the imbalance of sexual identities through the gendered linguistic system in the patriarchal social order. I believe that North Korea cannot and will not approach gender equality unless there is a change in the hierarchical linguistic system in which men and women address and converse with each other. I am not suggesting that this linguistic change is the definitive element that will enable the achievement of gender equality in North Korea. What I am suggesting is that fiction perpetuates the normative behavior that privileges men over women even in the way they communicate with each other.

Women in fiction not only honor men through the Korean linguistic system, but they also nurture men and show their affection through indirect expressions. For example, neither Chin-ho nor Mi-sun directly asserts love for the other person, but, instead, they speak indirectly. When Chin-ho says, "I feel strange walking with you like this," the strangeness he feels is his uncontrollable passion for Mi-sun, and yet he contains his excitement to present a refined gentleman-like persona to her. Likewise, when Mi-sun says that the books she saw at her uncle's house would help Chin-ho in his studies, she is revealing how her mind has been completely filled with him and how she is willing to find any excuse to be with him. Without having to state their feelings for each other directly, they each deciphered the linguistic codes of affection and prepared to kiss. This kind of dialogue between lovers follows the most common template in North Korean fiction.

In the February 1981 edition of *Munhwa'ŏhaksŭp* (Study of Cultural Language), North Korean linguist Ch'oe Wan-ho wrote an article titled "Nyŏsŏngdŭl'ui ryejŏlitgo kŏmbakhan mal" (Women's Courteous and Plain Language), where he argues that a mutual relationship among comrades—either in collective/individual or public/private lives—is derived from women speaking in courteous and plain language.[34] He provides several examples of how women ought to speak in the DPRK to show their well-mannered sense and sensibility:

> Instead of using direct expressions such as "Can I meet you right now?" indirect expressions such as "Are you busy right now?" or "Can you make some time for me?" reveal a clearer sense of desire to meet the other person in a more feminine way. . . .
>
> In the film *Nameless Heroes*, Sun-hŭi writes a letter to Yu-rim before she carries out an important duty. In the letter, Sun-hŭi confesses her love for Yu-rim. Instead of writing, "I love you," she writes, "I've been thinking about you," which shows a more feminine touch and sensitivity.[35]

Ch'oe Wan-ho claims that indirect language discloses a woman's deeper sense of affection and character. He discourages women from using eloquent and erudite words—particularly those derived from Chinese characters—as they make women appear superficial and bourgeois. He prefers that women use simple (*kŏmbakhan*) and innocent (*sobakhan*) words to describe their feelings. For Ch'oe, this is not a circumlocutory way of speaking or having to say more than necessary to express one's thoughts. Rather, it is a concise and meaningful way for women to reveal their femininity and sensitivity through linguistic codes of affection.

Ch'oe Wan-ho's suggestions are undoubtedly gendered, configuring a linguistic discourse to reconstruct and polarize gender identity in North Korea's culture. Ch'oe's short article reinforces a male-dominated gender politics, singling out women as the only ones needing linguistic discipline to maintain social decorum. It is, however, not only Ch'oe's article but also the majority of (if not all) North Korean fiction that constructs gender identities through linguistic utterances. Women are supposed to speak and act so as to preserve their honor and "virginity" as female subjects of the DPRK. Those who express their thoughts directly and openly (like women in Western culture, a typical target of ridicule in North Korea) are subject to public and private humiliation in narratives.

The linguistic codes of affection are not a prudish or repressive manner of speaking. Rather, they are more suggestive and inviting not only for the characters involved in the conversation but also for readers. Although Ch'oe Wan-ho is rather indirect about it himself, women's feminine way of speaking is for the listening/reading pleasure of male subjects. Addressing men in the honorific has been the normative discursive practice in North Korean fiction since the 1950s, which means that gender inequality in communication or linguistic structure has not been challenged. The imbalance in addressing the other in North Korea perpetuates male domination over women. And once the linguistic codes of affection have been deciphered, the lovers unite. In *Miners*, after their conversation, Chin-ho and Mi-sun gaze at each other under the moonlight. The text does not say Chin-ho drew closer to Mi-sun to kiss her; the text does not have to say that for readers to understand the passionate situation. Instead, the text says that Mi-sun was prepared to receive him, implying that she has parted her lips, tilted her head, and waited for contact with Chin-ho's lips. The linguistic codes of affection in North Korean fiction may excite the imagination more than visual mediums through which women are portrayed.

Although the management and regulation of sexuality by the state produce and codify the prescribed social behavior for men and women in North Korean political discourse, the words with which men and women engage in conversation, their bodily gestures, the spatial distance between characters, the specific moment when one praises Kim Il Sung, the verbal confessions that indicate the transformation of the character, and so on, are all performances that come undone, generating desire for the opposite sex rather than repressing it. In the following sections, I will further explain how North Korean fiction illustrates sexual interaction and erotic pleasures through linguist codes of affection.

Premarital Sex: Undoing the Political Consciousness of the Subject

In his sociological research work on North Koreans *Inmini sa'nŭn mosŭp* (The Way the North Koreans Live, 1995), South Korean writer Sŏ Tong-ik claims that North Korean universities strictly monitor sexual activities among students, and students have consequently faced expulsion. According to Sŏ, students have found ways to escape the ominous gaze of the university authorities by meeting in secret, vowing to marry upon graduation, and proceeding with their daily lives on campus as strangers.[36] Sŏ Tong-ik recognizes that a social institution where young men and women congregate to study and become future revolutionaries for the state creates an environment in which sexual activities are likely. The more university authorities place restrictions and laws against sexual activities, the more they generate the desire to engage with the other person and cleverer ways to navigate around the prohibitions. The issue that concerns me is not how the North Korean state—through its various socialized institutions—polices sexual repression and tries to obliterate it from the face of society, but rather how sexual desire is produced and reproduced with respect to the powers of the prohibitive law. In *The History of Sexuality*, Foucault says, "Thus one should not think that desire is repressed, for the simple reason that the law is what constitutes both desire and the lack on which it is predicated."[37]

In Foucault's view, the law does not prohibit one from speaking about his or her sexual adventures; rather it moves one to speak about them. The speaking subject has kissed, but, more important, the state inquires about the secret affair, to which the subject unabashedly responds. The secrecy of the subject is documented and treated like scientific evidence for experts to scrutinize and assess. In Paek Nam-nyong's *Pŏt* (Friend, 1988), a divorce judge carefully listens to Sŏk-ch'un's retelling of how he met his wife, Sun-hŭi, and engaged in premarital sex with her in the days of their youth. In *Friend*, it is all too clear who looks and who/what is looked at: Judge Chŏng Chin-u, a male magistrate, listens to Sŏk-ch'un's story of his premarital sex with Sun-hŭi, and the story itself is the object of erotic desire. The sexual experience is no longer a secret affair between Sŏk-ch'un and Sun-hŭi but a public one with a state-appointed judge intently listening to and reconstructing the scenario in his own imagination. In the Foucauldian sense, Judge Chŏng Chin-u is not simply the interlocutor but the authority who requires the confession, prescribes and appreciates it, and intervenes in order to judge, punish, forgive, console, and reconcile the couple's relationship.[38]

The state's moral authority figure does not reveal signs of disapproval of the couple's premarital sex because Sŏk-ch'un reassures the judge that the two were married within two months, implying that their premarital sex was not a moment's rapture but the result of a long-term commitment to each other. This reassurance is a necessary component in the narrative, as it operates as a confession and an admission of guilt that exonerates the couple from having breached the unspoken and unwritten codes of sexual behavior. Sŏk-ch'un understands the social and political ramifications of having premarital sex, and he complied with cultural decorum by marrying Sun-hŭi. Besides, he truly loved her. Their marriage contributes to Party morale, and the state reconfirms their matrimony as hope for the construction of a new cell in the revolutionary family of the DPRK.

Paek Nam-nyong uses Sŏk-ch'un's memories not only to explain past events but also to create a kiss and tell narrative that now involves the reader along with the judge. Sŏk-ch'un is a young technician who comes to a factory town in the countryside to educate and assist the workers with the latest technology. Sŏk-ch'un needs to fulfill his mandatory service to the state by working and residing with the factory workers for several months. On his bus ride into the town, he meets Ch'ae Sun-hŭi and immediately falls in love with her. Sŏk-ch'un's mind is preoccupied with thoughts of Sun-hŭi, and he decides to express his feelings for her in person. He invites her to meet him at a small park after work, but she does not appear. It begins to rain, and soon Sŏk-ch'un is drenched. The evening grows darker, and the workers' dormitory lights turn off one by one. There is still no sign of Sun-hŭi. It becomes very late and the streetlights are also turned off, leaving Sŏk-ch'un in absolute darkness. He begins to regret coming out to the park in the first place and realizes the absurdity of his infatuation with a woman who does not seem to care for him at all. But, then, in the midst of the pouring rain, he identifies a dark figure standing with two umbrellas. It is Sun-hŭi.

It is clear why Sun-hŭi waited until the last moment before she made herself visible: she wanted to meet Sŏk-ch'un in the dark while the rest of the town was sound asleep. The meeting after the lights have gone out closely resembles Jun-sang and Mi-ran's story in Barbara Demick's *Nothing to Envy*, except, in *Friend*, the lights are turned off not because of an energy crisis but for "energy conservation." The next night, when the town falls into a deep slumber and the lights have gone off as usual, Sŏk-ch'un demands that Sun-hŭi confess her love for him: "With the help of the bright moonlight, Sŏk-ch'un was able to see her blushed cheeks, the contours of her lips, her long eyelashes, and her timid eyes. Below her curvaceous shoulders, he also perceived her rapidly beating heart. . . . At that moment, Sŏk-ch'un was so driven by his impulses that he reached his hands out and grabbed Sun-hŭi's hands. She felt a little bashful, but she allowed him to hold her hands."[39]

In *The Way North Koreans Live,* Sŏ Tong-ik claims that South Korean men stereotypically choose their partners on the basis of physical qualities such as height, weight, facial complexion, facial features, and legs, whereas North Korean men stereotypically choose theirs primarily on the basis of socialist activities and potentiality for rearing children.[40] Sŏ Tong-ik's research was conducted in the late 1980s and early 1990s, about the time Paek Nam-nyong published *Friend.* However, this could not be farther from the truth for Paek's protagonist, Sŏk-ch'un, whose reasons for feeling sexually aroused by Sun-hŭi are based on the romantic ambience (their isolated, secretive meeting place) and her physical attributes rather than on her socialist activism or lofty political consciousness.

At that moment, there is nothing more important to Sŏk-ch'un than Sun-hŭi's desirable body, a material reality that destabilizes the trajectory of political and revolutionary consciousness. Sŏk-ch'un's sexual thoughts and his erotic gaze on Sun-hŭi move from her face down to her breasts. Sŏk-ch'un perceives Sun-hŭi's curvaceous shoulders—a distinct attribute of sexuality and a characteristic of beauty in many cultures. Sun-hŭi does not have her shoulders bare for Sŏk-ch'un to see, but he follows the curvature of Sun-hŭi's shoulders with his eyes, the *koksŏnmi* (literally the beauty of the curved line), imagining and eroticizing Sun-hŭi's body beneath her dress. But his gaze does not stop on Sun-hŭi's shoulders; he proceeds to examine her heart/breasts (*kasŭm*).

The ambiguous usage of the word heart/breasts (*kasŭm*) in the text opens up the possibility of transgressing into the restricted visual area of eroticism. The text, at this moment, says Sŏk-ch'un perceived Sun-hŭi's heart beating rapidly because of his advance toward her. His close proximity to her and the anticipation of what is going to happen next may have caused Sun-hŭi's heart to palpitate. Another way of reading Sun-hŭi's rapidly beating heart is as anxiety at the possibility of being seen by a passerby. She knows that there is always a chance of getting caught, and, if they were to get caught, it would become lasting gossip in the village.

However, this particular moment in the text is not describing Sun-hŭi's feelings from her own perspective but from Sŏk-ch'un's gaze. He is the narrator, the confessor, the kisser and teller, and he is describing what he notices about Sun-hŭi. Although the word *kasŭm* can mean both heart and breasts, particularly when referring to a woman, it is describing a man's lustful gaze upon a socially eroticized part of the woman. Sŏk-ch'un's eyes go from Sun-hŭi's physical shoulders to her physical breasts, or "perky breasts" (*pungkŭthan kasŭm*), as it is stated in the original text. This passage in the novel is not describing Sun-hŭi's breasts as sexually charged, but rather Sŏk-ch'un's gaze at her breasts as already being sexualized. In other words, the breasts are not naturally sexual; Sŏk-ch'un sexualizes the breasts by focusing on them as his object of desire. The passage describing Sun-hŭi's breasts is "put into discourse" (to use Foucault's phrase), or admitted to Judge Chŏng Chin-u, to render the particular body part as a sexual object. His impulse to grab Sun-hŭi's hand is not "original" desire or libido drive but the effect of sexualizing her and the intimate situation. The social, political, and cultural prohibitions against uncomely behavior toward the opposite sex create Sŏk-ch'un's impulsive reaction.

The operative word here is "impulse" (*ch'ungdong*), which poses a concern for social conventions that rely on collective consciousness or political awareness and self-control as opposed to individual spontaneity. Sŏk-ch'un's impulsive action is not intended to disrupt the harmony of the factory or the state, and, yet, it can be read as a form of threat to national security prevalent in North Korean fiction of the 1980s, where individuals exhibit schizophrenic tendencies of saying or doing one thing in public while thinking something else. Sŏk-ch'un's impulsive behavior is the physical manifestation of his emotional feelings toward Sun-hŭi. Although Sŏk-ch'un has to display his undying loyalty to the state in public, his love for Sun-hŭi suggests an antithetical kind of a North Korean man, who has forgotten for a moment his political duties and his transcendental love for Kim Il Sung. In this passage, Sŏk-ch'un's priority is neither the state nor to his political duties but Sun-hŭi. It has to be this particular evening for Sŏk-ch'un, a now-or-never situation, to release his pent up feelings and physically take hold of her.

Sun-hŭi is not simply the object of Sŏk-ch'un's sexual desire; she is the agent who destabilizes Sŏk-ch'un's subjectivity by presenting her body as an alternative reality to his immaterial drive toward political consciousness. She is the one who made Sŏk-ch'un wait for her in the rain and the dark. She is the one who presented herself before him. She is the one who is standing in front of him, obscuring the world of rationality and intelligibility, "coyly playing with a ribbon that hung from the front part of her one-piece dress."[41] This is perhaps the most sexually assertive gesture on Sun-hŭi's part, visually seducing her man by playing with a ribbon on her dress. The ribbon is meant to hold the dress together in the area of her breasts, but Sun-hŭi's playing with the ribbon directs the viewer's attention to her breasts and signals a come-hither erotic gesture. Her affective control over Sŏk-ch'un's emotions is an empowering performance that deconstructs or decenters his revolutionary subjectivity.

Through Sŏk-ch'un's detailed confession, the political subjectivity of the listening judge is also under duress from the imagination of the sexualized woman and the erotic storytelling. Despite his being a legal administrator, the judge does not use the law to condemn Sŏk-ch'un for his sexual behavior because it is precisely the judge who perpetuates the erotic story, desiring a resolution that gratifies his own subjugation of Sŏk-ch'un's discourse. The event is no longer only for Sŏk-ch'un's private pleasure; it has become an open discourse for the judge to project and inscribe in his own unmitigated fantasy. Sŏk-ch'un stands within inches of Sun-hŭi, but it is as if the judge is also present. The two lovers release the warm breath from their mouths moments before the anticipated physical embrace. Then, all of a sudden, the description shifts from the couple to their natural surroundings:

> Silver fog rolled down the mountains. The willow trees by the riverbank fluttered their leaves as though they had life. The moonlight reflected off the pebbles and the rocks by the rapids. Two large rocks stood close to each other as though they, too, came out to exchange their love for each other. The stream from the mountains flowed down boldly with life. It was a lyrical sound. . . .
>
> Foam from the eddies among the ripples reflected the moonlight. Large waves crashed on the bank with gusto, spread thin along the bank, and then silently flowed down the river. Another set of waves crashed, followed by the next as it continuously flowed.[42]

This intense moment in *Friend* juxtaposes the two lovers with the description of the natural scenery to avert attention from gratuitous physicality. Without explicit details of their sexual intercourse, readers imagine the lovers' sexual consummation from the depiction of their natural surroundings. The river rhythmically washing up on the banks is analogous to Sŏk-ch'un's body engulfing Sun-hŭi's. The glistening rocks represent the two lovers' sweating bare backs. The large tides repeatedly crashing on the banks are the sexual penetration. And the "lyrical sound" represents their orgasmic release. Sŏk-ch'un and Sun-hŭi are conveniently veiled by a "silver fog," obscuring the visibility of their sexual pleasure from the other villagers. The state not only has created a workplace where Sŏk-ch'un meets Sun-hŭi, but it also creates a space for their sexual union by conveniently (and romantically) turning off the streetlights for them in the name of "energy conservation." The only light provided to the lovers is the natural light provided by the bright moon.

Allusion to nature or metonyms for sexual acts or the genitals is a common literary trope dating back many hundreds of years and still used today in the East and West alike. In premodern Korean literature, *unujirak* (the pleasure between cloud and rain) and *unujijŏng* (the affection between cloud and rain) are euphemisms used to describe sexual intercourse between a man and a woman. Metaphors such as "wrapped in a wisplike cloud with a misty rain, a willow branch quivered, and the flower coquettishly whispered fragrant sobs" and references to a bee coveting honey and a butterfly loving flowers are all allusions to lovemaking found in a Chosŏn work of fiction called *Unyŏng-jŏn*.[43]

Euphemisms and allusions to sex in North Korean fiction are discursively coded in more or less universal literary tropes such as the season of spring. A spring evening suggests the season of rampant sexual desires that have been subdued by the repressive wintery nights. Unsurprisingly, the nights of lovemaking for Sŏk-ch'un and Sun-hŭi happen in spring, when the natural environment comes to life. Another North Korean author, Chŏng Ch'ang-yun, wrote a short story called "Pombam" (Spring Evening, 1985), about a worker secretly visiting his fiancée at night and satisfying her sexual needs. The sexual union between the worker and his fiancée is both the climax and the end of the short story. However, Paek's novel does not end just yet; the sexual consummation is only the beginning of Sŏk-ch'un and Sun-hŭi's relationship problems, which will be discussed in Chapter 4. But, for the moment, on this spring evening, Sŏk-ch'un's experience with Sun-hŭi by the riverbanks is riveting enough to propose marriage to her and recapitulate this sexual encounter to Judge Chŏng Chin-u.

Premarital sex is a deliberate act of subversion against the institution of marriage and the political instruction of preserving the sanctity of the virginal body and mind for the state and the leader. Erotic fantasies are not supposed to occupy the mind of an individual who is striving to achieve revolution. But, as men and women work together in the state-allocated spaces, the spatial and temporal working environment fosters the sexual attraction rather than repels it. Sŏk-ch'un and Sun-hŭi's premarital sex not only challenges the law, but it is also ratified by the law (Judge Chŏng Chin-u) through the "kiss and tell" narrative strategy. In other words, the confessional statement exonerates Sŏk-ch'un from having committed the cultural crime and frees him from the burden of guilt because the judge carefully records the confession as "evidence" that helps him resolve the couple's marital problems later in the novel. In *Friend*, the representation of sexuality and desire emerges from the discourse that tries to locate the revolutionary self within society. Such unsuspecting and unintentional discourse that competes with the correct discourse of becoming a revolutionary constructs a new discourse that reshapes the consciousness of individuals.

Scientia Sexualis: Medicalization of Sexual Love

The state is particularly concerned with sexual activities among young adults and keeps a watchful eye on them, attempting to enforce tighter restrictions and prohibitions. Kim Il Sung's passing comment about men marrying at the age of thirty and women at the age of twenty-eight has been an unwritten code of social practice for decades. In the DPRK Family Law, section 9, the legal marriageable age for men is eighteen and for women seventeen. However, there is an addendum to this section as follows: "The state will support the social spirit of marriage after a youth works effectively for the country, the people, society, and the collective." The North Korean state does not discourage marriage and dating as long as these activities do not hinder or obstruct the youth's labor for the country.

Young men and women are sent to remote areas of the country to fulfill their political duties and experience collective effort, but this deployment is also to disperse them so that they cannot forge lasting relationships and to make them work so as to exhaust their sexual energy. According to the South Korean writer Sŏ Tong-ik, the average North Korean worker begins the day at six o'clock in the morning and finishes at nine o'clock in the evening.[44] The tight schedule is designed to keep the bodies occupied throughout the day so that when the workers return to their dormitory room or home they sleep. The irony is that the young men and women find new partners and sexual relationships in the factory, farm, or village to which they are deployed regardless of the overwhelming work schedule.

In Kim Ch'ŏng-nam's short story "Naega saranghanŭn saram" (The Man I Love, 1978),[45] female physician Ryŏn-hŭi confesses her love for Hwa-sun to her friend in a letter. Her friend has teased Ryŏn-hŭi for having unrealistic expectations of a man and romantic fantasies of a knight in shining armor to sweep her off her feet. Ryŏn-hŭi writes to her friend that this is not true and that Hwa-sun is the man whom she loves dearly. Ryŏn-hŭi proceeds to write the story of how she met the man of her dreams at the hospital where she works.

Doctor Ryŏn-hŭi is trying to diagnose the medical condition of her male patient Hwa-sun. She cannot seem to locate his exact problem other than his gradual loss of hearing. One night, a forest ranger comes to the hospital with a child, looking for Hwa-sun. The forest ranger had found the child lost in the woods, crying for his uncle. It turns out that Hwa-sun had told his nephew to meet him in the woods but forgot about the meeting. Ryŏn-hŭi comes to believe that Hwa-sun's hearing loss is a minor condition compared to his frequent forgetfulness and negligent behavior, which she thinks might be attributed to a larger mental condition.

Doctor Ryŏn-hŭi orders Hwa-sun to visit the hospital for daily checkups, but he is constantly late for his appointments. Sometimes he fails to show up at all. When a nurse informs Ryŏn-hŭi that Hwa-sun has missed his appointments, Ryŏn-hŭi believes that his condition is becoming worse. Ryŏn-hŭi decides that Hwa-sun is not mentally healthy enough to carry out his job as a driver for the factory. She and her nurse run out to look for Hwa-sun. When they find him, Hwa-sun is talking with the manager at the factory.

Hwa-sun assures the manager that he is more than capable of driving the factory truck. The manager is reluctant to allow Hwa-sun to continue with the project because of his medical condition. As Ryŏn-hŭi listens to their conversation, she realizes that Hwa-sun has been forgetful not because of a mental condition but because he has been thinking about ways to improve the working conditions and the productivity of the factory as the Great Leader had instructed the workers to do. Ryŏn-hŭi is overwhelmed by Hwa-sun's commitment to the nation and discards the medical reports she wrote about him. Her love for him intensifies. Ryŏn-hŭi finishes her letter to her friend by determining to live a life worthy of the nation and the Great Leader.

Kim Chŏng-nam's "The Man I Love" reflects the social and economic climate in which North Koreans lived in the late 1970s and early 1980s. The Second Seven-Year Plan (1978–1984), much like the Six-Year Plan (1971–1976), called on the people to acquire the Three Revolutions—ideology, technology, and culture—and to apply them to heavy and light industries. Alongside the Three Revolutions in the early 1970s, the Party initiated the Speed Campaign (*sokdojŏn*) in 1974 to increase productivity in the agricultural, industrial, and cultural sectors across the country. The state media encouraged North Koreans to work tirelessly for the nation and claimed that the people's collective efforts were ways to please Kim Il Sung.

The Five-Year Plan (1957–1961), the First Seven-Year Plan (1961–1970), and the Six-Year Plan (1971–1976) that preceded the Speed Campaign equally called on the people to exert their energies for the economic productivity of the country. All of these economic plans overworked the people and subjected them to physical injuries and mental and emotional stress. The Party recognized but did little to rectify the sheer exhaustion from excessive manual labor and the low public morale. In *Kim Jong Il's Leadership of North Korea*, Jae-Cheon Lim says, "Officials were busy fulfilling economic goals in the shortest time with less care for the quality of the work. . . . Moreover, Kim's speed campaigns contributed to exhausting resources and the masses' motivation to work."[46]

"The Man I Love" depicts Hwa-sun as a victim of the Speed Campaign and Doctor Ryŏn-hŭi as the heroine deployed by the Party to assist the workers at local factories with any health conditions that they may have sustained from exhaustion. When Hwa-sun refuses to be hospitalized, Ryŏn-hŭi says, "The Great Leader is deeply concerned for the health of the comrades who are charging forward with the new Seven-Year Plan."[47] Overt political statements such as this one attempt to indicate Kim Il Sung's undying care and concern for his people during economic hardships. Though the Party may have sent doctors to local factories and farms to nurse the workers back to health, part of the motivation was so that the workers could return to work for another round of arduous labor.

The frame story of Kim Ch'ŏng-nam's "The Man I Love" begins with Ryŏn-hŭi's confession to her friend about the man whom she loves. She first meets her man in a hospital, the very social institution that sterilizes the human body, including the emotions. There is something Ryŏn-hŭi finds utterly attractive about Hwa-sun, but she writes, "I cannot fully express my love in words."[48] Perhaps words are not enough to reveal Ryŏn-hŭi's passion because they would be too sexual. Ryŏn-hŭi does not express her sexual feelings directly to Hwa-sun. She first needs to find a way to see him more frequently and develop a trusting relationship.

How convenient it is to construct a narrative around a medical doctor who can order her patient to check in every day for her voyeuristic pleasure. As a physician, Ryŏn-hŭi has the medical authority to treat Hwa-sun by asking him the most intimate questions without violating privacy codes; she can physically touch his body without infringing upon the state-prescribed gender codes of conduct between man and woman; and a doctor can order her patient to strip down for medical purposes while training her erotic gaze on him. Although North Korean fiction does not detail the nude body, Ryŏn-hŭi admits in her letter that "Hwa-sun's physique was sturdy, and he had well-toned muscles"—physical attributes that would only be visible when she has seen his naked body. In short, the production of desire is inscribed on the reference to nudity under the aegis of medical examination.

In the chapter "Scientia Sexualis" of his *History of Sexuality,* Foucault says, "Combining confession with examination, the personal history with the deployment of a set of decipherable signs and symptoms; the interrogation, the exacting questionnaire: all were ways of reinscribing the procedure of confessions in a field of scientifically acceptable observations."[49] Ryŏn-hŭi writes a single letter to her friend about Hwa-sun, but she has been writing about him for several weeks in her medical log. She prescribes daily checkups for Hwa-sun in order to record his behavioral patterns in her medical log—the daily entry of her expert analysis of the man of her interest. Ryŏn-hŭi's log, then, serves as her masturbatory ritual that reconstructs the erotic image of her man after each physical examination.

Each day's writing is an epistemic addition to the previous day's record. She conducts her observation under the auspices of medical science, but this medical log is only for her to see, as she never submits the medical report to a higher official or institution. When Hwa-sun forgets to come by the hospital, Ryŏn-hŭi feels gravely dissatisfied at not being able to observe her patient. Ryŏn-hŭi scolds Hwa-sun, "What is going on, comrade? Why aren't you following my instructions?"[50] Ryŏn-hŭi's ostensible anger toward Hwa-sun for not coming to the hospital masks her true concern for him.

Ryŏn-hŭi's scolding of Hwa-sun exhibits the coming undone of Ryŏn-hŭi's speech act, as her intentions are undeterminable. I have discussed how North Korean linguist Ch'oe Wan-ho argued for women to speak in an indirect manner to display their femininity. Ch'oe Wan-ho might consider Ryŏn-hŭi's speech act to be typical of a woman expressing concern for the other without saying it. "Why aren't you following my instructions?" can be read as the words of a doctor who is concerned about her patient. But it is also an expression of her intense erotic love for him. The hospital is not only a public institution but also an eroticized site where Ryŏn-hŭi entertains her private desires. However, without Hwa-sun, the hospital simply returns to being a sterile space with a sexually unsatisfied female physician.

"The Man I Love" first leads the other characters in the story to believe that Hwa-sun has a mental condition that will affect his work and the productivity of the factory. The other characters do not trust a worker like Hwa-sun, who is forgetful, negligent, and irresponsible. It is not until the end of the short story that the others, along with the narrator (Ryŏn-hŭi), understand that Hwa-sun never had a medical problem to begin with. It turns out that Ryŏn-hŭi and the other characters have had misconceptions about Hwa-sun, who has had his thoughts on the correct political ideology the whole time. The *anagnorisis,* or the recognition of Hwa-sun's true intentions and identity, is supposed to supply the narrative with an element of surprise. The question is whether or not this recognition is effective enough to designate Hwa-sun as the hero of the story.

North Korean literature from the beginning has constructed its narrative around the aesthetics of the *becoming* hero—similar to a character in a *Bildungsroman*—rather than the *already made* hero. Although there are exceptions to every rule, North Korean fiction has generally taken on the transformative method of writing narratives, as it conveniently adheres to the political and moral development of the individual who learns the strength and ethicality of the collective and what it requires to be integrated in the society. This narrative form is similar to what Nancy Armstrong says about Victorian novels in her book *How Novels Think*: "The figure could no longer generate expressions of excessive individualism that simultaneously detached the individual from a restrictive social category and made it possible for him or her to become more fully a citizen-subject.[51] According to Armstrong, novels in the nineteenth century shifted from imagining an amalgamation of individuals in the nation to reimagining the nation as that which required the individuals to achieve transformation and sublimation. The moral "lessons" in the novels, for Armstrong, are the self-cultivating signs that provide the cultural wisdom to transform the individual into a citizen-subject.[52] Likewise, North Korean literature delineates the hero or heroine as a transforming individual rather than an already made one. In this sense, Hwa-sun is not the hero of the narrative because he does not undergo an ideological transformation as is expected of characters in North Korean fiction. What began as a medical disorder turns out to be a healthy political consciousness that everyone at the factory is supposed to be inspired by and to emulate. By inference, Hwa-sun's healthy mental/political consciousness indicates that the other characters have had the disease of individualism—a mental "illness" that is considered to be one of the detrimental etiologies of socialist obstruction. The other characters (particularly Ryŏn-hŭi) have placed their individualism before their political consciousness, which is discursively rendered as "illness" in the DPRK. Through literature, North Korean citizens are constantly reminded of their political shortcomings and the need to work harder to eliminate the "illness" that hinders the pursuit of revolution.

"The Man I Love" shows the self-treatment, the sublimation, of the doctor with the disease of individualism. Doctor Ryŏn-hŭi's "illness" is identified dialectically through Hwa-sun, who is mentally and ideologically healthy. It is she who must overcome her individualism, undergo "medical treatment," and transform into the state-desired collective being. "The Man I Love" associates Ryŏn-hŭi's ideological disease with the disease pervasive among people in the DPRK during the 1970s: she lacked the correct political consciousness and, therefore, did not truly place the leader, the Party, and the nation above all else. The realization of what the Great Leader has done for the nation is the remedy that restores and renourishes the ailing body, mind, and spirit. While Hwa-sun speaks of the nation and seeks ways to please the Great Leader, Ryŏn-hŭi has been preoccupied with ways to gratify her own sexual desires. Ryŏn-hŭi's "illness" did not have a name or category until it was named (e.g., as bourgeois ideology, feudal-Confucian ideas, revisionism) and determined to be a medical/political problem by state political and social institutions. The state's discourse on sexuality identified its own problem and prescribed its own treatment.

The various types of political disease in society developed the need for a medicalization process, which in the 1970s DPRK was the systematic intake of political rhetoric as a social remedy. North Korean fiction uses political rhetoric as an institutionalized set of discourses that become the dominant state-administered "medical" performance, an ideological remedy for the individuals in the narrative to sublimate their consciousness toward the betterment of the state. The rehabilitative journey of Ryŏn-hŭi in the narrative brings about the transformation of her identity, which in turn provides a social and political prescription for readers in the DPRK. In such a way, the requirements of Sonia Ryang's concept of the "eternal triangle" have been met. The eternal triangle model reinforces the narrative strategy in which individuals in North Korean romantic fiction project their love toward Kim Il Sung. At the end of the story, Ryŏn-hŭi professes her newfound hope in living a life that is worthy of the nation and the Great Leader.

However, the transformation of a hero or heroine can be more of a literary artifice than an integral component of the narrative in North Korean literature. The trajectory of the narrative often finds its *telos* all too abruptly and incoherently, as if the story needs to end now or else it will be difficult to anchor the ending to the correct political ideology. Let us not forget that "The Man I Love" begins as a frame story with Ryŏn-hŭi explaining to her friend how she met the man of her dreams and not how she reconfirmed her love for Kim Il Sung. The emphasis in her letter is on the process of meeting Hwa-sun and falling in love with him, not on the kind of revolutionary Hwa-sun represents for Ryŏn-hŭi. Yet the story needed to end according to the state-prescribed narrative form. It could not allow Ryŏn-hŭi's individualistic and erotic desires to continue without constraint; it needed to ground her fantasies of her man to a rational understanding of true platonic love for the leader. This kind of spurious ending stifles the organic trajectory of the narrative with artificial rhetoric, a detrimental practice in North Korean literary culture. The incoherent beginning and ending of the story are not the result of authorial design or writing tradition in North Korea but rather the draconian imposition of strictures by a literary establishment that curtails imagination more than it fosters it. The story was forced to end. The requirement that platonic love be an integral component of the character's reality (as in nearly all North Korean fiction after the 1960s) inevitably generates ironic and schizophrenic individuals whose emotions, rationale, and bodies are divided and destabilized.

"The Man I Love" presents a dual confession: the first is Ryŏn-hŭi's love for Hwa-sun, and the second is Ryŏn-hŭi's love for the Great Leader. Neither one of these confessions is false or less sincere than the other. The dual confession does not suggest a hierarchical difference that prioritizes political confession over sexual confession. Sexuality *is* political in the DPRK, or in any nation-state.

One's sexuality must be made open to the public in order for the state to acquire, regulate, create, and disseminate new discourses in the literary, medical, and legal worlds. In other words, sexuality is never a private identity. Ryŏn-hŭi's political confession of love for Kim Il Sung does not mean that she overcomes her sexual desire for Hwa-sun; the prescriptive ending attempts to efface the secretive emotions that constituted her sexuality and to reconstruct her sexuality as that which purports her political subjectivity. In this sense, her love for Hwa-sun is to be taken seriously only to the extent that it reflects the state's gendered discourse on love. Ryŏn-hŭi does not love Hwa-sun; she loves a revolutionary who loves the state. Her love is thus allegorical and not human; she does not love another human being but the representation and the embodiment of the state in a man. This constitutes the figuration of the hero or heroine in North Korean fiction. But this figuration is also haunted by its own misunderstanding and unintentionality.

In the fictional world, there is never a task that is too burdensome for the heroes or heroines to overcome—the Kimilsungist revolutionary always triumphs. This literary strategy illustrates the hero's supernatural ability to transcend personal emotions and erotic desires for the achievement of pure political consciousness. Insofar as the narrative continues to contrive an artificial ending, the method of reading North Korean texts remains within a prescribed monolithic analysis. Rather than simply attributing this type of narrative construction to the empty signifier of socialist realism or propaganda, approaching the story as a "kiss and tell" narrative strategy says something additional about the generic characterization and plotline. The "kiss and tell" narrative creates fault lines of conflicting realities for the characters as they attempt to negotiate their competing desires in the process of developing their identities.

Competing Desires of the Schizophrenic Hero

The appeal of romantic narratives in North Korea lies in their seductive power to create alternative realities of the sexual act through confessions. The hero of the story does not keep his sexual exploits hidden from readers (or other characters in the novel). He makes them known to his readers, fulfilling the dual desire to "kiss and tell." The confession breaks the rules of discretion and transforms the listener/reader into the desiring subject, who needs to hear/read about the rest of the affair. Let us look at a passing but critical moment in Ri Hwa's novel *Sogŭmkkot* (Salt Deposits, 1984) in which the hero confesses his sexual desire for a woman. Then, he averts his eyes from gazing erotically at the woman and sings the praises of the Great Leader and the Party, which reveals the hero's unstable identity and competing desires.

In *Salt Deposits*, male protagonist Ri Yŏng-t'aek recalls his early days working at a salt mine in North Kangwŏn Province. He, like most men and women in the DPRK, has been deployed to a certain region of the country to fulfill his service to the country. At the salt mines, he complains about having to toil in a field of which he knows nothing; the one thing that keeps Yŏng-t'aek at the salt mines is his female coworker Ri Sun-gŭm, whom he finds attractive and sexually desirable. They exchange glances during work and smile bashfully, but nothing materializes until the miners hold a dinner party one evening. After dinner, one of the miners calls out Yŏng-t'aek and Sun-gŭm to stand before the salt miners and perform a duet. Yŏng-t'aek figures that Sun-gŭm had known that the miners would call the two out when she hands him a guitar that she has prepared. The following passage contains a sequence of events that requires close attention:

> Mrs. Ok-suk quickly got up and said, "Next, Comrade Ri Yŏng-t'aek and Comrade Ri Sun-gŭm will sing a duet that they have prepared." Mrs. Ok-suk made a mistake. We had not prepared a duet at all.
>
> But I knew what the miners were trying to do. They made us stand up there, clapping to encourage us to sing.
>
> Sun-gŭm seemed to have a keen sense of foresight. She had given my guitar to the kitchen maid for safekeeping. Sun-gŭm retrieved the guitar from the kitchen maid and handed it over to me.
>
> She protruded [*naemilmyŏ*] her perky breasts [*pungkŭthan kasŭm*] as she walked over to me and gently leaned her shoulder against mine.
>
> Elder U-ch'an nodded his head in satisfaction. For some reason, there were tears welling up in Mrs. Ok-suk's eyes.
>
> I held the guitar and began to sing.
>
> "Our father is the nation's leader Kim Il Sung / Our home is in the bosom of the Party."
>
> I sang the song with the purest intentions, and my heart and mind truly believed in the lyrics. This song could be considered the theme song of my life, as it impassioned my heart each time I sang it.
>
> Then, Mrs. Ok-suk sang a song that she used to sing as a teenager at her hometown called "Plowing Song" and Elder U-ch'an sang "Alright! It's Bumper Crop Year!"
>
> The festive reveries lasted deep into the night.[53]

This passage is an exemplary case of irony in a romantic plot. The hero's erotic gaze toward a female body conflicts with his platonic gaze upon Kim Il

Sung and the Party. The irony is that the protagonist claims to have his eyes set on the Great Leader and the Party while staring at Sun-gŭm's breasts. Yŏng-t'aek is stuck at the crossroads of two realities: physical life and political life. Physical life for Yŏng-t'aek is his daily interactions with the miners. He learns the value of labor, refines his rugged personality, and, most important, discovers erotic love. On the one hand, he confesses that he has had his eye on Sun-gŭm ever since he first saw her at the salt mine and that she has been the only thing on his mind. On the other hand, he claims that his thoughts were always on being a devoted worker for the state. The indeterminacy of meaning follows from the duplicitous nature of language. In *Allegories of Reading*, Paul de Man says, "Irony is no longer a trope but the undoing of the deconstructive allegory of all topological cognitions, the systematic undoing of understanding,"[54] and, in "The Concept of Irony," he claims that the reader is faced with an uncontrollable "polysemy of meanings" in which the text becomes an endless play of "the impossibility of understanding."[55] Much like Derrida and other poststructuralists, Paul de Man emphasizes that the text's resistance to any single understanding or enclosure is a testament to the instability of meaning already present in language. The arbitrary relation between the word and its designated meaning (signifier and signified) not only destabilizes or deconstructs the foundation of the structural language, but it suspends and defers any meaning from being decided once and for all.

There are multiple conflicts and realities embodied in North Korean heroes, conditioning the possibility of reading them as ironic/schizophrenic individuals. Schizophrenia is a psychological disturbance of the patient in relation to his environment or to reality in general. Although there is an aspect of the medical condition here, there are other conceptions of schizophrenia that are useful in discussing fiction. According to Rolf Beuer, it is particularly fruitful to consider schizophrenia in fiction as the response to certain kinds of interaction, namely to so-called untenable situations.[56] In the case of North Korean fiction, the hero's unwavering determination to find ways to please Kim Il Sung is not the only method of reading and analyzing North Korean individuals because the discourse that constructs the heroes and heroines is always already at risk of its own deconstruction. Derrida and de Man remind us that language and meaning are always at play, and so the logocentricity of the hero's unwavering concern or singular determination for the leader is put to the test with the very language that is used to venerate him.

The protagonist in *Salt Deposits* knows he must set his eyes on the Great Leader, but he cannot seem to avert his eyes from his lover's body. And yet ironically he claims that his gaze *is* on the leader. He then adds that he sang the song with the "purest intentions," which disrupts the speech act of intentionality in its very utterance. The protagonist uses his lips to praise the nation and the Great Leader, but those lips also transmit the desire to share his intimate sexual thoughts. Thus, the lips reciting the political rhetoric are not dependable in determining whether or not the subject is telling the truth. The identification of a schizophrenic subject does not necessarily mean that the protagonist cannot be trusted and cannot dwell in his community and among others. In "Schizophrenic Narrative," Lee R. Edwards says, "Schizophrenics come to us, then, always already de-centered. . . . They are, paradoxically, selves defined in dissolution."[57] North Korean narratives are schizophrenic in Edwards' sense. That is, they declare their own distress and proclaim their own desire to see a human face mirrored in the shattered subjectivity.[58] The hero is not reducible to a unified subject, totalized and completed by adherence to political determination. He opens up the enclosing powers of state-prescribed discourse through both his political rhetoric and his sexual confession—that is, irony resists closure.

Many North Korean individuals in fiction are subject to imperfect identity because of the destruction of the family (for example, through the death of a family member) or not having acquired the correct political consciousness. In *Salt Deposits*, Yŏng-t'aek has lost his parents to the Americans during the Korean War, so the only "family" he has is the salt miners. The only "parents" he has are Elder U-ch'ang and Mrs. Ok-suk. For Yŏng-t'aek, the notion of the family has to be reimagined and reconstructed within the material reality that affects him—those with whom he lives and interacts. The time has come for Yŏng-t'aek to express his love for Sun-gŭm before the presence of his newfound family of salt miners. It turns out that the dinner party is no ordinary dinner but an engagement dinner. It is a gathering to celebrate the couple's new future as a family. Sun-gŭm, too, has been waiting for this moment, as she approaches Yŏng-t'aek with the guitar. The pivotal moment in the narrative is the way Sun-gŭm approaches Yŏng-t'aek and the way he gazes at her. In Yŏng-t'aek's words as narrator, "She protruded her perky breasts as she walked over to me and gently leaned her shoulder against mine."[59]

Salt Deposits is narrated from Yŏng-t'aek's perspective. Readers follow his eyes, which, at this point, have fallen below Sun-gŭm's face and onto her eroticized body. As Sun-gŭm approaches Yŏng-t'aek with his guitar, Yŏng-t'aek does not describe her facial expression or features as Sŏk-ch'un does in Paek Nam-nyong's *Friend*. Instead, he focuses on the way Sun-gŭm protrudes her breasts for him to take notice of her. The only visible contour of Sun-gŭm's body is her perky breasts, using the same description (*pungkŭthan kasŭm*) Paek Nam-nyong uses in *Friend*. Yŏng-t'aek's gaze lingers for a short moment before he averts his focus from Sun-gŭm's bosom to the bosom of the Great Leader and the Party.

It is imperative to know precisely when and how such political speech acts are interjected as contrived artifices in the narratives of North Korean fiction. Here the sequence quickly shifts from Yŏng-t'aek's gaze to his singing: "Our father is the nation's leader Kim Il Sung / Our home is in the bosom of the Party."[60] Yŏng-t'aek's song choice is not the oddity in this sequence. The song choice is the correct one, as it demonstrates a Party-minded individual. The oddity is Yŏng-t'aek's deliberate accentuation of the lyrics of the song at this particular moment in the narrative. Of all the lyrics Yŏng-t'aek could have cited, he recalls the one and only lyric that would brand him as a true Kimilsungist revolutionary. He needs to assure his audience at the dinner party that his song is the verbal manifestation of his ideological mentality.

The second line of this lyric refers to the Party's "bosom," which in the Korean language is *p'um*. The word *p'um* refers to the bosom or arms, as in a child resting in the *p'um* of his mother. The word *p'um* alone in the Korean language does not have any tint of eroticism, and the metaphor of *p'um* for describing the Party is certainly not a sexual reference. In fact, *p'um* denotes warmth, security, safety, and intimacy—all characteristics that are thought of as motherly. For Yŏng-t'aek to sing of the Party's *p'um* reinforces the imagery of motherhood, and it also implies that the *p'um* of a real mother is only second to the deep sensitivity and true comfort of the Party. However, it is the context in which *p'um* is used that makes the word indeterminable and untranslatable. Two bosoms compete with each other—that of Sun-gŭm and that of the Party. But, of course, the reference to the bosom of the Party is supposed to veil Sun-gŭm's breasts because Yŏng-t'aek's "purest intentions" are on the Great Leader and the Party.

Yŏng-t'aek's confession of first gazing at Sun-gŭm's breasts and then singing a song about the Party does not demonstrate transcendental and austere self-control over his sexual desire. It is the ostensible display of a politically oriented hero. Considering that this is a dinner party—a public affair—it may be the proper code of conduct to sing praises of Kim Il Sung rather than to continue his voyeuristic gaze on Sun-gŭm's imposing breasts. In public, the Party and the Great Leader must be prioritized over personal desires in order for the hero to display the correct political consciousness. Yŏng-t'aek confesses that he sings the song with the "purest intentions" and truly believes in the lyrics: that is, he would rather be in the Party's bosom than with Sun-gŭm's breasts. However, Yŏng-t'aek's glorifying of the Great Leader and the Party can hardly be taken seriously. He is ultimately an unreliable narrator. There is no doubt that Yŏn-t'aek was aroused at the sight of Sun-gŭm's protruded breasts and by her leaning on his shoulder—why else would he mention it in his confession? While his eyes continue to gaze at Sun-gŭm, Yŏng-t'aek praises the Great Leader and the Party. The voluptuous bosom of the Party and the paternal love of Kim Il Sung overshadow Sun-gŭm's erotic body that is visible and made visible for Yŏng-t'aek. The choice of song that Yŏng-t'aek sings for his audience is his ostensible performance of Party-mindedness. In fact, it is precisely his claim of singing the song with the "purest intentions" that makes the reading more ironic and schizophrenic.

For whom is Yŏng-t'aek singing his song? Is it a love song for Sun-gŭm? Is it sung for himself so that he can reconfirm his true love for the Great Leader and the Party? Or is it for the miners to see his politically correct performance? Erotic desire and political desire diverge at the utterances of *p'um* and "purest intentions" in his confession. Why does Yŏng-t'aek even mention "purest intentions" after singing the song? Is it perhaps because Yŏng-t'aek could not focus on the Party and the leader with the purest intentions, that his subjectivity was already divided from the very beginning? Even his eyes cannot seem to fixate on one particular object as two sets of bosoms divide, distract, and divert his attention. His claim of singing with the purest intentions is an untenable response to the precarious situation of the two contradicting realities in which he is caught. Breuer succinctly says, "[Irony] is the paradoxical response to a paradoxical situation, as similarly, schizophrenia is a contradictory response to a contradictory situation."[61] The dialectics of overcoming his erotic emotions with political consciousness is not resolved, cannot be resolved, and resists resolution as the narrative suspends any certainty or decidability of meaning.

The story must go on; it cannot remain fixated on Sun-gŭm's breasts. It must deal with grander problems that concern the nation. After the dinner party incident, Yŏng-t'aek is appointed as the head manager of the salt mines—the position he had coveted. Once he becomes the head, Yŏng-t'aek begins to abuse his managerial authority and becomes a practitioner of bureaucratism (*kwallyojui*), a term Kim Il Sung used regularly to criticize his cadres. Yŏng-t'aek becomes a despised and power-hungry bureaucrat. In the early days of Yŏng-t'aek's career at the salt mines, he had labored alongside the workers. His hard work was evident in the sweat that formed under his armpits and on his back. The double meaning of the title of the novel, *Salt Deposits*, suggests the space he worked at (the salt mines) and also the temporality of his labor (the salty sweat formed on the body). As soon as Yŏng-t'aek becomes a manager of the salt mines, he no longer sweats or works alongside his miners. Instead, he finds comfort in his managerial position and abuses his authority.

The discursive strategy used in *Salt Deposits* is to redirect the conflict in the narrative from individual experiences of eroticism to national problems with middle management. In other words, the narrative tries to deflect Yŏng-t'aek's personal problems and his unreliability as a narrator to larger social issues that have persisted in North Korea for as long as there have been bureaucrats. After several decades serving as a manager, he reflects on how he has changed over the years and resolves to become a passionate revolutionary. Yŏng-t'aek reminds the reader how he gained the trust of the workers in his youthful days by displaying his Party-mindedness at the dinner party. He expects readers to believe in his "purest intentions" then and his intentions of transforming into a revolutionary manager now. However, what appeared to be his devotion to the Party in his youth turned out to be a manipulative performance or at the very least an ambiguous intention. He admonishes other cadres and managers to avoid falling into the trap of becoming too bureaucratic, which is a tactful method of diverting attention from himself. On the last page of the novel, Yŏng-t'aek provides his insight into what he has learned through years of being a heartless manager:

> When beautiful flowers are blossoming, it is a sign of heartfelt and hidden effort. Just as salt deposits are formed where the ocean meets the salt ponds, there are many faithful people. They are the rare and also creative flowers. . . .
>
> All of the people in managerial positions were once workers, farmers, and soldiers. I hope my story shows them not to forget their bygone years, and I hope that they unite with the workers they live with forever.[62]

In this passage, Yŏng-t'aek uses of the word "flower" (*kkot*) to imply the organic growth of one's political thought through effort and hard work, a labor that is "hidden" from the perception of others. Yŏng-t'aek professes that a worker ought not to fulfill his duty to the Party because he is forced to or because he has ulterior motives. Instead, a worker must display genuine loyalty to the Great Leader, the nation, and the Party. Yŏng-t'aek realizes that a true worker of the DPRK is one who labors behind the scenes, so to speak, without anyone acknowledging his efforts. Reading this novel at face value may lead to the conclusion that it is another "eternal triangle" narrative portraying the lives of young North Koreans devoting their energy to pleasing Kim Il Sung. It appears that Yŏng-t'aek achieves the correct Party consciousness by transcending his erotic gaze on Sun-gŭm and reprioritizing his love for Kim Il Sung, the Party, and the nation above all else, which is the correct method of reading *Salt Deposits* or any North Korean fiction. However, the entire novel is told from Yŏng-t'aek's perspective, which adds a layer of incredulousness and irony.

Salt Deposits reveals the indeterminacy between the divided self and his world, competing desires and their paradoxical utterances, and the disconnection between discourse/language from its speaker/narrator. The ironic discourse in *Salt Deposits* does not obscure the discrepancy between means and end, intention and result, but rather it exposes faults, fissures, and inconsistencies within the very structural discourse of the speaking subject. The ending of the novel opens up more questions than it answers and resists a concrete enclosure that justifies the unreliable narrator. *Salt Deposits* is an ironic text that suspends meaning and decidability throughout the narrative. The novel attempts to articulate a singular didactic message, but it stutters in its own utterance. It wants to assure readers that the hero has transformed into a Kimilsungist revolutionary, but this intention is forever suspended and caught in the web of indeterminacies.

In the next chapter, I continue to examine the fault lines that disrupt the teleology of North Korean fiction by looking at the doubts of women and competing visions of the conjugal family. Just as there are problems with heterosexual relationships before marriage, we will see the problems with maintaining a happy family and constructing a state-desired revolutionary in fiction. That is, women in these narratives question whether a happy marriage can exist when their husbands are ardent revolutionaries.

CHAPTER THREE

The Woman Question(s)

Desiring a Happy Marriage

> Do you actually think those thoughts as you endure the obstacles in life?
>
> *Kim Kyo-sŏp, Heights of Life*

> Do you think living like that will give you happiness and worth in life?
>
> *Ch'oe Sang-sun, Morning Star*

In Kim Kyo-sŏp's *Saenghwalŭi ŏndŏk* (Heights of Life, 1984), the female protagonist Yŏm-sun quietly but bitterly asks another female protagonist, Ch'un-ae, this all too forthright question to expose Ch'un-ae's dishonesty: "Do you actually think those thoughts as you endure the obstacles in life?" What are "those thoughts" that have put the two friends in a precarious situation? Ch'un-ae claims that her life has been devoted to serving the Great Leader and that she has held on to these thoughts passionately. Yŏm-sun does not believe her; she knows Ch'un-ae all too well. Yŏm-sun believes that Ch'un-ae speaks these words to gain the approval of the men at the research institute where they both work. Yŏm-sun also has strong suspicions that Ch'un-ae is having an affair with her husband, and she thinks that Ch'un-ae makes this claim to deflect those suspicions. Throughout the novel, Yŏm-sun questions the veracity and the intentions of Ch'un-ae as she recognizes the imminent threat to the harmony of her marriage. Then, in Ch'oe Sang-sun's *Saebyŏk pyŏl* (Morning Star, 1987), wife Chin-sun asks her husband if he truly believes that living for the state is the source of his happiness. Chin-sun continues, "If you *do* think like that, then I fear it will be detrimental to our family." For Chin-sun, the state is not the source of happiness but of pain for the family, especially women. The process of perfecting the political consciousness of individuals marginalizes women, silences the "woman question," and substantiates male dominance in society. In both novels, the women refuse to be sublated into the patriarchal social structure by doubting the very discourse that subjects them to the homogeneity of femininity.

North Korean fiction projects a fairytale-like image of conjugal couples, in which voiceless women are inscribed into the grand narrative. However, the couple in the fairy tale do not "live happily ever after." They still have a larger task ahead of them. Marriage, according to the *DPRK Encyclopedia*, is a political union between heterosexual couples and their engagement in fulfilling their duties for the Great Leader, the Party, and the state. In North Korean literature, happiness is not derived from married life but from political life, where individuals are weighed on an ethics scale to determine whether they have lived, are living, and will continue to live a devoted life to the state. A man's identity is that of a proud worker of the DPRK before he is a husband and father. A woman's identity is also as a worker before she is a wife and mother. The relationship between a husband and a wife is that of two workers rather than of two lovers. The ideal image of a married couple in North Korean fiction displays a wife willfully and happily supporting her husband in his revolutionary struggle for the nation. The couple never quarrels or disagrees with each other in this regard, and, more important, there is no romance between married couples either.

The intricate details of married life had a minimal role in North Korean fiction before the 1980s. The urgency to delineate proactive Kimilsungist heroes and heroines has dominated narratives since the late 1960s. In works of fiction before the 1980s, the threat to the solidarity of the nation had mostly come from external forces. Japanese colonialists, American imperialists, and South Korean lackeys were the typical villains who tested the political consciousness and national identity of North Korean heroes and heroines. A revolutionary husband or wife would not have been depicted as a problematic individual in the world of fiction. It was assumed that, once a man or a woman married, the matrimony irrefutably created a revolutionary family or, at the very least, was developing into one. Literary depictions of the conjugal family were not a serious site of contention until the 1980s, when the relationships between husbands and wives started showing signs of dysfunction and unhappiness—toward each other and, by extension, toward the patriarchal state.

In the 1980s, works of fiction revealed marital disillusionment, sexual discontentment between husband and wife, and a projection of married life different from the one the state has prescribed, all suspending the enclosure of the narrative form. Married couples began to pose the question of what happiness is, what happiness means to individual family members, and ultimately to undermine the state's deterministic meaning of happiness. In this chapter, I argue that Kim Kyo-sŏp's *Heights of Life* and Ch'oe Sang-sun's *Morning Star* question the illusion of a revolutionary family and disrupt the teleological narrative from ever projecting a harmonious unity. These two novels show suspension and deferment in the process of completing a revolutionary family through the disgruntled voices of wives. In so doing, their entire narrative content is also suspended and deferred from positing an ending, leaving the compulsory denouement to the story open-ended and the character development of the state-prescribed hero/heroine undeterminable.

Although North Korean fiction attempts to depict happy marriages of revolutionary individuals, a closer reading of these texts discloses the irony of this propaganda, as unhappy marriages are frequently found in overzealous Kimilsungist vanguards, particularly in husbands who neglect their wives at home. The hope for conjugal intimacy and a bright future together through marriage is described as illusory in these two novels, a description I argue is a metonym for North Koreans' recognition of the malfunctioning of the centrally planned system in their own country and the growing political and economic problems in the Soviet Union and Eastern Central Europe in the mid- to late 1980s. As these tensions abroad question the sustainability and the future of the socialist system, the North Korean state provides relief to its people by claiming that the leader will resolve all uncertainties as long as his people remain loyal to him. However, *Heights of Life* and *Morning Star* poignantly reveal that looking to the Great Leader for inspiration and comfort is not a panacea.

A discussion about the conjugal family in North Korean fiction is ineluctably connected to what I refer to as "the woman question." This is not only because North Korean women are socially constructed as dependents of their husbands, caretakers of the family, or representatives of the domestic space, but it is also because women pose the greatest threat to the stability of the state. Legislative changes regarding sexual equality within the Soviet Union, East Central Europe, and even China have affected the political, social, and literary climate in the DPRK. The contention between state politics and women's organizations was an ongoing struggle in these countries from the late 1960s to the late 1980s. As each of these countries revised their laws on marriage, divorce, and abortion to grant more freedom to individuals, the general trend has been a shift toward the ideal of the "traditional family." In *Cinderella Goes to Market,* Barbara Einhorn examines gender equality and women's empowerment in East Central Europe. She claims that the literature of the 1970s represented women speaking for themselves, rejecting prescriptive roles, and focusing on the real problems and contradictions faced by individualized and rounded female characters.[1] According to Einhorn, this was in response to the past iconization of woman as a national symbol, which had obfuscated the problems encountered by real women.[2] Thus, she identifies literature as the medium through which "passions, sensitivities, dreams and longings of men and women" are expressed. Einhorn's analysis of the "woman question" in East Central European literature of the 1970s is particularly relevant to North Korean literature of the 1980s because of the similar political discourse seeking to reinstate "traditional" femininity and motherhood along with individualized voices of women crying out for emancipation.

The title of this chapter, "The Woman Question(s)," raises more issues than the chapter answers. On one level, this chapter revisits the unresolved "woman question" (in the singular form) that has left the women in the two novels disenfranchised and unable to express their individuality and equality in the patriarchal society. On another level, the social, political, and historical problems women face in North Korea are not uniform—hence "the woman questions" (in the plural form). This chapter will also examine the verb form—"the woman questions, the women who question"—to show women's agency against the patriarchal state.

To be clear, I am not analyzing the actual social phenomena of women's fight for justice and equality in the history of North Korea, nor am I conflating the events in literature to social reality and the history of state oppression against North Korean women. What concerns me in this chapter is the way in which the "woman question(s)" emerges immanently from literary discourse that has been silent about the issue or has silenced and marginalized women from the centrifugal force of the state. The form and content of the narrative itself are already designed to produce the Kimilsungist hero/heroine, but there are also moments of slippages in the content; the very language of the discourse contains multiple readings beyond the telos of the state narrative trajectory. The "woman question(s)" in this chapter (and throughout the book) is threefold: first, it puts the male-centered state in crisis through questions of sexual difference; second, it questions the hegemonic monotony by forcing the state to rethink the *unthought;* and, third, it raises doubt or an ateleological trajectory of discourses without a definitive or prescriptive end. The woman does not disrupt the patriarchal polis from outside of its cultural norms but always from within, as she identifies irreducible differences through the language of the Same. She is not sublated, canceled, preserved, and lifted to the ethicality of a perfected state. The woman disrupts and suspends the closure of the prescribed narrative from within the linguistic system that has oppressed her. But before we analyze the woman question(s), we must explore the concept of the North Korean woman.

Womankind: The Everlasting Irony

The way North Korean literature portrays women and their role in the family and the state is closely related to Hegel's philosophical contemplation of individual consciousness in the community. In *Phenomenology of Mind* and *The Philosophy of Right,* Hegel identifies woman as that which functions as both the exemplar and problem of his philosophical argument. In *Phenomenology,* Hegel admits that, in the process of realizing the universality of the state, the state creates an "enemy for itself within its own gates, creates it in what it suppresses, and what is at the same time essential to it—womankind in general."[3] The next passage is Hegel's most notorious claim about the position of women in the state, a claim that feminist scholars have returned to time and time again. Hegel says, "Womankind—the everlasting irony in the life of the community—perverts the universal property of the state into a possession and ornament for the family."[4] For Hegel, these individuals must be suppressed in order for the state to realize its totalization of absolute spirit (*Geist*). The family produces individuals, but "the community gets itself subsistence only by breaking in upon family happiness."[5] The dissolution of the family, for Hegel, is the necessary precondition of the universalization of the community. But what Hegel perceives as a problem is when women fail to realize that the family does its part for the community insofar as it lets the individual go and allows the individual to realize the true potentiality that exists in the community. Hegel recognizes that women are driven by the laws of kinship to seek to maintain the harmony of the family. However, the woman must relinquish her individuality in the family to the state; she must transcend her selfhood for the universality of the community. This movement of transcending, lifting up, breaking out, moving forward and in doing so also negating, canceling, burying, and preserving is sublation (*Aufhebung*).

At the same time, Hegel recognizes that the woman cannot be sublated because she has to reproduce the next generation of individuals, which means that she falls back into the realm of the family. This is the irony of womankind for Hegel, which is in and of itself ironic because he never defines who is or what constitutes the woman, only that she is inferior to the man who enters the state. The woman only exists, for Hegel, in relation to the man, the state, the universal law of rationality. The negativity of woman is the positivity of man; thus, the privileging of man over woman is not only a natural hierarchy for Hegel but also a necessary one in order for the state to realize its unity and self-identity.

But even Hegel confuses essentialist and social constructionist arguments in *Philosophy of Right.* On the one hand, Hegel connects women to nature, the natural world, from which he derives the natural love between mother and child and her responsibility to educate the child in preparation for the community.[6] On the other hand, he recognizes marriage as a social and legal institution that establishes the conjugal relationship between husband and wife. In other words, Hegel naturalizes the mother and socializes the wife, but the two categories of women are embodied in the same woman. We may be all too familiar with Simone de Beauvoir's famous statement "One is not born, but becomes a woman,"[7] where she rejects essentialist determinations on the notion of sex. Whereas gender had been understood as a concept of social, cultural, and historical construction, sex had been determined as a stable and fixed category. For Beauvoir, along with other radical feminists, the concept of sex is neither fixed nor naturally definable. Instead, "woman" must be understood as what Beauvoir calls "myth of woman," or the production of social and political discourses that have been used to oppress women in the patriarchal, heterosexual society.

Irony is already at play when attempting to determine the concept or category of woman in North Korean literature. The performance of women as inscribed within the patriarchal state discourse is the precise site of contention that needs to be questioned. As Judith Butler aptly states, "Performativity is thus not a singular 'act,' for it is always a reiteration of a norm or set of norms, and to the extent that it acquires an act-like status in the present, it conceals or dissimulates the conventions of which it is a repetition."[8] In the case of North Korean fiction, the discursive construction of women reiterates the performance of their femininity in accordance with social and cultural norms, but the very discourse and performance of women conditions the possibility of irony and undecidability, which destabilizes the meaning of woman from the moment she is defined in relation to men. Just when the North Korean political system thinks it has "determined" the woman and attempts to enclose her in its totalitarian linguistic system, she evades the enclosure and works within the system in order to resist it, disrupt it, and prevent it from defining her once and for all. In *Feminism and Deconstruction,* Diane Elam argues that woman can only be understood as representation because there is no original meaning of woman. This representation of a woman, then, regresses into yet another representation—a *mise en abyme*—where women ultimately will never be determined as both object and subject within the male discourse. Elam says, "Women may be represented, but the attempt to represent them exhaustively only makes us more aware of the failure of such attempts."[9]

The way in which rationality is conceived and discussed in the North Korean state creates, in and of itself, the irrationality of women, who must be defined, repressed, and brought to order. Rather than allowing binary opposites to exist, the state constructs the image of the woman to meet the rational standards of the male-dominated social order, exemplified in the state's agenda to delineate motherhood. The presumption here is that the North Korean state (or any state, for that matter) considers itself to be a self-identical entity and that everything else is outside of it. So the state's efforts to rationalize women (make them into state-desired rational beings) are already working under the assumption that women are diametrically opposed to the masculine state, that binary opposites exist and need to be eradicated. Because such binarism exists, the state has privileged the man, the rational, the superior over the woman, the irrational, the inferior.

The North Korean state as the regime of the Same is not its own original self-identity but is already caught in the system of differences. That is, difference does not exist outside of the self but always already within the self, for that is how the self defines itself. In Saussurian linguistics, man defines himself in relation to woman; he sees in himself that he is not a woman, and so he concludes that he is a man. Derrida takes this linguistic argument further by introducing difference, or *différance,* whereby the man cannot be conclusively certain that he is a man simply because he is not a woman as the definition of man and woman is derived from the undecidability of determination. Beyond the identities and differences of man and woman, and before all notions of an original identity, there must have been some differentiating process that can only be known in its effects, only "known" to be other than any knowable binary.[10] For Derrida, all forms of identification and conceptualization escape themselves in language and through the irony in the uncertainty of language and meaning. In the sections below, I will analyze how *Heights of Life* and *Morning Star* show that defining women in relation to men does not secure the patriarchal state order of rationality and identity but rather puts it in question of its own self-identity.

Extra! Extramarital Affairs! Read All About It!

Kim Kyo-sŏp's *Heights of Life* ostensibly criticizes unfaithful characters for their bourgeois tendencies and reintegrates them into the state-desired family. The novel, which portrays several allegorical characters who undergo ideological conversion and end up committing to the political life, was recognized by the Party as one of the most ideologically consistent literary works published in the DPRK in the 1980s. Munye Ch'ulp'ansa (Literary Arts Publishing House) printed 100,000 copies of this novel, which is relatively high for a literary work in North Korea. Print runs of most novels range from 5,000 to 50,000 copies, as indicated inside the back cover of each work. For example, Ch'oe Hak-su's *Pyongyang sigan* (Pyongyang Time, 1976) received rave reviews in the *DPRK Almanac* (*Chosŏn chung'ang nyŏn'gam*), which reviews the important events and literary works of the past year. The almanac for 1977 praised Ch'oe's novel for portraying the brave heroes who reconstructed Pyongyang during the Chollima era under the gracious providence of Kim Il Sung.[11] However, even such a prominent novel was only granted 50,000 copies by the same publishing house that published Kim Kyo-sŏp's *Heights of Life*. It is not clear who or which bureaucratic department determines the number of novels published each year, how they are distributed across the country, and who gets to read them. I can only surmise that the number of copies printed depends largely on the ideological content of the novel as it pertains to the Party's directives and national campaigns at the time it was written.

The *DPRK Almanac* praised *Heights of Life* for its ideological content, and, in a separate section, a short blurb mentioned that the novel was the recipient of the June Fourth Literary Award. That section stated that over 10,000 novels, poems, dramas, and screenplays were conceived in 1984, but only 1,300 were published, and of those *Heights of Life* was chosen as the recipient of this literary award in the novel category. According to the poet Ch'oe Chin-i, formerly of North Korea, this award was given to novelists, poets, and children's book writers as incentives to create vibrant and exciting artworks. The Writers' Union proposed this award to Kim Jong Il in the early 1980s, and, on June 4, he approved and signed the proposal.[12] The award was officially announced to writers in the April 1982 edition of *Chosŏn munhak*. When the *DPRK Almanac* mentions a novel like *Heights of Life* or the novel receives one of the most acclaimed awards in North Korea next to the Kim Il Sung Literary Award, one can assume that the novel contains the most formulaic form and propagandistic content.

The narrative centers on two married couples who experience marital infidelity. The first couple is Ch'un-ae and Chun-ho, and the second couple is Yŏm-sun and In-sŏk. Ch'un-ae and Yŏm-sun are close friends who are engineers at a research institution. The first half of the novel details Ch'un-ae's dissatisfaction with her marriage; the second half elaborates on Yŏm-sun's suspicions of marital infidelity between her husband and Ch'un-ae. The novel portrays the deterioration and restoration of their friendship. More important, the novel celebrates the process through which characters transcend their individualistic motives for the solidarity of the collective.

The surface-level reading of this novel presents two women who understand each other and recommit to the state through the reevaluation of their political consciousness. Similar to most narratives in North Korean fiction, the conflict between the two women is resolved through a deep desire to please Kim Il Sung. In the end, they recognize that pleasing the Great Leader is the most important objective in their lives and the most meaningful way to construct the family-state of the DPRK. This kind of ending is not only a narrative convention in nearly every piece of North Korean fiction, but it is a necessary trope that promises the protection and preservation of the state. The homogeneous delineation of people striving toward a unified purpose reinforces the implications pervasive in the literary discourse of the state as a stable, strong, and solidified unit.

However, *Heights of Life* is anything but a typical formulaic plot. Even within such a seemingly impervious and overtly politicized narrative, the "woman question" or the "woman who questions" emerges and resists the totalization or the closure of the novel through woman's suspicions and doubts. The novel seemingly guarantees a happy ending with the characters rejoicing in the hearth of Kim Il Sung, but, at the same time, the novel cannot seem to forget the woman who, amid the celebration, continues to ask, "Do you actually think those thoughts as you endure the obstacles in life?" The four-hundred-page novel portrays complex individuals who desire and envision a different ideality of a happy marriage/family, which immanently questions and challenges the one proposed by the state.

The concept of the family as portrayed in North Korean literature itself puts the monolithic trajectory of the state discourse in question because of the various types of families with innumerable concerns, aspirations, and desires for which the state cannot account. Different educational backgrounds, stratified economic classes, hierarchical political positions in society, family members who live abroad or study abroad, wide-ranging occupations, differences in age, different standards of living, various geographic locations across the DPRK, and unconventional family members (for example, widowed, divorced, deceased, orphaned) are but a few examples of the multidimensional depictions of families in North Korean fiction, which are not particular to the 1980s but are accentuated in this decade. In short, the state's politicized notion of the family is far from being a homogeneous and unitary entity that can account for the diversity present in literature. For example, in *Sedae* (Generations, 1984), author Kim Sam-bok raises the concerns of a working-class agricultural family on the brink of falling apart as a result of the children desiring to work and live in the city. In Kim Sam-bok's other novel, *Hyangt'o* (Land, 1985), one of the protagonists, raised by a single mother from a well-to-do family, eventually leaves the countryside for the city to receive a better education, never to return again. Geographic location, migration, and economic status are important elements for Kim Sam-bok that create more complex conflicts in his narratives. In Kim Mun-ch'ang's *T'anbu* (Miners, 1986), a working-class family of miners faces a humiliating situation when the parents do not have enough money to pay for their children's wedding ceremonies. Paek Nam-nyong's short story "Saengmyŏng" (Life, 1985) addresses ethical problems among upper-class administrators who bribe a university dean to admit their children into the program. Wealth and political status have had an impact on interpersonal relationships in North Korean fiction throughout its history, but Paek's short story in particular portrays how material wealth and political prestige have constructed a problematic society.

The dynamic variations on the family have always been relegated to the margins of the narrative. North Korean fiction clearly reveals class difference, but it does not dwell on it or make it the central concern of the narrative. The novel must move forward and demonstrate how different families from different economic, political, and social backgrounds achieve the correct political consciousness of love for the leader, the Party, and the state. Families may begin at disparate social and political levels, but the denouement of the novel promises that such differences do not matter. But in fact they do matter because problems of difference have not been resolved. The all too abrupt and contrived endings in North Korean fiction reveal not only the obstructive limitations and impositions set by the state but also the state's inability to address pertinent issues that matter both in the fictional world and in reality.

One of the growing problems seen in literary works involved the rise of the intellectual class and its effects on the family. Since the 1970s, the DPRK had tried to improve the economy by encouraging its citizens to receive a higher education beyond the eleven-year compulsory schooling. The Party initiated a national campaign called the Three Revolutions movement, which consisted of ideology, technology, and culture. The idea of the campaign was to transform North Korean society into an industrialized nation worthy to compete on the international stage. The process through which North Korea envisioned success was by elevating the working class from performing manual labor to performing specialized, skilled labor, which entailed the need to acquire the latest technology. The predominant conflict in North Korean literature of the 1970s involved the disparity between those of the manual-labor generation and those of the intellectual generation. Manual laborers were no longer glamorized for their efforts, as they had been in 1960s fiction, but instead were criticized for remaining in the past and being unwilling to change with the present conditions of society.

From the end of the 1970s, many works of fiction portrayed an intellectual that outshined the other workers. The intellectual would typically be a skilled technician, architect, or engineer; he or she would likely be a researcher in the field of biology, chemistry, physics, or computer science. The common denominator among the intellectuals was that they refrained from manual labor. They would instruct, administer, and monitor the other workers, but they did not engage in that work themselves, exemplifying the stratified economic, social, and political class system in North Korea that prioritized and privileged the intellectual class. Although the working class remained the largest group depicted in North Korean fiction of the 1980s, it was as a nominal socialist emblem and an empty signifier in the political system, which always consisted of elite members of society. The intellectualization of the people through the Three Revolutions movement created an economic class difference between manual laborers and social elites, and this in turn affected the way in which narratives were formulated and characters were constructed.

The movement to intellectualize the people had a profound impact on the characters in Kim Kyo-sŏp's *Heights of Life*. Ch'un-ae and Yŏm-sun represent the intellectual class, and their socioeconomic status reflects the growing group of elites of the 1980s. These women, along with other researchers in the novel, are required to use their brainpower rather than their physical strength to create a hopeful future for the DPRK. However, what the novel really portrays is the way these women glamorize their elitist lifestyle as city dwellers, who refrain from toiling with their hands like farmers or industrial workers. They design blueprints in the quietude of an air-conditioned laboratory, but mostly they spend time gossiping and talking about topics unrelated to work. Their lab coats are not soiled from laborious work but rather neatly starched and ironed. Underneath their lab coats, these women wear tailored suits and high heels so that as soon as leave their office they can display their sense of fashion to the public as both the subject and the object of the consumptive gaze.

In *Illusive Utopia*, Suk-Young Kim notes a shift in women's fashion in the 1980s as a testament to North Korea's desire to update and modernize the sartorial image of women and increase production in the textile industry.[13] In *Heights of Life*, Ch'un-ae's and Yŏm-sun's clothes do not serve a functional purpose that enables labor performance. Instead, clothes for these women become a site on which feminine discourse of the elite class is produced, generated, and made desirable.

The elitist lifestyle of the intellectual class also lends itself to certain behavioral performativities that were rarely portrayed in works of fiction from previous decades. During one of the meetings of the factory's researchers, Ch'un-ae buries herself in a novel and isolates herself from her colleagues, somewhat similar to Jane Eyre reading *Bewick's History of British Birds* behind the curtains in her room—hiding from her abusive living conditions, taking flight from England in her imagination, and discovering her identity. Ch'un-ae falls deeply into the novel's fantastical world and walls herself off from discussion at the meeting. Author Kim Kyo-sŏp never identifies the book Ch'un-ae is reading, not because it is a negligible detail in the narrative but because it is the performativity of reading that is worth noting in this passage. Reading is a performance that conflicts with the spatiality and temporality of the subject and the book Ch'un-ae is reading. There are two spatialities and temporalities: the first one is Ch'un-ae's actual world, and the second is her virtual world. The book itself is aspatial and atemporal, as Ch'un-ae can always come back to the book at any given locality and temporality, as she does throughout the novel. In this particular passage, as the meeting is about to begin, Ch'un-ae picks up her book to read from where she left off, escaping from her present reality into her virtual reality. We can infer from her habitual reading that her book provides emotional gratification by supplying her vicariously with attention and nurturance she does not get enough of in her day-to-day existence.[14] For Ch'un-ae, the act of reading opens up a spatial temporality, where she lives a different life among different people in a different world.

Victorian scholars have associated the act of reading not only with the bourgeois culture of leisure and literacy but also with redefining political identity and the discourse of desire. In *Desire and Domestic Fiction,* Nancy Armstrong says, "The novel provided a means of displacing and containing longstanding symbolic practices—especially those games, festivities, and other material practices of the body that maintained a sense of collective identity."[15] The novel brought or kept the individual at home and away from public, collective activity. The rise of the novel, says Armstrong, challenged the existing political discourse of women and sexuality and produced a language of increasing psychological complexity for understanding individual behavior.[16] In more contemporary times, Janice Radway explores the culture of reading romance novels among women as "an activity of mild protest and longing for reform . . . to satisfy the emotional needs of women" who had been failed by the institutions of heterosexuality and monogamous marriage.[17] In *Reading the Romance,* Radway argues that romance reading can be seen as a "collectively elaborated female ritual" or a social performance through which women express, contest, and reevaluate their shared experiences as the appendages of men and "attempt to imagine a more perfect state where all the needs they so intensely feel would be adequately addressed."[18] For Radway, the act of reading is a form of escape in which women experience the imaginary world vicariously through the novel.

Likewise, in *Heights of Life,* Ch'un-ae's act of reading during the factory meeting is an expression of her agency and resistance to public affairs. Whether she is reading the Immortal History series, novels about the great heroes and heroines of the DPRK, risqué romance novels, or anything that would define her subjectivity as a woman is not the issue; the content contained within the book is not what defines her. Ch'un-ae defines her own political identity by establishing the parameters by which she wants to be defined. She chooses the kinds of work she wants to do at the research lab, and she chooses to participate in the collective activities that she finds interesting. Ch'un-ae's form of protest does not go unnoticed by her coworkers and supervisor, but that has been her intention all along. Her defiant behavior at a male-centered institution is a reflection of her marital dissatisfaction. Or, to put it in another way, discontent with her husband is the point of departure for her to exercise her apathy toward public activities by reading quietly, a form of resistance without voicing any particular objections.

The performativity of an intellectual family is evident in the way personal conversations between husbands and wives distinguish and demarcate the dichotomy of the private and public spheres. What Ch'un-ae and her husband discuss behind closed doors contrasts with what they ought to say and how they ought to behave in public. In public, Ch'un-ae and her husband Chun-ho maintain their dignity so that the perception of an elite family is not tainted. They prefer to save face in public than to expose their vulnerability. They understand the social codes of behavior that instruct them to speak words that edify the state. The wives in *Heights of Life* pretend to be in happy marriages at the cost of their unsatisfied need for sexual intimacy. They desire intimacy from their husbands more than participation in state affairs, and the lack of sexual attention derives from their husbands' zealous and at times questionable participation in their labor as revolutionary public servants.

When the novel begins, Ch'un-ae has felt empty and isolated from her husband for quite some time. She has always envied Yŏm-sun's intimate relationship with In-sŏk. This is because Ch'un-ae's husband, Chun-ho, is always away on a "research trip" for weeks or months at a time, leaving Ch'un-ae and her daughter alone at home. One night, as Chun-ho is preparing to leave again without advance notice, Ch'un-ae cries, "What? Leaving? At this hour of the night?"[19] Chun-ho is a geologist in search of rare rocks, but why he frequently leaves at night puzzles Ch'un-ae. She complains to her husband, "You no longer care for our family," as an attempt to convince him to stay.[20] When Yŏm-sun asks about Chun-ho's sudden departure, Ch'un-ae responds: "He's probably busy. What else would it be?"[21] Then, the narrator adds: "Ch'un-ae responded calmly, but, without her knowing, her voice quivered. This was because she did not believe in what she had just said."[22] Ch'un-ae does not disclose her private affairs in public (not even to her best friend) in fear of inciting suspicions and gossip from her female colleagues. For days, Ch'un-ae has not been eating well, functioning properly, and certainly not sleeping well. Her lack of marital intimacy is evident on Ch'un-ae's pallid face. On seeing Ch'un-ae's feeble body, Yŏm-sun suspects that Ch'un-ae is pregnant, to which Ch'un-ae curtly responds: "There is no way that could've happened!"[23] Ch'un-ae's brusque response reveals her lack of sexual intimacy with her husband. She suspects her husband is having an affair, has become indifferent to his family, or has become indifferent because he is having an affair. In the name of the state, he leaves a lonely, desperate wife unattended among male colleagues at work. Chun-ho's long absence from his wife and daughter is presumably for the sake of conducting "research" for the country, but Ch'un-ae has her doubts.

In *Heights of Life,* women's doubts are never cast away, even when the novel reaches the end. They haunt the individuals and the grand narrative of the novel. Doubts obstruct individuals from acquiring political consciousness; the novel itself seems to doubt whether fulfilling political duties can bring happiness to individuals. Ch'un-ae questions her husband's long absences from home, but she also questions her own identity as a woman. *Heights of Life,* in its entirety, is a story of doubts, skeptical characters, questionable actions/reactions, and an uncertain ending. To be clear, doubts in *Heights of Life* are not simply suspicions of lying but rather suspicions of every speech act. The intention or the truth value of the speaking subject is not what needs to be deciphered. Doubts displace and destabilize the very language in the narrative, revealing the possibility that the truth will always be deferred and estranged from perfecting individuals' political consciousness. For example, when Ch'un-ae responds to Yŏm-sun, "He's probably busy. What else would it be?" she doubts her own words and her husband's political intentions. Her question opens up endless possibilities that could provide an answer, an excuse for his frequent absences, except for the answer that would mark him as a revolutionary hero. Doubts in this novel disrupt the prescriptive narrative and by extension the stability of the male-dominated social system.

Ch'un-ae's question—"What? Leaving? At this hour of the night?"—demands that the man (the state) speak to answer for the violence he has committed against the woman, the violence of dissolving the family. The man does not speak; he just leaves the home, leaving the woman at the margins of the male-dominated social system. He needs to do "research," so what more does he have to say, *what else would it be?* The state rewards those who have acquired the male lexicon and are capable of bringing themselves out of the domestic space and into the public forum of men. In most North Korean fiction, a woman would never question or object to her husband's public duties. The woman's obedience is recognized as her tacit consent to national priorities, which in turn subjugates her to the state-desired iconography of wifehood and motherhood. In fact, she too is required to adopt the male linguistic system and perform her political duties alongside men. The North Korean state considers this sexual/gender equality. But Ch'un-ae disagrees. Ch'un-ae expresses her objection to her husband's obsession with his work, his need to become a revolutionary geologist in the middle of the night. Her discontentment toward her husband is her angst toward the state that is taking her husband from her and depriving her of the actualization of a happy marriage.

Through Ch'un-ae, *Heights of Life* divulges the conflict between a woman's vision of domesticity and the state's directives of family ethicality. Ch'un-ae stands at a crossroads of her divided desires. She understands that her calling in life as a researcher is designated to please Kim Il Sung, but she doubts whether working for the state can bring her true happiness in her marriage. For her it is only a job. Ch'un-ae's rationale is that her job comprises a portion of her identity and that her true selfhood is found in her domestic labor. She decides to quit her job and become a stay-at-home mother. Ch'un-ae claims that she recognizes the importance of staying home and supporting her family as a state-prescribed dutiful wife. In fact, she thinks that by becoming a more submissive wife she will rekindle her lackluster marriage with her husband. In other words, state-desired wifehood entails the woman's willingness to prepare the family for the public space, that is, to let her husband participate in his political duties.

However, Ch'un-ae's fantasy is short-lived. The research institute decides to pair Ch'un-ae and In-sŏk (Yŏm-sun's husband) on a project to design a new heater. The proposal for the project itself is innocent: it is to bring two bright and promising intellectuals together to design a heater for the factory, using the latest technology the DPRK has to offer. The two intellectuals, in this case, just happen to be a married man and a desperate housewife. The research institute creates the space for In-sŏk and Ch'un-ae to work closely on the new design late into the evening for an extended period of time. As it turns out, the working environment becomes a contested site of infidelity and doubt.

This is an important turning point in *Heights of Life*. The novel spends a considerable number of pages on the development of Ch'un-ae and In-sŏk's illicit relationship. Ch'un-ae recognizes that In-sŏk has the personality and characteristics she has been looking for in her own husband (warmth, tenderness, supportiveness, and love). Conversely, In-sŏk finds Ch'un-ae utterly attractive because of her innovative ideas and her skillfulness in drafting blueprints, qualities that are lacking in his wife. The irony of this situation is that the factory "broke up" the conjugal couples for work for the state, and, in the process of work for the state, a new, illicit couple is created. Ch'un-ae does not rediscover her true identity as a researcher for the state at the factory; she discovers another married man, who fulfills her every fantasy. When Ch'un-ae shows excitement about going back to the factory, Yŏm-sun is doubtful that Ch'un-ae is eager about designing a new heater. Yŏm-sun also recognizes the change in attitude of her husband, particularly in the way he talks about working with Ch'un-ae. It becomes more and more evident to Yŏm-sun that her husband, In-sŏk, is displaying his divided desire for the project and Ch'un-ae. In-sŏk spends less time with his own family, resulting in gradual estrangement.

Ch'un-ae perceives that Yŏm-sun is disturbed by the whole idea of the new project. When Ch'un-ae confronts Yŏm-sun about the matter, Yŏm-sun responds: "It's true that I am a bit uncomfortable with the whole thing. But it's not because you've decided to do the project. I may have been hurt, and I'm still worried about your project. But I am not worried that you have decided to complete the blueprints. Regarding this issue, you will not have to worry."[24]

Yŏm-sun is clearly not being honest with Ch'un-ae. In fact, Yŏm-sun is speaking rather incoherently. Yŏm-sun wants to say more, wants to be more straightforward with Ch'un-ae, and wants to shout, "Stay away from my husband!" At this critical moment when Yŏm-sun wants to utter a few more words to discourage Ch'un-ae from working with her husband, Ch'un'ae says: "If my blueprint could be a small bolt in the future plans that our Great Leader has set out, there can be nothing greater than that! . . . I will keep this thought with me as I work."[25]

What a timely moment for Ch'un-ae to claim her love for the Great Leader to diffuse Yŏm-sun's enmity toward her. In this situation, the political rhetoric of loving the leader is used to control and abate Yŏm-sun's suspicions of Ch'un-ae's intentions in working with In-sŏk. Yŏm-sun knows Ch'un-ae all too well; she does not believe that Ch'un-ae believes in the words that she has just spoken. Yŏm-sun thinks that Ch'un-ae's political rhetoric is intended to make her project nobler and loftier than it actually is and to make other characters in the novel believe that Ch'un-ae is a Party-minded heroine at the research institute. Ch'un-ae's use of such rhetoric infuriates Yŏm-sun even more: "Yŏm-sun silently glared at Ch'un-ae with doubting eyes. After a while, Yŏm-sun let out a sigh and asked, 'Do you actually think those thoughts as you endure the obstacles in life?' "[26]

Yŏm-sun is not convinced that political thoughts are Ch'un-ae's motivation for completing the assigned task—"those thoughts" that are the answers to all life's problems; those thoughts that are supposed to define happiness for all North Koreans; those thoughts that compel the individual to live his or her life only to please the Great Leader; those thoughts that reconfirm Kim Il Sung, Kim Jong Il, and Kim Jung Un as the sole provider of hearth, shelter, food, family, and life. Political rhetoric in North Korean literature is supposed to control, discipline, and compel individuals to look beyond their personal problems. However, Yŏm-sun thinks there is an underlying motive in Ch'un-ae's excitement to complete her blueprints, and she believes that Ch'un-ae's display of Party-mindedness is intended to win the approval of men who surround her at the lab. To Yŏm-sun, Ch'un-ae is an attention-hungry, lascivious woman who has already forgotten about her absent husband in the company of another man. Ch'un-ae's use of her sexual body to receive male attention is Yŏm-sun's greatest remonstrance.

Heights of Life shifts from narrating Ch'un-ae's desperation to acquire a happy marriage to Yŏm-sun's desperation to maintain a happy marriage. This shift occurs because the "woman question(s)" does not concern only one woman in the narrative but multiple women. Just as the teleological narrative is about to resolve Ch'un-ae's identity/femininity crisis, Yŏm-sun emerges with doubts and suspicions that destabilize the trajectory of the narrative yet again, suspending it from foreseeing any conclusive enclosure. This shift is a critical one; it erects a dissatisfied woman without finding a resolution to her problems. Yŏm-sun asks the question "Do you actually think those thoughts as you endure the obstacles in life?" at the precise moment when Ch'un-ae seems to have acquired the language of the Same. The very language that Ch'un-ae contested at the beginning of the novel seems to be the only language she knows. Yŏm-sun believes neither Ch'un-ae nor the semantics of Ch'un-ae's confession.

Yŏm-sun's doubts resonate throughout the novel, subverting and destabilizing the rhetoric of individuals' political commitment to the state. She does not just doubt Ch'un-ae; she doubts the state discourse that nearly every North Korean hero or heroine utters in fiction. Yŏm-sum exposes Ch'un-ae's rhetoric as displaying a spurious connection between what she says and what she believes. In other words, Yŏm-sun's suspicions reveal the disjointedness of Ch'un-ae's statement and her intention, the signifier and the signified, and the utterance and the meaning. Yŏm-sun does not claim to know Ch'un-ae's actual intentions, but what she does know is that Ch'un-ae's political rhetoric is ritualized practice that individuals in the state are supposed to recite, repeat, and perform in order to display their Party-mindedness. Yŏm-sun's faith in her friend, her husband, and the entire state is destabilized as she recognizes her alienated identity within the community. She can neither force herself to comply with the political rhetoric nor believe in it. Comrade-love is supposed to encourage friends, lovers, and spouses to live a life worthy of the state, but, for Yŏm-sun, her husband's words are far from giving her physical, emotional, and psychological solace.

Yŏm-sun has been suspicious of In-sŏk ever since he and Ch'un-ae began working late nights on the new project for the factory. One night, in an effort to rekindle their love, Yŏm-sun prepares a lavish dinner for In-sŏk and invites his friends. In-sŏk does not come home from work although his shift ended hours ago. Embarrassed for his friends, Yŏm-sun goes out to the bus stop to wait for him in the cold. When the last bus of the evening finally arrives, Yŏm-sun sees In-sŏk get off the bus with Ch'un-ae, who is wearing In-sŏk's blazer. Both In-sŏk and Ch'u-nae are shocked to see Yŏm-sun at the bus stop. Ch'un-ae bids good night to In-sŏk and hurries home. In-sŏk tries to give his blazer to Yŏm-sun, but she refuses it. It pains Yŏm-sun to see her husband eagerly spending time with her friend. But it pains her more to see her closest friend from college betray their friendship by disrupting the harmony of a once happy family. Yŏm-sun advises her husband to be discreet about having an illicit affair with her best friend. She says, "I cannot stop you from loving others. But, please be discreet about it so that others will not see."[27] In-sŏk does not deny Yŏm-sun's allegations.

Yŏm-sun's advice to In-sŏk is unexpected and uncharacteristic of wives in North Korean fiction. This striking admonition from Yŏm-sun differentiates between one's inner thoughts and outer decorum. In *On the Art of the Cinema,* Kim Jong Il instructs his writers and filmmakers to create heroes and heroines whose actions and dialogue conform to their correct ideological thought: the outer is the direct manifestation of the inner.[28] As the private sphere is not supposed to exist in communist societies, one's inner, personal thoughts are to be made public or to conform to collective thought, uniting individualism with Party-mindedness. Yet Yŏm-sun warns In-sŏk to store his feelings for Ch'un-ae in the depths of his private chambers, his private fantasies, while presenting the performance desired of a worker in public.

The binary opposites of inner/outer, thoughts/utterances, private/public, and leisure/work, are not blurred but dissociated in *Heights of Life.* The former in each pair is represented through or manifested in the latter, but *Heights of Life* shows the impossibility of the latter ever totalizing, enclosing, or even making sense of the former. Yŏm-sun values the façade of family stability, the appearance of a happy family, even if it means having to maintain an unsatisfied marriage. She cannot prevent her husband from loving Ch'un-ae, but she warns him against making her family a public mockery. She desperately desires others to think that she is in a healthy marriage. Yŏm-sun clearly understands the binary opposites that exist in her world. She understands that if she were to disclose the private to the public or if the public were to discover what has been occurring in private, it would have harrowing ramifications for her social status as a middle-class intellectual woman. In order to save face in public, Yŏm-sun keeps these binary opposites separated and reluctantly allows her husband to engage in his sexual pleasures behind closed doors despite her disapproval.

The illicit affair puts the harmony of the state-desired family into crisis as sexual issues question women's identity in the state. Ch'un-ae desires the fantastical ideality of a "happily ever after" story, but she never finds it. Yŏm-sun thinks she's been living in a fairytale-like marriage, but she discovers a different reality. However, the novel needs to come to an end in the "happily ever after" narrative convention. It cannot keep the two women unsatisfied with the state.

It must transform the irrational women into rational beings that meet the prescriptions of the state. Yet the story ends too abruptly, showing the ending to be contrived and artificial. Like most North Korean fiction, *Heights of Life* finds a way to resolve a problematic situation through an overdose of reciting Party directives and honoring Kim Il Sung. Ch'un-ae finds her college diploma hidden in her closet and remembers how she once loved her nation and the Great Leader. She commits to drafting her design and unsurprisingly completes it with great success. Yŏm-sun abandons all suspicion of Ch'un-ae, and she, too, commits to her research. Yŏm-sun and her husband rekindle their love and forget about his extramarital affair. Ch'un-ae's husband returns from his trip at the timeliest moment, and notices how Ch'un-ae has recommitted to her political duties. He says that he has been away to provide time for Ch'un-ae to redefine her love for the nation and the Great Leader. The novel has somehow managed to formulate the "happily ever after" ending with the loving guidance of the parental leader Kim Il Sung.

Heights of Life presents multiple metaphors of heights (*ŏndŏk*) that individuals in the novel have to overcome. The meaning of *ŏndŏk* as a hill or a slope in Korean refers to problems in society. Chun-ho lectures Ch'un-ae during one of their many quarrels: "I believe there ought to be hills in everyone's life. Once we climb that hill, we must designate another hill to climb. But what have we done in our lives?"[29] Chun-ho's definition of a hill refers to one's goal that needs to be achieved for the state to please Kim Il Sung. The apex of the hill represents one's award or sense of accomplishment, which for Chun-ho is not the end of one's journey but a continuing excursion to find the next heights in life to perform greater achievements for the state. However, for Ch'un-ae and Yŏm-sun, the hill refers to the challenges and obstacles that obstruct their married lives and question their identity as women. For Ch'un-ae, the lack of sexual intimacy with her husband is the unbearable obstacle in her life, causing her to shift her eyes to other men in search of much-needed affection. Ch'un-ae does not find her fulfillment as a revolutionary researcher for the state, but rather behind closed doors with male workers. For Yŏm-sun, the factory's new project becomes the intolerable obstacle in her life as her marriage is torn asunder by the national campaign to increase productivity and by having In-sŏk work closely with Ch'un-ae. Yŏm-sun quietly resents her husband, her best friend, Ch'un-ae, and the state. The soap opera–esque plot and tone of *Heights of Life* delineate the emotional and psychological problems of the women in their earnest attempt to hide their innermost secrets from each other and from the gaze of the Party.

Heights of Life is not a story about a harmonious family that faces problems only to return to being the same family it once was, but rather it is about the indeterminable definition of what a family is and what it means to exist in the state. The novel opens with two women discussing insurmountable problems that question the stability of their marriage and their identity as state-desired wives. The two women understand their duty to express their love for the Great Leader in public. They know the expected decorum, the appropriate gestures, and the ideological rhetoric that mark them as loyal subjects of the Great Leader. *Heights of Life* is ostensibly a novel that delineates the lives of women who reconfirm and reaffirm their devotion to the Party and Kim Il Sung. If, on the one hand, the novel is to be read simply as an educational tool, then it teaches readers to recite the correct political rhetoric that they are supposed to use in critical situations.

On the other hand, if we read the novel as a schizophrenic and ironic text that always contains the possibility of doubt and disbelief, then the novel resists any certainties of meaning and definition. The conjugal problems are never resolved in the novel but are only deferred or deflected away from the grand narrative. The real marital problems are obscured, marginalized, and subsumed into the overbearing voice of the male-dominated state discourse. However, the novel cannot forget, efface, or exorcise the woman who questions: "Do you actually think those thoughts as you endure obstacles in life?"

He Said, She Said in Ch'oe Sang-sun's *Morning Star*

It is not an overstatement to assert that the North Korean literary culture is a male-dominated institution. Novels portray the establishment of the nation by men, the achievements of men, and the nation as a community of men. Women are also represented in literature as noble characters of virtue and political consciousness. However, women who participate in the forum of men are required to become men, to exist for men and through men. The public space was never meant for women to dwell in, and it was certainly not a place for women to design according to their desires and thoughts. The violence of disenfranchisement toward women is at times implied in literature and at other times clearly evident. But no novel in the 1980s shows the violence toward women as severely as Ch'oe Sang-sun's *Saebyŏk pyŏl* (Morning Star, 1987), in which the woman is completely effaced from the conclusion of the narrative, as if she never existed in the story and as if her story never mattered. Below is a summary of the novel.

Chin-sun and her young daughter eagerly wait for her husband, Sŏk-jun, to return from his research trip. Sŏk-jun is a high school teacher at the district Agricultural Institute. He has been researching the potentiality of a fertilizer for over ten years. He visits Professor Son Sŭng-p'il at the Agricultural University to gain more insight into the fertilizer. Son Sŭng-p'il wrote his dissertation on this particular fertilizer, so Sŏk-jun believes that Professor Son can assist him. Son Sŭng-p'il immediately rejects the idea that the fertilizer is of any use and sends Sŏk-jun away. However, Sŏk-jun is still determined to complete his research.

Sŏk-jun struggles with his research, and his assistants leave him. Despite the dire conditions, he presses on and prepares to give a lecture on his new findings. The day of the lecture arrives. He stands before teachers, professors, and farmers from the area. After his presentation, the audience begins to debate Sŏk-jun's research. Professor Son Sŭng-p'il is one of the first to criticize Sŏk-jun. Pak Chun-t'aek is another researcher who doubts Sŏk-jun's research results. Both Son Sŭng-p'il and Pak Chun-t'aek had worked together earlier on this fertilizer to no avail. The problem escalates to the point where Sŏk-jun is asked to leave his teaching position.

Several months later, Sŏk-jun picks up a science journal and discovers that his research on the fertilizer has been validated and published. However, the credit is given to Professor Son Sŭng-p'il. The professor plagiarized Sŏk-jun's findings and submitted the report to the journal under his name. A few of Sŏk-jun's friends urge him to confront Son Sŭng-p'il about this matter. However, Sŏk-jun feels that it does not matter who wrote the report as long as the new findings benefit the nation. Meanwhile, Pak Chun-t'aek has also read the journal and realized that Son Sŭng-p'il copied Sŏk-jun's research. Pak Chun-t'aek changes his opinion about Sŏk-jun and considers him a legitimate researcher.

The Agricultural Committee holds a lecture on the successful findings regarding the fertilizer, and Professor Son Sŭng-p'il is the keynote speaker. Sŏk-jun receives an invitation to attend the lecture. When Son Sŭng-p'il finishes his lecture, the audience asks its questions to Sŏk-jun instead of the keynote speaker. The audience knows that it was Sŏk-jun who had discovered the potentiality of the fertilizer. Later Sŏk-jun discovers that Pak Chun-t'aek had invited him to this lecture to be acknowledged and vindicated by the community. A few days later, Sŏk-jun returns to his teaching position at the district high school and continues to teach with much pride and self-esteem.

Morning Star begins with the concerns of a wife, but these concerns are never fully addressed or resolved in the rest of the novel because the narrative trajectory rationalizes the action of the husband as that which constructs the nation. Author Ch'oe Sang-sun wrote her novel *Morning Star* to depict the kind of hero that reflected the Party's new national campaign. The Hidden Hero (*sumŭn yŏngung*) campaign began in the late 1970s and continued throughout the 1980s.

One of the first headlines to commemorate a Hidden Hero appeared on October 13, 1979, in *Rodong sinmun* (Workers' Daily): "Heart for the Party and the People." In this article, the female biologist Paek Sŏl-hŭi was honored with an award from Kim Il Sung for her outstanding achievement in advancing the field of science and technology. Thereafter, three others received an award from Kim Il Sung for their unparalleled achievements, Kim Sang-ryŏn, Pak Yŏng-ch'ŏl, and Chang Chae-san, followed by the headline "Let's learn from the Hidden Heroes who have shown their passionate devotion." Fictionalized short stories were written about these four heroes along with other nonfiction stories about ordinary people in the DPRK in a three-volume anthology called *Uri sidae'ui yŏng'ungdŭl* (Heroes of Our Generation, 1988).[30] The purpose of this collection was to raise the consciousness of the workers and to encourage them to emulate these characters so that productivity, technology, and Party-mindedness would increase throughout the nation.

This movement was not the first to recognize citizens for having accomplished feats in the community. *Rodong sinmun* had reported on everyday heroes across the country to showcase the strength and success of socialism in the DPRK since its inception. The difference between past heroes and the hidden hero of the 1980s was the discursive reconstruction of political rhetoric that revered Kimilsungism as the guiding principle through which the hidden hero performed his or her duties. Although heroes in the past had also praised and thanked Kim Il Sung for his providence in addition to articulating their visions of a perfected socialist country, for hidden heroes, glorifying Kim Il Sung was not an additional component to their vision but the only one.

The hidden heroes in fiction symbolize the Kimilsungist nation, and, therefore, to disseminate this discourse of a leader-centered nationalism in the 1980s, the state penetrated into the protagonist's personal life to justify whether or not one is living his or her life for the Great Leader. The nuclear family was a topical choice to inscribe the Hidden Hero campaign in literature because such narratives divulge the state's penetration into the domestic space to disclose private conversations between married couples and unveil the intimate relationships of lovers in order to show the transformation of the sexual protagonist into a desexualized hidden hero. The state's penetration into the individual's intimate life was designed to discipline and punish under the aegis of the Hidden Hero campaign. There was nothing the hidden hero should or could hide from the state's gaze.

One of the indicative traits in hidden hero narratives is the phrase "without anyone knowing" that had never appeared in stories of previous decades.[31] Unlike the Three Revolutions heroes and heroines in the 1970s, hidden heroes in the

1980s conduct their research, carry out their political duties, and assist the collective "without anyone knowing." The rhetorical effect of such discourse in hidden hero fiction is intended to motivate readers to continue with their work for the nation and for the leader with the foreknowledge that nobody is watching their performance. The hidden hero does not wait for the country to assign tasks but takes the initiative to find tasks that will benefit the greater good. In his presidential inaugural address, John F. Kennedy called on the American people to do something similar: "Ask not what your country can do for you, ask what you can do for your country." Amid the growing anxiety of Americans over the Cold War, Kennedy's rhetoric was that of optimism and solidarity. The use of chiasmus in his speech produces the desired efficacy through the symmetry of two imperative questions—ask (not) what your country can do for you, and ask what you can do for your country—in which the latter question is weighed more favorably over the former. Likewise, the rhetoric of "without anyone knowing" for hidden heroes impresses upon North Korean readers the need to emulate the mindset and initiatives of such heroes no matter how exhausting and frustrating the nation's political situation may be.

Scholars have suggested that North Korea's economic decline occurred when the Party declared a self-sufficient economic model and placed its highest priority on heavy industries for the domestic market rather than for the international market. In his article titled "The Political Economy of Economic Reform in North Korea," Yong-Soo Park argues that this economic strategy diminished North Korea's foreign trade and forced North Korea to take out a huge number of foreign loans from the West during the 1970s.[32] Its closed-door policy in pursuit of a self-sufficient economy caused North Korea not to import capital and technology, which then led to stagnation in exports.[33] In "North Korea's Closed Economy," Hy-Sang Lee surmises that, for a number of years leading up to the 1980s, productivity growth in North Korea was actually less than zero (-1.7 percent).[34] This undoubtedly had an adverse effect on heavy and light industries, factories, cooperative farms, and, of course, the people. North Koreans in the 1980s suffered from the state's insistence on continuing the national agenda to fortify domestic production while neglecting to open up markets and integrate its economy with those of the West. Paradoxically, the DPRK maintained its economic dependence on the Soviet Union and China from the end of the Korean War.[35]

The North Korean state needed to stabilize the growing tension among its own citizens as the failing economy of the country and the Soviet bloc became evident. With Gorbachev's political reforms in the mid- to late 1980s, the DPRK found itself in a precarious political, economic, and ideological situation as the

Soviet Union made efforts to normalize relations with China and open up trade relations with Japan and South Korea.[36] Changes happening among the DPRK's allies were too liberal and posed a threat to Kim Il Sung's political power. In terms of domestic policies, the DPRK held steadfast to its centralized government under a single-family regime and tightened the Hidden Hero campaign to monitor the people closely.

Unlike other national campaigns such as Chollima (the national reconstruction era of the 1950s and 1960s) and the Three Revolutions movement of the 1970s, the Hidden Hero campaign neither rewarded North Koreans for their efforts nor projected a goal for the people to attain. During the Chollima era, the Party's objectives were clear: to reconstruct the DPRK (particularly Pyongyang) from the devastation of the Korean War, to establish a stronger collective spirit through participation, and to achieve socialism for the benefit of the nation. The Three Revolutions movement replaced the political ideology of Marxism-Leninism with Kimilsungism, increased the productivity of small and large industries to compete with the international market, and educated North Koreans with a new set of cultural discourses that venerated the nation's leader. Both of these campaigns had a distinct purpose and a systematic approach to enforcing power over the people to achieve the end result. However, the Hidden Hero campaign created an entirely different power mechanism for disciplining the people. It did not have a materialist objective with physical evidence of society's advancement and accomplishments; rather, it was intent on completely normalizing the state's omnipresent gaze on each individual of the DPRK. Through the Hidden Hero campaign, the North Korean state dispersed its surveillance over the people by empowering mid-tier officials, local cadres, and others in positions of management to report on the people's performance (or lack thereof). The campaign sought to identify not only the hidden heroes in society but also the miscreants and those who expressed dissatisfaction with the political situation in North Korea.

The discursive power of the Hidden Hero campaign resembles the disciplinary mechanisms in Bentham's design of the Panopticon, which Foucault discusses in *Discipline and Punish.* Foucault argues that Bentham's prison architecture ensured two principles of power: visibility and unverifiability. First, the prison inmate had to be visible to the prison guards at all times, and the central tower had to be visible to the inmate at all times. Second, the inmate must never know whether he is being watched at a given moment, but he must be sure that he may always be so.[37] In other words, the guards may not be present in the central tower to watch the inmate, but the inmate must believe that the guards are there. Verification of knowing is a one-way street: only the prison guards can see and know the actions of the inmate. From the inmate's perspective, the uncertainty of whether the guards are present is irrelevant as long as the central tower exists. The mere presence of the central tower itself is the disciplinary instrument that enables the exercising of power over the inmate. Foucault says, "He is seen, but he does not see; he is the object of information, never a subject of communication."[38] For Foucault, the Panopticon is a visual aid that enables the production of knowledge through disciplinary mechanisms of surveillance. The effectiveness of executing this power of surveillance is found in its ubiquity and capability of watching, observing, and recording everything while remaining invisible. Furthermore, the inmate is convinced that he is being watched and therefore behaves accordingly, which results in the dispersion of disciplinary powers over the object of the panoptic gaze.

The Hidden Hero campaign in North Korea operates under the same disciplinary techniques. The very name of the campaign itself is premised on the ubiquity of the political gaze and the visibility of the citizens living in their private and public spheres. Identifying the hidden hero in local communities is paradoxical and ironic from the very initiation of the campaign because the hero is never actually hidden. Statements such as "We must find the hidden hero" or "You are the nation's hidden hero" or "Let's learn from the hidden heroes who have shown their passionate devotion" are contradictory, sending mixed messages to the people about the entire political agenda. These heroes are always discovered by someone (local informants, colleagues, local cadres, or the secret service) or some institution (factory, farm, school, or organization groups) in order for them to be recognized as hidden heroes. For protagonists in fiction to receive recognition as hidden heroes, they have to be made visible for others to see, observe, and report to authorities. Travis Workman, in his essay on North Korean films on the hidden hero, says, "The hero's only acceptable desire is to want to be seen, to have one's personal struggle and suffering be recognized by the leader's gaze."[39] The desire to be recognized is not a natural impulse in these heroes and heroines, but is created through the discourse of the Hidden Hero campaign. In short, the hidden hero is discovered and made into a hero by consigning the characteristic of "hiddenness" to such individuals in fiction.

North Korean fiction celebrates the success of the nation rather than the success of the individual. The trope of the Hidden Hero campaign is evident in *Morning Star* as Sŏk-jun has been researching a particular type of fertilizer for over ten years without any formal recognition. His greatest satisfaction comes when he discovers his research published in a science journal. This validates his research, but, more important, the journal article indicates that someone took serious notice of his research. He has received acknowledgment from his colleagues and community. However, he is not promoted from a high school teacher to a university professor, which is the typical denouement of hidden hero narratives. Instead, he returns to his high school and continues to teach the way he has always done. The novel ends: "[Sŏk-jun] looked as simple and ordinary as in the past. The only difference was his confidence and dignified demeanor."[40] The narrative trajectory of *Morning Star* reinforces the idea that a true hidden hero does not work for self-aggrandizement or for self-promotion; he works only to improve the nation.

Morning Star can be (and is supposed to be) read as a story about the nation, a man who strives to construct a better nation, and a man who finds himself in the nation. The hero's energy must be exerted toward the improvement of the nation, even if it means sacrificing his body. Sŏk-jun says, "It's not only dinner that I haven't eaten. For the past couple of days, I've been running around without a concept of time."[41] Indeed, the hero loses his sense of time when his mind is only on achieving something great for the nation. Sŏk-jun is so preoccupied with his research that his colleagues rebuke him, but he says, "I have to do what my heart tells me to do. It is something that we all must do, even if it is stressful and tiresome."[42] What the hero dislikes most are people who work for their self-interest and who think that their social position matters. Sŏk-jun criticizes Professor Son Sŭng-p'il regarding this: "Your position as a professor is respectable. But your position alone does not shape your identity."[43] Sŏk-jun says something similar to Pak Chun-t'aek: "I am not doing my research to become a professor or a hero. I just want to do my part in supporting the nation."[44] The true hidden hero's political obligation and ethical duties must replace the self: his identity belongs to the state; he represents the state; he lives for the state; he is the state. He must be willing to sacrifice everything to do his part. Sŏk-jun convinces his wife to assist him with his research. He says, "If we do this together, then we can hold our heads up high before the state. When I finish my research, I will do everything for you."[45] The story of the hidden hero prioritizes the nation above his family. There cannot be any obstacles for the hero, even if his family desperately needs him at home. The hero may face a critical dilemma, but this is only temporary. North Korean fiction colors its pages with the hero's monochromatic love for the nation. This is what he says. But what about his wife? What does she say?

In *Morning Star,* the voice of the doubting wife disrupts the romanticism and glamorization of the Hidden Hero campaign. The woman questions the illusory campaign that has subjugated her husband to become a heartless and faceless worker for the state. The woman doubts whether her husband's pursuit of the Hidden Hero campaign will ever bring happiness to the family. Chin-sun is Sŏk-jun's wife. As a farmer, she has devoted her entire life to the collective farm in her village. She feels that she has contributed to building the nation by living a simple life of a farmer and raising her daughter. However, she cannot understand why her husband exerts all of his energy and time researching a fertilizer rather than teaching at his high school and caring for his family. The novel opens with Chin-sun and her daughter waiting for Sŏk-jun to return from his research late in the evening. Chin-sun thinks to herself, "Does he have to work this hard every night?"[46] Then, the narrator adds, "Chin-sun sighed without knowing it." Her husband has been fruitlessly researching the fertilizer for over ten years, which Chin-sun cannot understand. She does not valorize her husband for his tireless efforts. Instead, she sighs without knowing it.

The woman who questions, the woman who doubts is also the woman who sighs. Underneath the surface of the state's celebration of the Hidden Hero campaign lies the concerned, frustrated, and embittered sigh of the woman. If *Heights of Life* is a novel of doubts, then *Morning Star* is a novel of sighs. Chin-sun sighs consistently throughout the novel, which is represented in various literary metaphors and allusions to indicate the immeasurable distance she feels from the male-centered state. The novel describes Chin-sun's emotional and psychological feelings toward the patriarchal social system as "heaviness of the heart," "emptiness," "loneliness," and "mumbling." It opens with Chin-sun walking in an empty field at night, looking at the stars that are beyond her reach. Between her and the unreachable stars is darkness or emptiness.[47] The metaphor of the stars represents the hidden heroes that have brightened the DPRK with their astounding scientific discoveries, and yet for Chin-sun that recognition is beyond her reach. In fact, she has no desire to become a hidden hero. Her husband, who is adamant about succeeding, is also beyond her reach. The state, the national campaign, and her husband—all that are male-centered—have inflicted irreparable damage and pain on Chin-sun.

If *Heights of Life* is about an intellectual elite family in the city that has the luxury not to face financial problems, *Morning Star* depicts a working-class family that worries about day-to-day finances. Sŏk-jun receives a salary from teaching, but he has not been able to bring home his wages because of his research. Chin-sun says, "Sŏk-jun, I have to sell our pig. I need the money. It's to buy you new clothes for work."[48] Chin-sun makes the excuse that she is going to use the money to buy Sŏk-jun new clothes, but it is actually her euphemistic way of saying that the family is in financial destitution. Her work at the collective farm is not enough to support the family, especially when Sŏk-jun is not bringing home his salary. Chin-sun cares about the nation as does her husband, but she cares more about her family and the family's livelihood, as these are the material realities in her life. If Sŏk-jun is the romantic hidden hero of the state, then Chin-sun is the pragmatic heroine of the family.

Morning Star offers two legitimate points of view about the desirable image of a happy family. For Sŏk-jun, the ideal family of the DPRK is one in which the wife willfully and joyfully supports her husband in state affairs. For Chin-sun, the ideal family derives from a happy marital relationship. *Morning Star* presents these two views about the family to demonstrate Chin-sun's process of acquiring the understanding to live for the state. But what Chin-sun expresses in the story is that Party-mindedness comes at the expense of the general welfare of her family. That is, the basic necessities to operate a family such as food, clothes, and other expenses are disregarded to support a husband who has his mind on the nation. For Chin-sun, the two idealities cannot converge and satisfy both the state and the family equally. When Sŏk-jun demands that Chin-sun join him in his research, their marital problems escalate. Below is the conversation between the two:

> "I can only do my research if you help me. I would like for you to start as soon as possible," said Sŏk-jun.
>
> Chin-sun was shocked.
>
> "Is that so?" replied Chin-sun indifferently. She uttered something that was different from what she was really thinking.
>
> Sŏk-jun continued, "I'm not asking you to quit your job. I'm asking you to assist me with my research. At times you will have to conduct experiments. At other times you will have to do some research at the library. If we do this together, then we can hold our heads up high before the state. When I finish my research, I will do everything for you." . . .
>
> Chin-sun said, "Do you think living like that will give you happiness and worth in life?"
>
> Chin-sun continued without skipping a beat, "If you *do* think like that, then I fear it will be detrimental to our family."[49]

Like the women in *Heights of Life,* the woman in *Morning Star* casts doubts on her husband who claims that living for the state is the only true form of happiness for both of them. Chin-sun questions whether her husband truly believes in what he has said. She doubts his intentions to be a humble scientist for the nation; she is convinced that he desires prestige and public acknowledgment—against the creed of the Hidden Hero campaign. More important, Chin-sun makes her position clear: her husband's overzealous concern for the state is threatening their marriage.

North Korean heroes and heroines rarely take the pragmatic approach to building the nation; there is always some kind of risk or danger involved. The idea of being a hero or heroine requires counterbalancing the imminent problem with daring actions—the greater the problem, the riskier the action needs to be. Pragmatic characters in North Korean narratives are never the hero or heroine precisely because their circumspect and sensible actions are not idealistic. North Korean heroes and heroines are romantics in the strictest sense, whose view of society is detached from reality. For revolutionary romantic heroes and heroines, the perfected nation exists not in the present reality but in the near future. The nation is always becoming, in the process of developing into the ideal state rather than a reflection of the ideality. The current condition of the state is always unbalanced, distorted, and problematic, which requires Party-minded revolutionary heroes and heroines to lead others to the perfected state.

In *Morning Star,* the wife poses a critical dilemma to the husband as she stands against his romantic pursuit of a groundbreaking scientific discovery. To be clear, she is not asking her husband to turn from his political duties. She wants him to take a different approach. Chin-sun says, "Why can't you be like others and just focus on your lectures? You may get promoted and get a raise. Then our lifestyle will improve."[50] As a pragmatist, Chin-sun focuses on tangible realities that would benefit both the country and her family. Her advice to Sŏk-jun is to continue working as a paid science teacher rather than as an unpaid researcher. Chin-sun reminds her husband that his teaching position is a service to the state and to the family. He has the responsibility of educating the next generation of the nation's greatest scientists. For Chin-sun, the prospect of Sŏk-jun succeeding in his research is minimal, which means that his selfless sacrifice for the country will have been in vain. Although Sŏk-jun claims that his service to the nation requires greater sacrifice and devotion, Chin-sun suspects that he is conducting research primarily to receive recognition; he wants to be seen and not hidden. The unseemly ambition of becoming a hidden hero blinds his ethical sensibility toward his family. In *Morning Star,* the woman question emerges from the state discourse in the form of a pragmatic wife who is denied any sense of nationalistic pride and self-worth for lacking the romantic impetus of her male counterparts.

Wives in North Korean fiction are the ones who show true self-sacrificing devotion to both the state and their family with the premonition of the eventual dissipation of the family. Chin-sun reluctantly decides to join her husband in his research while continuing her job as a farmer. The dual tasks take a toll on her body. She is physically and mentally exhausted from supporting her husband. She feels embittered toward her husband for forcing her to do laborious work for his research. On one occasion, Chin-sun advises a young female colleague, Yŏng-gŭm, to rethink the concept of marriage. Chin-sun offers three pieces of advice:

> "Yŏng-gŭm, don't ever get married."
>
> "If you must get married, then enjoy your single life when you're still young."
>
> "After you've enjoyed your single life, then get married."[51]

Chin-sun's marital advice contradicts that of the state on all three counts. Chin-sun's first piece of advice is an attempt to protect another woman from the patriarchal strictures of marriage in the DPRK. For Chin-sun, the woman can articulate her agency by not participating in the state-desired institution of marriage. Abstaining from marriage means the woman will not have to submit to her husband, procreate the next generation of family members for the state, and give the members up to the state. For Chin-sun, refusing to marry is an obstruction to the state's efforts to normalize, enforce, discipline, and impose its powers over individuals.

Her second piece of advice redefines the state's definition of youth. For Chin-sun, unmarried men and women should take advantage of their youthful years. She tells Yŏng-gŭm, "Just thinking about how I can never go back to those days saddens me." Chin-sun equates her youthful days with individual freedom and agency. Dating, spending time with friends, traveling around the country, and working are what Chin-sun considers the highlights of youth. Chin-sun suggests enjoying the simple pleasures in life. Happiness in life is living for oneself rather than for the state.

Her third piece of advice is for Yŏng-gŭm to get married after she has exhausted her energy as a single woman. Chin-sun claims that marriage disenfranchises the woman from expressions of freedom. The married woman has to answer not only to her husband but also to her mother-in-law and the other members of her husband's family. She will no longer live her life for herself. In the novel, people do not call Chin-sun by her name. She is always referred to as Chŏng-ok's mother (Chŏng-ok is Chin-sun's daughter) or Sŏk-jun's wife, which is a cultural practice in both North and South Korea. An unmarried woman maintains her identity through her name, but a married woman loses her personal identity and assumes the state's identity of wifehood and motherhood. In short, Chin-sun argues that marriage enslaves the woman and depletes her of happiness, which contrasts with the state's prescriptions regarding marriage.

The state does not restrict youths from getting married but prescribes that they marry after a certain age. Kim Il Sung made a passing remark that men should marry at the age of thirty, and women should marry at the age of twenty-eight. However, youths should exert their energy for the state rather than for the opposite sex. The state does not encourage them to enjoy their single life or lead a hedonistic life but to please the Great Leader through their labor. The youth's pleasure in life should derive from finding ways to please Kim Il Sung. Furthermore, the state does not claim that married life is less satisfying than single life but that married life is the beginning of one's true happiness. After all, the literary discourse of wifehood in the DPRK is modeled after the two exemplary wives, Kang Pan-sŏk and Kim Chŏng-suk, who found their happiness in supporting their husbands and the revolution.

The acquisition of the revolutionary lexicon within the male-dominated political system is what the state expects from women. A woman who lacks the correct Party ideology is considered irrational or not yet rational; conversely, a woman who understands the political system is glamorized as a rational being. In *Morning Star,* Chin-sun is reeducated about the ideology of marriage in the DPRK and the prospects of the ideal wife when she accidently breaks some of her husband's flower pots while conducting research and, in fear of her husband, goes to see her mother in her hometown. There, she meets a friend, Sim Chŏng-ch'ŏl, who says, "Comrade Song is my wife, but I do not consider her as a wife only. She is a revolutionary comrade who has endured all the trials in life with me. She is mentally stronger than I am and a revolutionary vanguard. That is why I respect her as a comrade and not as a wife."[52] Later, Sim Chŏng-ch'ŏl's wife, Song Chi-ye, talks with Chin-sun. Chi-ye says, "What makes a man so beautiful is his faithfulness and devotion to the state."[53] Both Chŏng-ch'ŏl and Chi-ye articulate the state-desired definition of a happy marriage. Husband and wife are supposed to consider the other as a comrade and nothing beyond that. The political rhetoric claims that there is nothing more attractive in a person than one's faithfulness and devotion to the state. Chŏng-ch'ŏl and Chi-ye both criticize Chin-sun's irrationality for running away from her revolutionary duties of supporting her husband.

Works like *Morning Star* demonstrate that political statements reinforce the hierarchical design of the male-dominated society. Author Ch'oe Sang-sun does not portray the wives as comrades to their husbands but as victims of the patriarchal structure. Chin-sun is enraptured by her friends' lecture, and she recognizes her mistake of leaving her husband. When she returns to her husband, he is pleased to see her. However, they do not exchange a deeper conversation about how they are to work as comrades. Sŏk-jun puts Chin-sun right back to work as his inferior assistant. *Morning Star* shows that the wife must transform *her* political consciousness in order for the family or married life to improve. Or, to put it in another way, the husband was never at fault to begin with. The husband's political duties are always justified and rationalized, whereas the wife's voice (unless it reflects the correct political rhetoric) is irrational.

State-sponsored fiction like *Morning Star* never denigrates a husband like Sŏk-jun who works assiduously for the nation. According to the Hidden Hero campaign, everyone in the DPRK ought to learn from Sŏk-jun and criticize Chin-sun for leaving her husband. Sŏk-jun accomplishes his work for the nation but does not share the credit with his wife. Chin-sun recedes to the margins of the narrative, and Sŏk-jun receives the coveted title of the Hidden Hero. He is the morning star that shines brightly in the dark evening sky. In the Korean language, morning star (*saebyŏk pyŏl*) refers to the planet Venus (*kŭmsŏng*), which is the brightest star in the evening sky. It also indicates a great achievement. Sŏk-jun is analogous to Venus because of his hopeful and bright success in a grim and dark social environment. Amid North Korea's dire economic problems in the 1980s, fictional works like Ch'oe Sang-sun's *Morning Star* attempted to uplift the dispirited morale of the people. As a North Korean writer, Ch'oe needed to urge her readers to continue their political duties for the nation in spite of the dark and ominous conditions at the time. Whereas *Heights of Life* celebrates the bright future of the intellectual class, *Morning Star* venerates the hidden heroes in the countryside who work tirelessly to uphold the pride of the nation.

Yet *Morning Star* proceeds without the wife. Once she returns to her husband, she is no longer part of the narrative. The last five chapters of the novel do not mention Chin-sun. She is neither standing by her husband nor in the background; she is effaced from the story as if her existence as a character never mattered. The last five chapters of the novel are not about the reconciliation between husband and wife, the projection of a happy marriage, or shared visions of building the nation. Instead, the last five chapters celebrate the success of the man in his scientific discovery that displays his Party-mindedness. The wife in the novel is relegated to the margins of society yet again.

Or perhaps she wishes to remain in the margins, refusing to celebrate with the men. As the novel opened with Chin-sun feeling physically, emotionally, and psychologically distant from the stars in the sky, she disappears at the end of the story to symbolize her incompatibility and dissociation from the patriarchal society. Perhaps Chin-sun refuses to transform her "irrationality" to the "rationality" of the male discourse because it is, after all, male discourse that has dissolved the conjugal family. Chin-sun's friends remind her of the importance of comrade-love and the transformation of her irrational behavior, but the typified political rhetoric so common in North Korean fiction is not enough to prevent Chin-sun from sighing and asking: "Do you think living like that will give you happiness and worth in life?"

Much like her contemporary Kim Kyo-sŏp, Ch'oe Sang-sun delineates the woman as the one who perpetually puts the state in question with her doubts and incessant sighs. The woman may be absent in the narrative, but her skepticism toward the patriarchal social structure is ever so present. Both *Heights of Life* and *Morning Star* portray the conjugal relationship as one that is supposed to fortify the identity of the state via the state-desired happy marriage, but instead the two novels present the interminable conflicts that exist within the public/private binary opposites and, by extension, the conflict that represents the state's tenuous economic and political problems in the 1980s. In the next chapter, I will discuss a novel in the 1980s that rejects the institution of marriage altogether through a woman who not only fights to divorce her husband but, more important, refuses to participate in the male-dominated society.

CHAPTER FOUR

Women, Divorce, and the State

No, no. I can't do that. I can't stand it anymore!

Paek Nam-nyong, Friend

Women in Paek Nam-nyong's *Pŏt* (Friend, 1988) elude and resist the oppressive patriarchal state order that dictates the construction of female subjects of the DPRK. In the majority of North Korean fiction, the narrative trajectory and conclusion not only promote the Party and offer "eternal optimism,"[1] but also explicitly reinstate a male-dominated sociopolitical order. Whether the narrative takes place in a factory, farm, army, school, or any other social institution, the methodology of reading North Korean fiction is to understand the immanent role of the Party or Kim Il Sung that leads the trajectory of the narrative to the rationalization and legitimacy of a patriarchal society.

Although North Korea officially eradicated sexual inequality by the inception of the nation-state in 1948,[2] even after forty years (when *Friend* was published), the portrayal of the state-desired submissive women continued to be reproduced in literature. As I demonstrated in the previous chapter, women's participation in the public space was not a promise of their agency but an absorption and submission to the patriarchal state order. North Korean literature is supposed to render a unitary reading, a univocal meaning that complies with Party thought, where *difference* or *otherness* is disregarded, eliminated, or simply *unthought*. However, Paek Nam-nyong's *Friend* shows otherwise.

"No, no. I can't do that. I can't stand it anymore!" are the words of female protagonist Ch'ae Sun-hŭi, who confirms and reminds herself that she is unwilling to compromise with her husband, the judge presiding over her divorce case, and the social model of a submissive wife. The double negation ("No, no") affirms her resistance ("I can't do that. I can't stand it anymore!") to a social prescription that attempts to mold women physically and spiritually (*chŏngsinjŏkin*) into state-desired subjects. *Spiritually,* what a harrowing term for Sun-hŭi! The term is used to refer to a systematic design to transform individuals into rational beings, which is nothing more than making all individuals think and act in accordance with the masculine state. Sun-hŭi refuses to be *interpellated* into a rational subject of the patriarchal state in two ways: first, her double negation of resistance ("No, no. I can't do that. I can't stand it anymore!") and, second, her response without a response, which I will detail toward the end of this chapter.

In the first instance, Sun-hŭi speaks out against the state's prescriptive discourse of constructing subjectivity: "I can't do that." It is not that she does not want to be a wife or a mother, but rather she cannot continue to be the state-desired wife and mother. The law (male protagonist Judge Chŏng Chin-u) diagnoses her with a disease of irrationality and attempts to mold her into a rational subject that complies with the Party prescription of womanhood and motherhood, a discursive practice in North Korean fiction to discipline individuals. Sun-hŭi takes a stance by claiming that she cannot stand it anymore, that she is no longer willing to submit herself to the patriarchal design. Her double negation reveals both her pent up anger against the hegemonic society and her imperative resistance to the state, affirming her decision to file for divorce in the opening passage of Paek Nam-nyong's *Friend*.

This chapter will analyze the dual power struggle that a woman confronts against her male counterparts—she confronts, first, the state's controlling efforts to tailor and construct a subject according to Party directives for revolutionizing the family and, second, the subject-making force that delimits her individuality—as an affirmative expression of her agency. Sun-hŭi initially struggles to divorce her husband, whom she finds to be an incompatible partner, but the novel further divulges her struggle with Judge Chŏng Chin-u, her director at the Provincial Performing Arts Theater, and even her son, who sympathizes with his father more than his mother. Sun-hŭi's male counterparts surround her and suffocate her very existence as an individual, demanding her submission to the patriarchal state order. But the narrative does not render a promising enclosure of her individuality; she does not become the ideal citizen, woman, and mother. The seams of the narrative come undone at the end of the novel, opening up the condition of possibility for multiple readings and multiple interpretations that disavow the novel's allegiance to a singular meaning and depart from the predictable endings expected in North Korean literature. In Chapter 2, I discussed a particular moment in *Friend*. Below is the basic plot of the novel.

Ch'ae Sun-hŭi comes to Judge Chŏng Chin-u's office to file for divorce. Sun-hŭi is a celebrity singer at the Provincial Performing Arts Theater, and her husband, Sŏk-ch'un, is an ordinary factory worker. She claims that her husband is a stubborn and an incompetent worker who cannot win awards for inventing a new machine as other workers have. She complains that her husband has used his income to reimburse the factory for all his failed attempts at his new machinery, which he has been working on for the past five years. Chŏng Chin-u has already divorced a couple (Ch'ae Rim and his wife) and is reluctant to see yet another broken family. He, therefore, sets out to rectify the couple's marital problems.

Chŏng Chin-u pays a visit to Sŏk-ch'un and Sun-hŭi's house only to find their son, Ho-nam, standing alone outside the house in the pouring rain. Chŏng Chin-u decides to take Ho-nam to his apartment, where he can rest and wait for his parents to pick him up. Sŏk-ch'un is the first to arrive at Chŏng Chin-u's apartment. There, Chŏng Chin-u gathers information on how Sŏk-ch'un and Sun-hŭi met and fell in love. The judge learns how the two got married and how the turbulence in their marriage has brought them to the brink of divorce.

Chŏng Chin-u visits Sŏk-ch'un's factory to gather more information from the elderly manager. Chŏng Chin-u learns from the manager that Sŏk-ch'un has been working on the same project for the past five years without any progress, which he attributes to Sŏk-ch'un's stubbornness and refusal to change with the technologically advancing times. The manager tells the judge that the couple's relationship has been deteriorating for quite some time. Sŏk-ch'un has resorted to both physical and verbal domestic violence. Sun-hŭi is not completely innocent either. Her celebrity status has made her arrogant and vain. She has been degrading her husband in public and ridiculing his incompetence.

Chŏng Chin-u pieces the accounts together and concludes that Sŏk-ch'un is at fault for not improving his technical skills and advancing his position at the factory, and that Sun-hŭi's arrogance derives from her husband's incompetency as a man of the new generation. He critiques Sŏk-ch'un for falling behind and suggests taking evening classes at the technical institute. He also critiques Sun-hŭi for not abiding by the ethical principles of what a wife ought to be doing for her husband and her son.

Meanwhile, Chŏng Chin-u deals with another problematic character: Ch'ae Rim. There are two characters named Ch'ae Rim in the narrative. The first Ch'ae Rim, a manager at the Electrical Hardware Factory, is the one who has divorced his wife; the second Ch'ae Rim is Sun-hŭi's second cousin, the chairman of the Provincial Industrial Technology Commission Board and the one who is causing grief to Judge Chŏng Chin-u. (At first, Chŏng Chin-u confuses the two, but he soon clears up his confusion as he recalls the court trial of the first Ch'ae Rim and his wife.) While Chŏng Chin-u tries to restore Sun-hŭi and Sŏk-ch'un's marital health, the second Ch'ae Rim stands on the opposing side, urging Sun-hŭi to divorce her husband. Ch'ae Rim is a local cadre with much influence and social power, but Chŏng Chin-u has maintained his legal authority by not conceding to Ch'ae Rim's bribery. Additionally, he has discovered that Ch'ae Rim embezzled government funds—which were given to award workers for inventing new machines—for his own personal profit. Chŏng Chin-u charges Ch'ae Rim with financial fraud and threatens to imprison him. Ch'ae Rim confesses his wrongdoing and promises to return the cash prize to the rightful winners.

Chŏng Chin-u, then, rectifies the couple's marital problems by reminding them that their duty as citizens is to continue the nation's revolutionary struggle. Chŏng Chin-u also counsels his neighbors on their marital problems and makes amends with his own wife, whom he has regretted marrying because of her long absences from home and from her domestic duties. In the end, Chŏng Chin-u proves to be more than a legal advisor and more than a marriage counselor; he is the exemplary friend of the community.

The Literary World of Paek Nam-nyong

Paek Nam-nyong's *Friend* was published in 1988 and had made its way across the DMZ and into the hands of some South Koreans by 1992. After reading the novel, one of South Korea's renowned writers, Hwang Sŏk-yŏng, said this: "The first time I went to North Korea, I came across Paek Nam-nyong's novel, and I was deeply impressed. In this novel, the characters' individual concerns and circumstances were well described, which shocked me. Through this novel, I realized that there are people living in the North."[3] Another South Korean writer, Yun Chŏng-mo, said, "Paek Nam-nyong's novel is not only the most extraordinary of all North Korean novels that I've read so far; it contains such shocking realities that it overturns our distorted knowledge about the North."[4] Their genuine shock over Paek's *Friend* may not have been based simply on its theme of divorce but on a deeper level of reading and understanding the tenuous narrative structure and the complex theme of the individual versus the state. In the 2000s, the DPRK sponsored a television drama series based on Paek's *Friend* called *Kajok* (Family). There were supposed to be ten episodes, but the series did not televise the last episode for reasons unknown, according to the South Korean reporter Kim Hyŏn-kyŏng.[5] If the television drama series had wanted to remain faithful to the novel, then I can only surmise that the last episode would have provided an ending that the DPRK had never seen before.

This novel makes divorce its central motif, which was extremely rare in North Korean literature before its publication in 1988, as divorce threatens the dissolution of the family-state. Turbulent marital problems, issues with raising children, and the desire to live a comfortable life devoid of Party directives are some of the concerns found in *Friend,* and none of the characters are without problems. That is, a model citizen is not already made in the narrative but must be perfected through interpersonal relations and self-reflection (or self-criticism).

Sŏk-ch'un and Sun-hŭi want a divorce because of personality conflicts. The second couple, Ch'ae Rim and his wife (who makes an appearance without a name), have divorced because of irreparable personality conflicts. The third couple, a coal factory worker and a schoolteacher, have been faithfully married despite myriad personality conflicts. Finally, the fourth couple, Judge Chŏng Chin-u and his wife, Ŭn-ok, also face marital problems because of her long absence from home to conduct field research.

It may appear as though the novel polarizes two sets of couples to distinguish the ideal family (coal miner and schoolteacher) from the antirevolutionary one (Ch'ae Rim and his wife). The clear dichotomy of the different couples is supposed to provide readers with a framework that maps the superimposition of the Party's ethicality of a politically driven family. For example, in Ri In-ch'ŏl's short story "Mangne ttal" (My Youngest Daughter, 1980), the polarization of political ideologies perpetuates the good/bad, white/black, right/wrong binary oppositions.[6] In that story, the first daughter is married to a morally depraved capitalist, the second daughter is married to a poor socialist, and the third daughter is about to marry a socialist young man. The short story reveals that the eldest daughter has been living in an unhappy marriage as a result of falling into the trap of capitalism, and the second daughter has been living in a joyful marriage as a result of participating in socialist activities for the DPRK. When the father realizes this, he decides the youngest daughter should marry the socialist young man. This story does not take place in the DPRK but in Japan among Korean residents, which would explain the first daughter's being married to a capitalist businessman. But, despite the geopolitical aspects of the story, the pretense of there being a "choice" as to which couple lives the happier life is the narrative strategy in stories like "My Youngest Daughter," in which the correct moral values are in fact predetermined. This technique not only depicts the individuals as being flat and undeveloped, but it also limits readers' options for making their own choice. In other words, the choice is obvious and prescribed for readers by the Party.

Paek Nam-nyong's narrative strategy is not to provide a choice between the ideal couple and the antirevolutionary couple. Instead, Paek focuses on each couple's marital problems to show the transformational process of a dysfunctional family into a revolutionary one. In *Pukhan munhaksa* (North Korean Literary History), South Korean coauthors Sin Hyŏng-gi and O Sŏng-ho argue that Paek's *Friend* shows the revolutionary love of the couple (Sŏk-ch'un and Sun-hŭi) and that no other novel in North Korea has portrayed love as such.[7] The novel certainly raises issues of revolutionary love between couples and how this love ought to be materialized for the nation. Still, all characters in North Korean fiction must arrive at an understanding that the family-state is the projection or completion of an individual's rationality, and thus it is no coincidence that a judge—a legal administrator of the state—is the hero of *Friend.*

Yet the novel portrays a woman who questions, resists, and undermines the very seams of the typical narrative formula that inscribes the wholesome order of the family unit and its prescribed devotion to the state. *Friend* ends with ambiguity as to whether the married couple on the verge of divorce will remain unified. The novel demonstrates that human emotions and interpersonal relationships between married couples resist prescriptivism. This novel, along with *Heights of Life* and *Morning Star,* discussed in the previous chapter, creatively explicates raw, undisciplined human emotions and desires in individuals who struggle to negotiate between their public (external, generally superficial, obligations to the collective) and their private lives (internal ambitions for themselves).

Although the conflict between individual and state is a recurring theme in North Korean literature, *Friend* stands out, among Paek's works and even among other novels published in the 1980s, for its inability to seal off individualistic tendencies in its female characters. The "utopian" ending in the novel is artificially contrived to meet the demands of the state; it is a formality. What makes *Friend* unique is its implication that love and loyalty to the state cannot be forced on or demanded from individuals. Although the novel is supposed to present the divorcees' ability to transcend their differences and instantiate their obligation to the state, it pursues larger thematic problems between presiding judge Chŏng Chin-u and Ch'ae Sun-hŭi, where Sun-hŭi resists the enclosure of her individualism and thus reasserts the "woman question." Sun-hŭi's voice, the marginal voice that utters "I can't stand it anymore," poses a threat to the state-desired conjugal family.

I am not suggesting that *Friend* is an antithetical text in North Korea or what one might call a dissident work. *Friend* can be read as a didactic narrative that instructs its readers to develop rationality from their irrational impulses, to acquire the prosthesis of Kim Il Sung, the Party, or the state as the rationalization of the dysfunctional family. That is, the rationality of the nuclear family finds its completion in the family-state through the process of *prosthetization*—a foreign extension that is artificial to individuals. It is not surprising to readers of North Korean literature to find the prosthesis of Kimilsungism and Party directives in fictional narratives. The prosthetic element is supposed to reveal the necessity for each individual in the narrative to act as loyal citizens of the DPRK no matter how contrived or artificial it may appear. The prosthesis is supposed to be taken seriously as a vital (but artificial) extension of the individual's life.

As such, the dysfunctional couple in *Friend* must learn to accept Judge Chŏng Chin-u as the prosthesis that will enable them to recognize the much needed state-ordered and Party-minded rationality. The utopian future of the DPRK is fulfilled by the recognition and acceptance of such prostheses. According to South Korean scholar Ko In-hwan, the portrayal of the problems between Ch'ae Sun-hŭi and Ri Sŏk-ch'un is not intended to show how one overcomes the other but, rather, how the two acknowledge their mutual problems in order to create a better future for both of them.[8] The achievement of this "better future" is fulfilled through gestures of individuals to maintain a harmonious family-state, which in the 1980s was orchestrated by the Hidden Hero campaign.

The Patriarchal Semiotics of the People's Friend

Nearly all of Paek Nam-nyong's stories center on the middle management tier of the social and political hierarchy. His other stories, such as *Pokmujadŭl* (Servicemen, 1979), *Il-t'ŏ* (Workplace, 1979), *60 Nyŏn-hu* (After Sixty Years, 1982), *Chŏlmŭn Tang-bisŏ* (The Young Party Secretary, 1983), and "Saengmyŏng" (Life, 1985), all depict cadres who struggle to improve living and working conditions for the collective, as they have the ethical duty to administer and control the political commitment of individuals to the state. Much like other North Korean stories, Paek's narratives create a fictional world where the directives of the Party are channeled through cadres. According to Tatiana Gabroussenko, North Korean fiction portrays the "caring cadre,"[9] which is a physical embodiment—a living, walking, talking, and emotional being—of Party directives.

The rhetoric of the Hidden Hero campaign reinforces the patriarchal state's disciplinary governance over the people in *Friend*. Sŏk-ch'un and Sun-hŭi's marital problems are presumably resolved by the incorporation of a new member into the couple's family: Chŏng Chin-u, a male judge of the municipal court who administers divorce proceedings. Throughout the novel, Paek Nam-nyong alternates between calling him "Judge Chŏng Chin-u" and "Chŏng Chin-u" as appropriate to the narrative. Paek shows the transformation of Chŏng Chin-u from an impersonal and bureaucratic cadre of society to a personal, paternal friend of Sŏk-ch'un and Sun-hŭi's nuclear family. Judge Chŏng Chin-u watches, observes, records, and administers the law to the couple as a close member of the family.

Friend creates an entire lexicon around Chŏng Chin-u as a companion and a pseudo-fatherly figure rather than an indifferent bureaucrat who administers the law from a distance. For example, when Sŏk-ch'un and Sun-hŭi leave Judge

Chŏng Chin-u's apartment with their son Ho-nam, the narrator says, "The judge wasn't their relative or a friend, but to invite the family over to his house and offer this kind of hospitality was out of the ordinary. The three left the judge's apartment."[10] Later, also at Chŏng Chin-u's apartment, he criticizes Sŏk-ch'un saying, "I'm advising you not as a judge but as your elderly friend."[11] Finally, toward the end of the novel, Chŏng Chin-u asks if he may visit Sŏk-ch'un and Sunhŭi on the day of their anniversary: "I want to go over to your house not as a judge but as your friend. Ho-nam will also greet me like his pal."[12] The access code that the novel uses to have an elderly bureaucrat penetrate the domestic space is "friend," which is far less imposing, threatening, and obstructive.

The family revolution campaign asserts that the nuclear family is only a cell of the society but that proper care and discipline are required to prevent the cell from turning into a cancerous one. In the novel, Chŏng Chin-u cultivates vegetables during Ŭn-ok's (his wife) absence. Chŏng Chin-u's nursing of the vegetables in the greenhouse reflects the micropolitics of maintaining and monitoring the nuclear family. He controls the humidity level, measures the temperature, and clears away any weeds that may deter the health and growth of the vegetables. Although he grumbles at his absent wife for leaving him with all the household chores, Chŏng Chin-u faithfully tends to the vegetables as if they were his own. His attitude toward the vegetables mirrors the way he nurses Sŏk-ch'un and Sunhŭi back to their marital health. His tenderness toward the couple as their friend allegorizes Chŏng Chin-u as a parental figure rather than a faceless bureaucrat.

North Korean fiction delineates the hidden hero through his work ethic and tireless efforts to overcome obstacles even at the expense of physical pain and emotional distress. In one instance, when Chŏng Chin-u discovers that Sŏk-ch'un's experiments have been fruitless because of a shortage of the proper type of sand, he goes to the deepest part of the river and digs up a backpack-full of quality sand. This comes with the cost of public humiliation, as locals passing by the river have witnessed Chŏng Chin-u rolling up his sleeves, taking off his trousers, and wading into the icy river. As a result, Sŏk-ch'un is overwhelmed by Chŏng Chin-u's willingness to help him with his project. Moments like this show the discursive construction of Chŏng Chin-u as a qualified hidden hero of the narrative. This particular moment in the novel does not distinguish Chŏng Chin-u from other heroes and heroines in North Korean literature. It is a common or perhaps even an overwrought portrayal of the hero who extends compassion to his comrade in times of distress.

What makes *Friend* unique in this respect is not the hero's extended service to his people and the community but the hero's failure to provide the correct kind of assistance. It must be noted that it is Chŏng Chin-u's effort to help

Sŏk-ch'un with the sand that moves Sŏk-ch'un and not the quality of the sand itself. Typically, in North Korean fiction, when a hero assists another worker the way Chŏng Chin-u does Sŏk-ch'un, the moral encouragement and the material object with which the hero has helped the worker both prove to be successful. This narrative technique indicates that the hero not only has the passionate heart to uplift the downtrodden spirit of the worker but also knows precisely the right kind of material object needed to help the worker. However, in *Friend,* this is not the case. Chŏng Chin-u tries to encourage Sŏk-ch'un (which he does) by retrieving the sand from the river, but unfortunately it is the wrong type of sand. Although Chŏng Chin-u has good intentions of helping Sŏk-ch'un, the sand proves to be useless. This moment in the novel shows a narrative pattern in *Friend* that is different from the other prescribed short stories and novels from the 1970s and 1980s. Although Chŏng Chin-u still represents the hidden hero who imbues the correct political consciousness in the dysfunctional family members of his community, the novel shows that the correct consciousness alone does not determine one's heroism. In other words, the novel makes a distinction between the discursive construction of the appellative hidden hero and the performative gestures of heroism. North Korean fiction in the past had conflated these two into a singular trope, in which the two are interrelated and causal. However, in *Friend,* the delineation of the hero goes beyond a mere heroic performance and considers the hero's spatial and temporal locality in society and the way in which the hero affects and is affected by his community and his own family.

The family cannot be perceived as an individuated entity that simply exists within society. Much like the phrase "family is the fundamental cell of society," the family exists in relation to the affectations of social intersections—the interlacing of interventions and withdrawals of the state. Policing of individuals, as Jacques Donzelot argues, takes place *through* the governmentality of the family rather than by enforcing regulatory powers on it. He says the mechanisms of governmentality—the complex web of relations of dependence and allegiance—"induced the reorganization of family life by promoting the new norms as being so many advantages favoring a more complete realization of the family's goal of increased autonomy."[13] Gilles Deleuze, who wrote the preface to Donzelot's *Policing of Families,* adds, "Marriage is less a matter of preserving the order of families than of preparing people for married life."[14] For both Donzelot and Deleuze, the family exists within the intersections of state power, family tradition, social institutions, and judicial action, affecting and being affected by these intricate relationships.

The hidden hero, then, moves along these intersections of private and public spheres, the family and the state, the self and the other, as his identity affects and is affected by social apparatuses. The hidden hero goes to the family, is found in the family, works through the family, and affects the family in his pursuit of heroism. *Friend* illustrates the culture of the legal system in North Korea as Judge Chŏng Chin-u makes unexpected (and often undesirable) visits to individuals' homes. For example, Chŏng Chin-u goes to Sun-hŭi's house with the excuse of discussing the divorce issue with her husband, Sŏk-ch'un, knowing that he is still at work. There is no doubt that Chŏng Chin-u earnestly intends to talk with Sŏk-ch'un, but he is more interested in investigating the living conditions of the quarreling couple: the cleanliness of the inner quarters, the way their son, Ho-nam, is raised, and the way the couple interacts with each other at home. The narrator says, "Although Kang'an District house number 19 was a bit out of the way, he could stop by on his way home from work."[15] The domestic space is never too far from the state's reach. It may be "a bit out of the way" for Judge Chŏng Chin-u, but the distance is only a minor problem in comparison to the impending task of rehabilitating a dysfunctional family and its misguided individuals. Guiding individuals to the correct state-oriented rationality entails entering into the premises of their living space both literally and metaphorically.

In *Friend,* the legal representative of the state not only physically enters into the private quarters of Sun-hŭi and Sŏk-ch'un to identify the source of their marital problems, but he also enters into their psyche, their inner thoughts, in order to transform their irrationalism and to provide them with the Party's directives. Toward the end of the novel, Judge Chŏng Chin-u asks Sun-hŭi if he may visit her family on a Sunday afternoon, which is her wedding anniversary. The judge wants to visit the couple to share the joyous event, hoping that the anniversary will rekindle the dying embers of their marriage. As marriage is a political and social institution in North Korea, the judge feels justified in celebrating the couple's anniversary with them.

It is not unusual for communist societies and their literature to expose the domestic space to the public, showing the porous nature of the binary. According to Article 86 of the revised DPRK Civil Procedure Code, the court may dismiss divorce litigation if the married couple can reconcile their differences and project a hopeful future together through the arbitration of the judge.[16] The operative word is "arbitration," not in the sense where the prospective divorcees stand before the judge in court but during the "on-the-spot" investigation procedure where the judge gathers evidence. The judge is not to advise reconciliation passively to the couple, but, rather, he is to expose the faults of the litigants, bring the couple to a mutual understanding, and assign a division of labor regarding the raising of their children among other things by actively persuading the couple.[17] In this sense, Paek Nam-nyong's delineation of Judge Chŏng Chin-u as what

South Korean scholar Kim Chae-yong refers to as the *people's friend* (*inminui pŏt*) is not an unusual way to characterize judges in the DPRK.[18] It is Chŏng Chin-u's legal duty to penetrate into the domestic space and into the private thoughts of the couple in order to reconcile their differences and reassert the family revolution.

His antithetical position toward the antagonist Ch'ae Rim, who is self-serving rather than serving the needs of the people, further secures his position as the hero. Ch'ae Rim's obese body symbolizes his opulent lifestyle and power. His silk suits and fashionable neckties display the economic class disparity between elite cadres and workers. Ch'ae Rim is accused of falling into bureaucratism and formalism—the two most deleterious ideologies to the construction of the Kimilsungist state.[19] He is also charged with embezzling government funds. After Chŏng Chin-u threatens to indict and imprison Ch'ae Rim for criminal activities, Ch'ae Rim confesses his misconduct and promises to restore the funds properly. Unlike villains in the past, the "enemy of the state" in the literature of the 1980s is no longer found outside the Edenic society of the DPRK but rather inside, disrupting the movement of the state toward its socialist perfection.[20]

The portrayal of the figure "Chŏng Chin-u" as the sympathetic people's friend who transforms the nuclear family into revolutionary members by eliminating familial discord and the figure "Judge Chŏng Chin-u" as the unerring law enforcer who proceeds to prosecute and attack the cancerous individuals in the society runs parallel with the Party's family revolution. In this respect, Chŏng Chin-u assumes the category of the prototypical hero in North Korean socialist realist fiction as discussed in Kim Jong Il's *On the Art of the Cinema* (2001), where everything is subordinated to the positive figure, including the fate of the entire dramatis personae.[21] In other words, the hidden hero is the embodiment of the imagined state with moral virtues that constitute the desired modern subject. The hero learns that he has always been a national subject, and it is this realization or recognition that determines his heroism rather than his performance.

Kim Chae-yong discusses Chŏng Chin-u as the hidden hero of *Friend,* a hero from among the common folk, unlike the militant guerrillas during the colonial era or soldiers on the battlefield during the Korean War. Kim says, "[The hidden hero] must be able to show his objective development as a prototypical hero."[22] In *Friend,* Judge Chŏng Chin-u is a common civil servant who certainly appears to embody the magnanimous virtue of the state-desired hero. Yet this description of Chŏng Chin-u reduces him to the typical hero or heroine as seen in North Korean literature from previous decades. What makes Chŏng Chin-u the hero of the novel is not his strong moral qualities, unbureaucratic attitude, and keen sense of revolutionizing the family; in fact, it is the opposite.

Friend makes a great effort to reconstruct the image of flat heroes from previous decades in North Korean fiction so that a hero is no longer an unattainable force of absolute virtue and perfection but rather a human being who also displays shortcomings, weaknesses, and character flaws. Even in comparison to representations of other hidden heroes in 1980s fiction, *Friend* elaborates on Chŏng Chin-u's psychological and emotional transformation, providing a sense of humanity to his otherwise magnanimous and infallible character. Chŏng Chin-u is by all means not a flat hero who only emits Party-desired virtues. Then again, he is not a rounded character like a papier-mâché figure composed of layers and layers of Party slogans. In *Friend,* the hero suffers from the revenants of anger, hatred, frustration, and regret. *Friend* delves into the monstrosity of human emotions to show the ambiguity of the novel's prescribed resolution. That is, rather than posing a materialist problem for the hero to resolve, *Friend* poses human emotions as the object of dilemma and fright. The image of the hero metaphorically wrestling with his own emotions produces the aesthetics of a literary character that had been overshadowed in literature by the infallible heroes of the 1970s, whose heroism was mostly based on overcoming their physical environment. The extent to which a literary hero struggles with himself in *Friend* suggests a shift in the aesthetics of depicting heroism in fiction of the 1980s. The hero's formidable enemy is himself, his decentered self, his divided allegiance to the state, and his delinquent moral attitude. The irony in *Friend* is that, in the midst of resolving other couples' marital problems, Chŏng Chin-u cannot seem to manage his own marital problems, which results in his entertaining thoughts of divorcing his wife: "He had to raise his son from kindergarten to the day he went to the military because his wife was gone most of the time. He complied with every one of his wife's requests and desires. However, now he is frustrated and has been complaining about his wife and their family life. He has become indifferent toward his wife's research experiment."[23]

The judge consigns domestic responsibilities to the woman's "natural" role as the nurturer of the family. Chŏng Chin-u is frustrated with his wife's extended absences from her domestic duties. When he comes home to an empty apartment, Chŏng Chin-u thinks to himself: "Why do I have to do all the housework? She should be the one doing it; she's the wife. It's not like her research is groundbreaking. It's just cultivating vegetables."[24] Chŏng Chin-u has a sexist perspective on women's role in society and in the nuclear family. Although he encourages women to partake in national responsibilities outside of the home, he feels that it is also the duty of women to manage the domestic space. For Chŏng Chin-u, these include raising the child, cooking for her husband, cleaning the house, and standing by the side of her husband. His complaints toward his wife come from her nonconformity to the societal demands of a housewife. In the later stage of his married life, Chŏng Chin-u has come to expect his wife to assume gendered roles and refers to these specified roles as the woman's ethical response to her basic nature. For example, when Sun-hŭi comes to Chŏng Chin-u to file for divorce, he sends her away saying, "Take care of your husband and your son. Divorce is one thing, but fulfilling your ethical responsibility as a wife and mother is another."[25] Chŏng Chin-u conflates Sun-hŭi's national duty with domestic work as the single embodiment of what all women ought to do in the DPRK. This enduring North Korean cultural code of imbalanced gender roles is manifested in much of Paek Nam-nyong's writing.

Paek Nam-nyong portrays Chŏng Chin-u, an honorable judge and a state representative, as the caretaker of domestic duties in order to elicit sympathy from his readers. The image of Chŏng Chin-u carrying his son on his back is supposed to be seen as an emasculated patriarch rather than a supportive husband. It is not "normal" for a man to have a child hanging on his back in the Korean culture, as this duty is typically attributed to women. The novel adds that Chŏng Chin-u has had to raise his son from kindergarten to the age he entered the military, which is well over ten years of rearing his son by himself. The portrayal of Chŏng Chin-u's "domestic" duties does not imply that he has learned the difficulty of raising a child and working at the court or that he understands the double labor, or "second shift," women have had to face and still face in the DPRK.[26] In this sense, *Friend* maintains the strict dichotomy of gendered roles as prescribed by the patriarchal social codes of conduct. Any crossing or inversion of gendered duties in *Friend* is described as a temporary substitution rather than a reconsideration and rebalancing of gender identity.

In *Friend,* the patriarchal social dynamics do not come undone with a man doing what is perceived as woman's duties. But Chŏng Chin-u comes to recognize the importance of his wife's research for the community and that a healthy family must overcome personal interests for the advancement of the state. He, therefore, transcends the limits of his personal angst toward his wife and supports the agricultural endeavors of the collective for which his wife works:

> Sometimes I complain and vent my frustrations. But it's been a rewarding life. This is beyond the expectations of our wedding night. To be honest with you, a few days ago, I was not able to think with such a pure and sympathetic heart. I began to envy other families where the wife stayed at home and lived a normal life. Don't be discouraged. Radishes and cabbages have to be considered a success. Don't you think the villagers at Yŏnsudŏk will be able to enjoy the cabbages and radishes by next year?[27]

Chŏng Chin-u's ability to accept his wife's research indicates he has resolved his emotional and psychological struggles that are not readily overcome with only the correct political consciousness. He does not undo his sexist views because this is not the story of the transformation of a patriarchal hero. Instead, he is a projection of a malleable subject that absorbs and manifests a virtuosity of compassion for his wife. Unlike most of the gung-ho, flat, and prescribed heroes in narratives of the 1970s and even the 1980s, Chŏng Chin-u's heroism derives from the understanding of his subjectivity and his surrounding conditions. He resists retaliating against his wife or complaining; instead, he accepts his fate of isolation and emasculation as a husband who needs to perform the domestic duties. His magnanimity as a hero in the novel is a result of a shift in recognition: he does not fight to change circumstances; he endeavors to change his perspective of the existing circumstances.

Very much like Hegel's Absolute Spirit (*Geist*), spirit in North Korea is self-consciousness recognizing itself in relation to other self-consciousnesses. Through this dialectical process (*Aufhebung*), self-consciousness becomes aware of the fundamental unity of its rationalized reality. North Korean literature, then, demonstrates the process of self-consciousness recognizing itself amid its social environment. The protagonist begins as a conscious being who is simply aware of his surroundings. Through the course of the story, the protagonist comes to recognize his own identity and desires through the presence of another character. The protagonist is now self-aware in relation to another self-conscious being. As the two (or more) characters in the story conflict and resolve their personal issues, they come to recognize their true identity, which is in the identity of the collective.

The regime of the Same in the North Korean context established the spirit (*chŏngsin*), rationality, and absolute patriarchal tyranny at the center of all epistemological apparatuses that make up the political society. Spirit is supposed to be devoid of sexed/gendered bodies, as women were desexualized in the discursive construction of motherhood. Spirit relates only to self-consciousness. Through fiction, the North Korean state has been asserting the unisex nature of thought, the "unsexed" discourse that does not differentiate between male and female ways of thinking. The state is correct in that there is a unisexual thought; however, the uniform thought it has adopted is masculine.

The family revolution campaign through the elevation of the hidden hero has engendered a patriarchal, phallocentric, logocentric, and misogynistic prerogative of the Same, reinstating state-orchestrated hierarchies: man/woman, husband/wife, and father/mother. The male-centered discourse creates its own territory in which women are subjected, drawn into the regime of the Same under the guise of sexual and gender equality. But the discourse turns out to be a tyrannical institution of oppression, discipline, and reconfiguration. Women in North Korean literature find themselves at the mercy of the political linguistic system. The sexual difference of women is effaced, elided, and displaced from the totality of the state, which paradoxically claims that there is no sexual difference in the realm of political consciousness. Within the parameters of the masculine state politics and epistemology, women are required to become "rational" beings and to disregard any sense of ontological differences.

By the 1970s, the spirit of the socialist collective had faded into the forgetfulness and the patriarchal spirit of Kimilsungism had found its home in the regime of the Same. Kimilsungism became the logocentric, phallocentric, and patriarchal center through which every aspect of North Korean society is governed and subjugated. In establishing Kimilsungism at the center of thought, behavior, and performativity, the regime of the Same reconstructs and normalizes the epistemological understanding of society, culture, and politics, particularly in its relation to women. The regime of the Same is a male-centered political system that proscribes women from recognition, consideration, and participation in the political forum of men. In *Friend,* Judge Chŏng Chin-u criticizes only the men in the narrative; he does not articulate the Party's directives to the women. This is because the narrative is about the transformation of men. *Friend* appears to follow the formulaic structure of typical North Korean fiction on families with the restoration of men as the patriarchs of the family and by extension the stronghold of the nation. Chŏng Chin-u compels Ch'ae Rim to confess his fraudulent misdeeds; he criticizes the director at the Provincial Performing Arts Theater for not maintaining social and ideological harmony at work; he convinces the coal miner to quit drinking and to pursue his long-lost passion; he transforms Sŏk-ch'un into a "new man" (*sae in'gan*),[28] helping him to acquire the latest technological skills appropriate to the Party's demands; and, most important, he undergoes his own state-desired transformation, qualifying him as the hero of the narrative. For Chŏng Chin-u, the family is structured with the male as the head of the family and everyone else subordinate to him. The husband and wife share a balance of power according to the DPRK Family Law, but, in practice and for Chŏng Chin-u, the man is the ultimate administrator of power within a socially contrived patriarchal system.

However, there is an unresolved issue in the novel. The end of the novel does not fulfill its enclosure of the narrative as in most cases in North Korean fiction. The story does not ensure that the men indeed have transformed. The contrived ending seems to resist closure or, at least, suspends the completion of the novel. Readers are left with the thoughts of Chŏng Chin-u, who claims that Sun-hŭi and Sŏk-ch'un will resolve their differences and build an optimistic family: "Chŏng Chin-u looked at Ho-nam and tried to quell his envious thoughts. Don't worry, child. Your parents will remarry. They may not have a wedding ceremony, but they will prepare a new family. It will be a spiritual wedding."[29] For Chŏng Chin-u, a "new family" is built not only on conjugal relations but more importantly on the spiritual (*chŏngsinjŏkin*), or the recognition of the Kimilsungist ideology. Indeed, the spiritual wedding does not refer to the reformation of the nuclear family but to a new commitment to the patriarchal state, a political vow to the Great Leader, and a reincorporation into the regime of the Same. The nuclear family is supposed to elevate itself, sublate itself, go beyond itself to and for the state. Meanwhile, where are the women in the novel?

Apolitical Tears of Women

At face value, *Friend* appears to typify the commonplace narrative pattern in North Korean fiction where a male authority figure brings contending individuals to a better understanding of what the state desires from each of them and thus restores the harmony of the conjugal family, and by extension the community. Although this is accurate for the men in the novel, the women offer a different perspective of the patriarchal social structure. Each woman in *Friend* contests, resists, and questions the oppressive discourse of the Same through the shedding of tears, which diverge from the metaphoric conventions of tears in other North Korean literature.

The trope of tears in North Korean fiction exemplifies the external manifestation of a character's determination to live a life wholly committed and devoted to the state. The most important and prevalent kind of tears women shed (and in some cases men as well) in North Korean fiction is a reflection of their ineffable emotions on encountering Kim Il Sung. For example, the leader comes to a factory or a collective farm, and the overzealous people respond in the form of tears. The mere presence of the leader evokes tears. Another kind of tears is tears of disappointment, shame, regret, memory, and joy shared among characters. For example, a woman is frustrated with her coworkers; a worker is shamed before his comrades for not living up to Party standards; a man regrets his days of not abiding by the Party's directives; an elderly man remembers the day when Kim Il Sung liberated Korea from Japan; men recall a nurse who sacrificed her life during the Korean War; a woman is overjoyed at the success of machinery at her factory; a mother is proud of her children fighting for the revolution; a soldier returns home after military service—the list goes on. The common denominator in the majority of the narratives that have characters in tears is the understanding of one's love (or lack thereof) for Kim Il Sung, the Party, and the state. Tears in North Korean fiction are metonyms of collectivity that respond to social, political, and historical events; they do not pertain to the crying individual.

When Kim Il Sung died in July of 1994 and when Kim Jong Il died in December of 2011, many DPRK citizens wailed along the streets as the funeral procession drove by. At Kim Il Sung's mausoleum, numerous North Koreans shed tears as they observe the embalmed body of their leader. The death of Kim Il Sung was called the Great National Bereavement, as the entire nation mourned the loss of its one and only leader. Heonik Kwon and Byung-Ho Chung state that the image of collective lamentation was at once familiar and deeply alien to South Koreans, who viewed the event on television news: "It was familiar to the extent that the way in which individual mourners expressed their grief was akin to how Koreans would express grief at family funerals, according to the custom of public lamentation. The spectacle in Pyongyang's public squares appeared alien, however, because public lamentations in traditional Korean custom are usually for the loss of a close kinsman rather than a political leader."[30]

The public display of lamentation for the deaths of Kim Il Sung and Kim Jong Il was a political response to the people's solidarity and collectivity. The veracity of one's true emotional response was of little concern in the public space. The very fact that the individual was present in the public square—whether out of one's own volition or because one was forced to be present—demonstrated his or her political participation. In the public sphere, the individual's emotional response was part of a shared response demonstrating how the nation felt, grieved, and displayed its loss. Kwon and Chung claim that the death of Kim Il Sung was akin to the death of a father for many North Koreans, that it was a *family affair*.[31] The exhibition of tears was a participatory gesture of paying respect to the father of the nation. Whether or not a citizen of the DPRK cried at the announcement of the deaths of Kim Il Sung and Kim Jong Il in the solitude of one's private sphere was a political statement in and of itself—unresponsiveness was also a response.

Although tears for Kim Il Sung or Kim Jong Il *interpellate* the crying individual as a subject of the state, at times those very tears are indecipherable and uncertain as to whether they are representing the spirit of the state or undermining it. The four female characters in *Friend* produce tears that are radically different from the conventions of shedding tears in North Korean fiction. The tears of these women reveal that individual emotions dwell beneath the surface of collective political utterances. Ch'ae Rim's wife, the schoolteacher, Ŭn-ok, and Sun-hŭi are worth examining, as their tears are directed at the injustice of the patriarchal system in the DPRK.

The tears that Ch'ae Rim's wife exhibits in court are of regret for supporting her callous husband over the years while he was a university student rather than living for herself. The novel does not provide the reader with the name of Ch'ae Rim's wife—she is simply referred to as the "wife." Her nameless character is already marginalized from the main narrative and the correct political life she is supposed to live. She is a passing character, not even a secondary character. She is given neither a name nor a voice in the narrative—she has no spoken lines. She only dwells in Chŏng Chin-u's memory, and, in that memory, she only cries. But her tears move Judge Chŏng Chin-u more than words.

The wife had been working for a reforestation company to support her two children and her husband, who is away at a university in the city. Her hands had become calloused from planting trees, her skin burnt from staying out in the sun for extended hours, and her body emaciated from lack of nutrients. She never spent her hard-earned wages on herself (e.g., to purchase new clothes or eat well). She wired most of her wages to her husband in the city. When she would visit him, he would mistreat her and embarrass her in front of his city-slicker friends. He never appreciated her but took advantage of his submissive wife. She finally filed for divorce, and Judge Chŏng Chin-u approved the case. At first, Judge Chŏng Chin-u was concerned for the wife's well-being, but he saw the wife's determination to live a healthier life without her husband:

> She stated quietly that she could no longer live with her husband. She began to cry incessantly. These were tears of regret for having lived a life of misery. Although they could be perceived as the tears of a frail woman, they were tears of a firm determination for a new day ahead of her. She was the kind of person who worked harder when her hands hurt from planting trees in the mountains. Like a wild chrysanthemum, she will emerge from the undergrowth of the dead forest.[32]

This passage reveals the emotional and psychological strength of the wife, and her determination to live independently from the constraints of marriage. Her strength derives neither from community support nor from her platonic love for Kim Il Sung. Her focus is on her new life journey without her husband and without the social construct of wifehood. The divorce verdict releases the wife from the bondage of marriage, which the text describes as a "dead forest" that has been obstructing her identity as a woman in a tightly structured patriarchal society. The divorce is not only from Ch'ae Rim but from the institution of marriage on which her entire life painfully hinged. Now she has the ability to redefine her identity as a woman and to utter the one word that has been so alien to her: *freedom*.

The novel does not explicate what the wife does with her newfound freedom. On one occasion, Chŏng Chin-u runs into her in the city, but the wife lowers her head and walks past him without greeting him. The wife has decidedly distanced herself from engaging in small talk with the judge. Divorce in the DPRK may be considered a shameful act of violence against the nuclear family as it affects the harmony of the Great Family, but the wife's attitude toward Chŏng Chin-u transcends the social stigma against divorcées. The wife refuses to speak to a male authority figure. She breaks the code of etiquette to her elder and to a hierarchically positioned legal administrator. The state has granted her the divorce and has empowered her as a human being, and she no longer feels the need to succumb to social authority by reengaging with Judge Chŏng Chin-u.

The second instance of tears comes from the schoolteacher, who lives in the apartment below Chŏng Chin-u. Her tears represent disdain for the court's decision to divorce Ch'ae Rim and his wife, leaving the children confused by the adults' selfish reprisal of their happiness. The schoolteacher tells the son, Ch'ae Yŏng-il, about the divorce. She has noticed that Yŏng-il has changed for the worse since his parents' divorce. One day, the schoolteacher meets Chŏng Chin-u on a road, confronts him about the court's decision to divorce Yŏng-il's parents, and expresses her disappointment in a law that cares little for victimized children.

The schoolteacher appears to be the most passive character among the women in *Friend*. She waits in front of the apartment complex every night for her husband to return home from work. Chŏng Ching-u respects the schoolteacher for doing this and often wishes his wife would do the same for him. The schoolteacher appears to be the ideal housewife who caters to the needs of her husband. She neither reprimands her husband for being an alcoholic nor complains about his complacent attitude toward his work. The schoolteacher is supposed to exemplify the image of a submissive housewife and an upright member of society.

However, the novel does not simply delineate her as a flat character for the purposes of polarizing good and bad, moral and immoral, and submissive and defiant characteristics. In fact, the schoolteacher is the only character in *Friend* who reprimands Judge Chŏng Chin-u directly to his face, causing him to regret his decision to divorce Ch'ae Rim and his wife. Chŏng Chin-u is supposed to be the people's friend and the hero of the narrative. Yet the schoolteacher has been harboring disdain toward the law and toward Chŏng Chin-u, waiting for the appropriate moment to confront him. When she meets the judge on the road, she proceeds to tell him about her student Yŏng-il. During lunch at a school picnic, she had gathered all of the students but recognized that Yŏng-il was missing. She searched the entire park, but Yŏng-il was not to be found. She finally went to the riverbank and saw Yŏng-il, sitting by a large boulder. As she approached Yŏng-il, she noticed that he was not sitting alone but with his sister, Yŏng-sun. They were sharing lunch. They hid from the other students and from their teachers in order to avoid public scrutiny. They chose not to participate in the collective school activity but to take a short moment to remind each other of the strength of their family bond. The schoolteacher says: "No matter how much a teacher loves her students and would, therefore, do whatever it takes to help her students succeed, I realized that the love of a teacher wanes in comparison to the love between blood-related siblings. And it's precisely these kids, whose parents have kept apart their love for each other, it's precisely these kids who suffer most."[33]

The schoolteacher is incorrect in her statement. The parents have not kept the siblings' love apart, but rather the law has separated the siblings. The law has determined that the siblings will no longer live under the same roof with a single parent. However, the schoolteacher is correct in saying that neither the siblings' parents nor the law can sever the love between the siblings. The schoolteacher recites the proverbial "blood is thicker than water," stating that neither a state institution such as school nor any comrade from that institution can supplant the familial bond that exists between the siblings and their biological mother.

The argument essentializing family members as a natural bond contrasts that familial bond with the artificial political bond with the Great Family of the DPRK. *Friend* illustrates that the love between siblings outweighs state-prescribed emotions toward the Great Leader, the Party, and the nation. Judge Chŏng Chin-u's divorce verdict is not enough to keep the siblings apart, as Creon's verdict was not enough to keep Antigone away from her brother. The law may advise or direct people to live a certain way, but it cannot fully control human emotions and human experience. Upon discovering the siblings, the schoolteacher does not admonish the two for alienating themselves from the collective. She, too, understands the strength of their love for each other and allows them to enjoy the precious moment together. The siblings' love overwhelms the schoolteacher and causes her to doubt the law's verdict on their parents' divorce. In short, the schoolteacher articulates a humanitarian cry to Judge Chŏng Chin-u that prioritizes family commitment above legal or political commitment. "Whether the divorce was done legally or not, I feel that separating these kids was a crime. Comrade Judge, why did the court permit the divorce? Was it for the adults' new life, their newfound happiness? Can there be happiness for parents who have stripped away the happiness of their children?"[34]

The schoolteacher's words are strong and visceral. For the schoolteacher, the law may be rational and may legislate the best interests of the citizens of the DPRK, but, if it has no compassion for the people, it is utterly criminal. She feels that separating the children from each other and from their parents is a "crime," regardless of the legal rhetoric of child welfare. Judge Chŏng Chin-u has divorced Ch'ae Rim and his wife, thinking that he was doing the wife a favor. But he now realizes that the children have been negatively affected by the divorce, and this, in turn, has affected the schoolteacher. She expresses the law's inhumanity toward the people whom it is supposed to serve. Although there is nothing Judge Chŏng Chin-u can do about the divorce at this point, he can feel the embittered tears of the schoolteacher that are directed toward him.

Through the tears of the schoolteacher, Paek Nam-nyong reaches into the depths of human love. Although the legal system of the DPRK is supposed to provide civil rights, freedom, and happiness for its citizens,[35] the schoolteacher criticizes it for its lack of true compassion and love for the people. The schoolteacher questions the ethical fiber of the court's all too easy verdict of guilty/not guilty without recognizing the consequences of such a decision. The schoolteacher may have appeared passive and submissive throughout the novel, but it was only a matter of time before she confronted the judge. The schoolteacher has worked all her life for her country, but, on this day, on this road, in the face of Judge Chŏng Chin-u, she turns her face with disapproval. This is a not a sign of rebellion or anger toward the state. Instead, she is expressing her sincere desire for her beloved country to improve the sociopolitical infrastructure and living conditions for its citizens, including the children.

The third set of tears comes from Chŏng Chin-u's wife, Ŭn-ok, whose mind is constantly on her field research back in her hometown rather than on her role as a housewife. Ŭn-ok studied biology in order to research a hybrid vegetable that can withstand the rough terrain of her hometown farm. At first, Chŏng Chin-u promises to support Ŭn-ok with her research plans. But he never anticipated her long absences from him and from her duties as a wife. On the night of their marriage, Ŭn-ok stares out of the window with tears in her eyes, longing to be with the villagers in the place of her true residence: "I can't help but recall my childhood. I feel like I'm still in that place. It feels like some other woman got married. I'm scared. I feel guilty for leaving Yŏnsudŏk over there while living over here. In that village, there are the old-timers and comrades whom I grew up with."[36]

Chŏng Chin-u mistakenly perceives her tears as joyful tears at being married to him. Although Ŭn-ok is supposed to be overwhelmed with the thought of starting a new revolutionary family with her husband, she is unable to depart emotionally and psychologically with her hometown family members, whom she grew up with and whom she cares for more than her husband. Ŭn-ok's longing for her villagers must not be understood as a desire to live among the collective or an expression of the correct political consciousness by desiring to assist her hometown village for the sake of the country. In other words, her desire to go back home must not be read as unfailing political commitment where she will sacrifice even her husband for the Great Leader. Instead, Ŭn-ok's tears of nostalgia are indicative of her yearning for an imagined community that lies beyond her political reality.

Ŭn-ok is never home throughout the narrative. At the beginning of the novel, Chŏng Chin-u returns to his empty home to find only a short letter from Ŭn-ok saying that she has had to return to her village because of an emergency. He resents Ŭn-ok for prioritizing her research before her family. Meanwhile, he is the one who raises their son, and her long absences make Chŏng Chin-u a self-sustaining man. Of course, Chŏng Chin-u changes his resentful attitude toward Ŭn-ok through the course of the narrative. At the end of the novel, Chŏng Chin-u expects his home to be empty but is pleasantly greeted by Ŭn-ok. After the two have dinner, Ŭn-ok softly asks permission to leave for her hometown again.

Ŭn-ok is constantly moving from one location to another; she is never settled in one particular place for any length of time. The only place that is stable and unchanging is her hometown, which is the creation of her imagination. She creates the space and makes the time to leave for her hometown. Her research to improve the vegetation of her hometown will never be successful (she is aware of this as well), but she returns to the place of her youth and memories because that is where she finds her identity.

Ŭn-ok is not a defiant character in the novel. However, she may be the only female character in all of North Korean fiction who fails to conform to the strictures of what a housewife ought to do from the beginning to the end of the narrative. She is never reprimanded for her domestic negligence but is accepted has having duties beyond the parameters of domesticity and femininity. She is not an antagonistic character who is evil in the eyes of the other characters or readers. She appears to be performing her national duties as an intellectual assisting her technologically and agriculturally less advanced village. There is nothing erroneous about her actions in the narrative. But Ŭn-ok unassumingly breaks all the social and cultural codes of a housewife. She does not change or even attempt to conform to the role of the state-prescribed housewife. Instead, Chŏng Chin-u undergoes a transformation from a chauvinistic to an open-minded husband.

The character delineation of Ŭn-ok is arguably the most creative in all of North Korean fiction. Ŭn-ok is literally the most elusive character in *Friend* because of her perpetual absence in a narrative that tries to cement the family revolution to the responsibility of women. Even at the end of the narrative, Ŭn-ok does not come home to celebrate success in her research as the majority of North Korean narratives typically would have her do but rather claims that she must return to her village for more tests. It is evident that Ŭn-ok's research will be continuous, well beyond the scope of the narrative. The story does not end "happily" for Chŏng Chin-u, and the family revolution will not be completed. Ŭn-ok must return to her hometown and be among her friends and villagers. This is the only way to dry Ŭn-ok's tears and keep her happy. She is the missing link in the unity of the family revolution, but she would prefer to maintain her connection with her childhood memories than with a politically institutionalized formation of the nuclear family. She is not alone in thinking this. In the next section, I will closely analyze Ch'ae Sun-hŭi's tears, which, unlike Ŭn-ok's, carry a resounding and thunderous cry against the patriarchal state.

Song of Sun-hŭi: A Different Linguistic System

Sun-hŭi imagined divorce would be as swift and easy as her performances on stage. She imagined her unhappy marriage would end with her plea to the judge. She imagined leaving the courthouse as a new and liberated woman. She imagined never seeing Sŏk-ch'un toiling over his invention again. She imagined starting a fresh life with only her son. She never imagined her divorce would be a struggle against a most formidable opponent—Judge Chŏng Chin-u.

Although the main conflict in *Friend* appears to be between the two antagonistic cadres Chŏng Chin-u and Ch'ae Rim, the implicit conflict is between Chŏng Chin-u and Sun-hŭi—a power struggle between the state and an individual. Ko In-hwan allegorizes Sŏk-ch'un as the state and Sun-hŭi as the family, and argues that the harmony of the state and the family represents the fulfillment of the family revolution promoted by the Party.[37] Ko's observation is correct in its prima facie reading of the married couple and perhaps captures the reading the Party expects from the readers. The view that Chŏng Chin-u represents the failure of the state, the one who is unable to stem the individualistic tendencies in Sun-hŭi, thus creating fissures in the community, may be an iconoclastic reading. However, it is this reading that resists the novel's optimistic enclosure and allows difference and multiple readings—a *new linguistic system*—to become visible from the margins of the narrative.

Sun-hŭi pleads for divorce not for the purpose of disrupting the harmony of the state but simply because she cannot live with Sŏk-ch'un anymore.[38] Her cry "I can't stand it anymore" refers to her intolerable relationship with Sŏk-ch'un. Sun-hŭi's initial request for divorce derives from her incompatibility with her husband—from her private marital affairs. But Sun-hŭi quickly recognizes that her contention with her husband has become a larger issue beyond the limits of her private world, an issue that involves the state. "Marriage is a legal binding" are the words of Chŏng Chin-u, indicating that Sun-hŭi's marriage to Sŏk-ch'un irrefutably belongs to the state. Sun-hŭi learns that her private affairs have been in the public purview from the moment she stepped into the contractual agreement of marriage, an institution that is protected by the state. The narrator says: "When a man and a woman fall in love and decide to marry, it's their freedom. But, they have to register their new family. The law protects the entity of a family. Divorce is disconnecting the relationship between a husband and wife; it's not a personal matter. The family's fate as the fundamental cell of society is concerned with the greater family of the society and sociopolitics."[39]

In *Friend,* a wife's marital problems with her husband are a metonym for her dissatisfaction with the institution of marriage, her resistance to becoming a state-desired woman, wife, and mother. The notion of the family revolution devises standard protocols by which husband and wife ought to behave. The rhetoric of the family as the fundamental cell of society is the state's method of controlling and administering power over the people so that each family can reflect and recite the Party directives for emulating the members of the Great Revolutionary Family. Sun-hŭi is aware of this subject-making discourse and asserts that she has made efforts to be the state-desired wife: "I have been faithful to my husband's demands. I have stood by him and his work, the one thing he considers more important than me! I've been submissive to him while he has been working on a single project for the past five years. I didn't care if he did not bring home a salary or if he didn't help me with house chores. I've endured it all and continued to live with him."[40]

Sun-hŭi's attempt at being an ideal wife proved to test the limits of her agency and individuality. It may have been her choice to love and marry Sŏk-ch'un, but it was not her choice to become a manufactured product of the state-prescribed wife. Her faithfulness and submission to the patriarchal order has reduced her and forced her to conform to the state against her will. She is the oppressed and disenfranchised victim of the patriarchal state. This is because the concept of "woman" marks a point of dispute and problematizes language itself so that her injustice cannot be registered in the grand narrative of the DPRK. She cannot appeal her injustice to the court of men not because she does not have a legitimate case, but because she does not belong to the linguistic rules of men. The patriarchal state has inscribed the woman into its discourse and has oppressed her through its sexist semantics. If she speaks, she has to use the language of men to make her case. Sun-hŭi is frustrated with Judge Chŏng Chin-u because he cannot seem to understand her plea. The conflict between Sun-hŭi and the judge is about the legitimacy of her divorce petition, but it is more about rationalizing the woman who refuses to be rationalized under male standards of consciousness.

Sun-hŭi feels the more she speaks "rationally" to the judge about her case, the more she loses her identity as a woman. She is caught in an *aporetic* situation: she cannot express the wrong done to her by the male-centered social system unless she articulates the language of logocentrism, which would then subjugate her back into the hierarchical structure in which women are at the mercy of the men. The woman is the victim of North Korea's patriarchal discursive conditions, in which she cannot express her loss or suffering as "damage" that deserves restitution. Lyotard calls this a *différend,* which is when something "asks" to be articulated but then suffers from the wrong of not being able to be put into words right away.[41] Lyotard says, "A *différend* is born from a wrong and is signaled by silence"; when there is a *différend,* damage has already occurred.[42] A wrong takes place when one's loss or suffering cannot be given a determined meaning (a value) and cannot be reified in the language of exchange, or, if it can be reified, the exchange is blocked for lack of currency—the damage cannot be rectified. Sun-hŭi is the victim of a *différend* in the jurisdiction of her male counterparts, but, at the same time, she perpetually questions the ontology and epistemology of the grand narrative of the state as the permanently contested site of meaning.

Sun-hŭi faces an additional problem when the state orders her to "let go" of her child and become the ideal self-sacrificing mother. Sun-hŭi realizes her powerlessness before the law. She has given birth to her son, but she realizes that her son was never hers to begin with. The law does not decide what is best for individuals but what is best for the state: "As soon as she grabbed Ho-nam and pulled him into her arms, Judge Chŏng Chin-u reprimanded her as he had at his office. 'Comrade Sun-hŭi, let the child go.' She realized that the law supported her son's welfare over hers."[43] The law tries to reduce Sun-hŭi to a mother whose duty is to "let go" of what is *rightfully* hers to the state like the mother in the film and novel *Sea of Blood.* The state instructs her to give up what is *legally* the state's and expects her to become reabsorbed into the discourse of the Same.

The law is more concerned for Ho-nam not only because he is an innocent victim of disputing parents but because he is the future of the state.[44] In a previous divorce hearing, Chŏng Chin-u had remanded a boy to his father's custody for the benefit of the boy's future, which was related to his physical and mental growth.[45] It is the state that "establishes" the child's patriarchal identity, while the mother "raises" and "lets him go." This logic asserts that children need to be well fostered in order to pass from the family to the state in Hegelian terms. "The family attains completion in the bringing up of children and the dissolution of the family."[46] For Hegel, ethical life derives from the family but soon suppresses, interferes, preserves, and sublates the spirit of individualism. Though each individual originates from a family, the ethical calling for the individual is not to remain in the family but to break away and even dissolve the immediate family for the state in order to become a *completed* individual. Hegel says, "The youth goes forth from the unconscious life of the family and becomes the individuality of the community."[47] The family is a temporary space, the realm of the unconscious, before the individual (most notably men for Hegel) secures his identity in the state. Motherhood, then, as Suzy Kim discusses, is the selfless channel that allows for the son to enter into the state.[48] While Sun-hŭi tries to hold on to what is hers, the ominous administrator of the law orders her to "let the child go," reminding her that the tug of war is not with her husband but with the state.

Even Sun-hŭi's best friend at the Provincial Performing Arts Theater advises Sun-hŭi to "let go" of her stubbornness and submit to the patriarchal order. On her way to work, Sun-hŭi runs into Ŭn-mi, her best friend, who says, "Sun-hŭi, it's about time that you let it go."[49] Ŭn-mi, with the best intentions, tries to assuage Sun-hŭi's anxiety by attempting to sympathize with her marital problems. Ŭn-mi shares how she deals with her own husband: "I just shut my mouth, bite my tongue, and take it all in."[50] Ŭn-mi represents the submissive, rational wife in *Friend* whose individuality has been subsumed in the patriarchal system.

However, Sun-hŭi continues to assert her agency to the political order. When her director at the Provincial Performing Arts Theater blames Sun-hŭi's marital problems for interfering with the business, Sun-hŭi says, "If I am bringing shame to the company, then I will quit."[51] Sun-hŭi's claim is initially aggressive and threatening to the status quo. The prospect of quitting her job at the Provincial Performing Arts Theater, which is under the aegis of the Department of Propaganda and Agitation, reveals an antagonistic attitude that indicates her lack of the correct ideology. Sun-hŭi is faced with an indeterminable choice between her career and defending her individuality against the patriarchal state. As soon as she utters these words, Sun-hŭi realizes her consequent fate: "In order to persist in her desires, she would have to sacrifice her fame and all that came with her future as a singer. And she would be ostracized from the large family called society."[52] Author Paek Nam-nyong carefully describes this crucial moment in Sun-hŭi's life as a decision that generates unutterable pain and agony for Sun-hŭi. Sun-hŭi's torment is intended to show that such decisions are not "ready-made," prescribed, or resolvable by the application of the state's formulaic directives. Although Sun-hŭi may be willing to abandon her career and fame to resist the male discourse, "all her frightening thoughts derived from her anxiety and despair at accepting the fact that she would be a wretched being."[53]

Sun-hŭi would be left without a job, a family, her son, and, most important, her dignity as an individual. Her wretchedness derives not only from the prospect of her deprivation of society but also from her inevitable absorption into the very social order she has tried so hard to resist. Sun-hŭi has nowhere to turn, no one to depend on—her best friend Ŭn-mi urges her to remain married, her director nearly fires her, Chŏng Chin-u refuses to divorce the couple, and even her son seeks his father. Where can Sun-hŭi find refuge?

Memories. Although Chŏng Chin-u asks Sŏk-ch'un to recall the romantic days to tenderize Sŏk-ch'un's calloused feelings toward Sun-hŭi, the judge does not solicit Sun-hŭi's past. The narrative does not dwell on her side of the story. Her voice is not part of the grand narrative of the patriarchs. Sŏk-ch'un's story is brought in to reestablish his responsibility as the head of the family, where even the idea of memories serves the construction of the patriarchal state.

Memories in North Korean literature are supposed to function as the operative trope to reconstruct a new identity for the protagonist. Most memories recall the messianic deliverance of Kim Il Sung in the arduous days of the colonial period or the indelible trauma of the Korean War. Sometimes memories of Kim Il Sung visiting a factory or collective farm or of how the workers have sacrificed their lives for the construction of the nation determine the positive outcome of individuals' actions. However, *Friend* is exceptional in that individuals do not recall the nation's past but their own personal pasts. Of course, these memories serve as a narrative strategy to contextualize the couple's relationship in the logic of the narrative. In that sense, even these so-called personal memories contribute to the construction of the dominant patriarchal order as they fail to tap into the unconscious level of the storyteller but remain at the conscious level.

Chŏng Chin-u attempts to constitute memory for Sun-hŭi by reminding her of her tenth wedding anniversary. He hopes that thoughts of her anniversary will somehow move her and compel her to accept the social norms that are expected of her. The judge's attempt to reinforce social and cultural norms in Sun-hŭi's life proves to be futile when she responds: "Those kinds of days are only meant for normal families."[54] For Sun-hŭi, celebrating her wedding anniversary is a state affair since marriage is institutionalized by the state. To partake in commemorating her wedding anniversary would normalize her selfhood to that of a state-desired wife. Sun-hŭi asserts her agency before the face of the law in one last act. When Judge Chŏng Chin-u asks if he may participate in Sun-hŭi's anniversary celebration, she responds with a nonresponse:

> "Would it be fine for me to stop by your house on that day?" asked Chŏng Chin-u.
>
> "Please, who can stop you, Comrade Judge," responded Sun-hŭi.
>
> "No, I'm not going to your house as a judge but as a friend," said Chŏng Chin-u.
>
> Sun-hŭi left without saying a word.[55]

Sun-hŭi's nonresponse is a tacit refusal to acknowledge Chŏng Chin-u's "friendly" gesture. It extends beyond their dialogue and encroaches upon the disavowal of the entire patriarchal system. She refuses to participate in or be incorporated into the discourse of the Same—the unitary voice of state-prescribed individuals. Sun-hŭi offers neither tacit consent nor a verbal refusal to the judge. She is not exhibiting a submissive docility to the state's legal administrator. Instead her (non)response is a demonstration of her affirmative agency against the tides of the dominant and oppressive system of patriarchs. It is a (non)participatory act of ultimate defiance, a defiant act without words using a language that is foreign to the language of the Same. Her deafening silence disrupts the discourse of the Same, throwing it into confusion and chaos.

To Judge Chŏng Chin-u, Sun-hŭi is acting irrationally: she adamantly refuses to remain married to her husband and she breaks the social codes of conduct by leaving the court without bidding farewell to an elderly man. She no longer perceives herself to be a docile participant in this systematic patriarchal order but as an anomaly to the family-state. Her words, any words, would have been considered as the participatory kind of rationalism that the state seeks, a rationalism that recognizes the other in Sun-hŭi and attempts to sublate her. Instead of allowing herself to fall prey to such rationalism, she chooses of her own volition to exercise her individuality by disregarding the judge's imposition and by making herself *unrecognizable* to such rational logic. For Sun-hŭi, the judge's actions (no matter how innocent they may be) infringe upon her identity, causing her to become more defensive rather than to yield to his directives.

But who can stop the law from entering into the premises of Sun-hŭi's house? Even on her wedding anniversary, the state watches the couple through the gaze of Chŏng Chin-u. The judge attempts to approach Sun-hŭi not as a cold and impersonal bureaucrat but as a gentle and trustworthy friend. The state imposes itself through the threshold and into the domestic space with familiarity and a smile. It urges Sun-hŭi to *let go* of her resistance and conform to the normality of her social conditions.

However, normality, for Sun-hŭi, means the effacement of her individuality and the denial of her selfhood. Sun-hŭi understands "normal families" to be those that abide by the dictates of the law, perform the set of practices instructed by the state, and conform to the unitary language governed by the totalizing power of patriarchy. Her attempt at distinguishing herself from normal families does not indicate a claim to sever all ties or to leave the community but to proffer a different linguistic possibility—albeit a scandalous or marginal claim—from the normalizing discourses of the social order. It is a claim that conditions the possibility of otherness, a resistance that does not become reabsorbed into the Same.

Sun-hŭi's voice is not heard at the end of the novel. The conclusion is in the voice (or narration) of the judge. Although reading practices in North Korea may instruct readers to accept that Sun-hŭi resigns her obstinate individuality and goes on to forge a new family, the narrative of *Friend* does not dictate such an ending. It is an inconclusive conclusion. Chŏng Chin-u projects his own utopian imagination at the end of the novel. It is the state's forceful and contrived imagination that cries for the abnormal to become normal, the irrational to become rational, and women to become wives and mothers. But such binary oppositions do not compel Sun-hŭi to conform to the state directives. She retains her own language, a *natural* language (not an *originary* language), a language inextricably tied to her individuality and identity as a woman. Sun-hŭi's *natural* language is found in her reveries and not in memories mandated by the state.

Sun-hŭi's refuge is in imaginings that transgress the limitations set by the subject-making law. Sun-hŭi's memories are of her childhood and not of the time she dated and married Sŏk-ch'un. Her childhood memories are fused with her imagination, making it difficult to decipher truth from fantasy:

> During her carefree childhood days, her dream-filled teenage years, and her pure blossoming adulthood, nature had blessed her with warm and beautiful memories. The dripping sound of rain from the eaves had been an enchanting, vibrant sound. Sun-hŭi thought that each drop of water contained the universe and was the fountain of life. At first, it had dripped like a stringed instrument, but soon it made the sound of a symphony orchestra, producing harmonious melodies as it fell on the pear tree leaves, barn roof tiles, wooden fences, flower gardens, clay pots, and on the dirt path. It seemed that the neighborhood children, who were also listening to the sound of the falling rain, were soon going to all gather at Sun-hŭi's house. A song was heard. Sun-hŭi's clear voice joined the voices of the neighborhood children.
>
> "Mom?"
>
> What a familiar voice. That voice was now pulling at her shirt, dragging her away from the reveries of her youthful days.
>
> Sun-hŭi was tossing and turning in her bed as she returned to reality, leaving her youthful days with the neighborhood children in her ephemeral dreams.[56]

This is the only account of Sun-hŭi's private, unconscious moments in the novel, the only moment in which gender, class, and the Party do not determine her identity. Sun-hŭi's reveries open up the realm of the unconscious that suspends temporality from progressing along its teleological path. Her reveries open up a space that is devoid of temporality. It is uncertain at which point in Sun-hŭi's life this memory occurred. She is not recalling a specific time but an atemporal space that suspends and dissociates any enclosing narrative. Sun-hŭi's memory is essentially a nonnarrative. A story is not being told to any particular reader, but rather the narrative of the nation often found in North Korean fiction through memory is being untold by this still frame of Sun-hŭi's reveries. The state cannot own or become the proprietor of Sun-hŭi's imaginings. But it will try its best to "pull" and "drag" her away from ungrounded, unconscious, and unideological reveries, which is the dangerous ground on which Sun-hŭi stands. Sun-hŭi inevitably, against her will, must return to reality, to the conscious level, to her ethical and societal responsibilities as her son—the future of the state—gently beckons her.

We must remember that Sun-hŭi's occupation is as a singer for the Provincial Performing Arts Theater, a bodily medium through which the state's ideology is reverberated. She is a musical propagandist, an animate instrument of ideology, a vocalist who is supposed to sing in unison with Party directives. Her singing is not only a performance on stage but is supposed to move her audience members to conjoin their sentiments with the state ideology. In this sense, she is a representative of the state much like Judge Chŏng Chin-u. She also has been speaking the discourse of the Same, the very language that she tries to resist. The difference is that she has managed to disrupt the regime of the Same through her affirmative resistance to the male discourse and, moreover, her resistance to the enclosure of the narrative form in North Korean literature that decides once and for all the definition of woman.

Sun-hŭi's reveries are musical; they are a song from nature, perhaps the only song in which she wholeheartedly enjoys participating. Sun-hŭi becomes one with nature as she sings along with its melody. Nature allows her to imagine a universe beyond her social conditions. It is nature that allows her to imagine, that empowers her to think beyond the scope of patriarchal rationality and produce new thoughts, new voices, and new linguistic systems. Her imagination escapes from the patriarchal economy in which she is supposed to participate. She is not interested in dominating or mastering nature, as the creed of communism would suggest. Instead, she learns from nature the power of self-becoming. After all, nature (*chayŏn* 自然) contains its own implicit definition of self-becoming. The song of Sun-hŭi is not a *Bildungsroman,* where a prescribed image (*Bild*) of a character constructs the teleological narrative. No, Sun-hŭi articulates her thoughts clearly on this issue when she says, "I can't stand it anymore." Sun-hŭi's song is more organic than that. She sings of the unpredictability of human nature, self-becoming with no clear direction or ideological teleology like that to which characters in fiction are subject.

The narrative trajectory of *Friend* is structured in three "acts": Act 1 is called "Their Love" (Kŭdŭl'ui sarang), Act 2 is "Two Lives" (Tu saenghwal), and Act 3 is titled "Family" (Kajŏng). "Two Lives" suggests the bifurcation of Sun-hŭi and Sŏk-ch'un's marital relationship in the second act. Sun-hŭi's reveries begin and end on the same page in the opening of Act 2. They are a flickering moment in the novel, much shorter than in Kate Chopin's *The Story of an Hour,* where Mrs. Mallard experiences "freedom" from her marriage for only an hour. But Sun-hŭi's reveries are enough to suggest that perhaps *Friend* is referring as well to the two separate lives that coexist within Sun-hŭi, her bifurcated life for the state and for herself. This bifurcation is nevertheless a porous relationship, where she negotiates her two lives on a daily basis in public and at home. Sun-hŭi's reveries do not indicate how an individual ought to behave as a citizen of the DPRK; instead, she indulges in a space where imaginings that enable her self-becoming dictate her behavior, her ethics, and her being.

Sun-hŭi establishes herself as the agent that decenters and destabilizes the rhetoric of state-desired womanhood, wifehood, and motherhood—she is abnormal in every way. Paek Nam-nyong does not categorize or generalize the aberrant symptoms of Sun-hŭi in the same way Hegel determines the place of Antigone. Antigone, in committing her crime against the state, becomes Hegel's person of interest and an allegorical figure for all womankind. Hegel categorizes Antigone's act of resistance as pertaining to the divine law that women uphold (the law of kinship), which is in opposition to human law or the ethical life (*Sittlichkeit*) that produces the norms of social intelligibility and political rationality. As Hegel maps out his philosophy on reading *Antigone,* woman stands in opposition to the state and therefore disrupts the completion of the state. However, according to Judith Butler, by supplanting Antigone with "womankind," Hegel performs the very generalization that Antigone resists.[57]

In *Antigone's Claim,* Butler finds the binary model of man/woman and state/kinship problematic, as it already establishes an essential relation between them. Butler says, "[Antigone] absorbs the very language of the state against which she rebels, and hers becomes a politics not of oppositional purity but of the scandalously impure."[58] Unlike other feminist scholars, who consider Antigone to be a feminist heroine, Butler refutes this claim because Antigone dies at the end of the play. For Butler, Antigone neither makes a strong affirmative claim against the state nor does she live to witness the effects of her claim. Rather than viewing Antigone as a feminist representation, Butler reads the heroine as the "political possibility that emerges when the limits to representation and representability are exposed."[59] In other words, for Butler, the relationship between family and state is not diametrically opposed and firmly established in its own right but rather implicated in one another in ways that suggest that there is no simple opposition between the two.[60]

How much of Sun-hŭi's resistance has been successful or has materialized? Can her voice stand against the thunderous voice of that which she contests? Unlike Antigone and Mrs. Mallard, Sun-hŭi does not die in the end. Sun-hŭi's tragedy may be the fact that she will have to continue to live in her patriarchal society without any recourse to a law that will empower her womanhood. She is put back in her place, the domestic space. At the end, when Chŏng Chin-u, who comes to the train station to welcome her back from her tour, asks Sun-hŭi how her trip went, she does not reply. Sun-hŭi's nonresponse to the judge's question reflects her position of disassociating herself from the oppressive linguistic hegemony.

The narrator speaks for Sun-hŭi: "She felt the utmost respect and humility before the representative of the law. Her heart grew warmer, and the hope of starting a new life enraptured her."[61] It appears as though (or it is supposed to be understood that) Sun-hŭi has finally given up and has "let go" of her obstinacy and submitted to the existing social order. But Paek's choice of the words "new life" (*saengsinhan sam*) suggests new resolve regarding how she will live and practice her individuality within her social conditions. It does not suggest that she has absolutely submitted to the judge's directives, and the narrator does not suggest that this new life involves her husband—it is undeterminable. After this encounter, Chŏng Chin-u takes Ho-nam to a park to leave Sŏk-ch'un and Sun-hŭi alone. Chŏng Chin-u hopes to reignite the couple's love for each other. The novel ends as such: "A family is where the love of humanity dwells and is the beautiful world where hope flourishes."[62] Will his hope be transferred to the stoic couple? Does this "family" also include Sun-hŭi?

The state's agenda is precisely to convert an aberrant individual like Sun-hŭi to a *normal* state-prescribed woman. Although the law may have legitimized Sun-hŭi and Sŏk ch'un's marriage and although Judge Chŏng Chin-u may have brought the couple physically together by the end of the novel, there are no concrete indications to suggest Sun-hŭi has chosen the path to normality. Sun-hŭi sings her song in her own language with her own melody and her own rhythm. She is not a woman, a wife, and a mother—everything that locates, categorizes her, and fixes her as the complementary and specular other of man—but rather a complex and multilayered embodied subject who has opted to distance herself from the institution of femininity.[63]

The song of Sun-hŭi does not threaten the stability of community because the narrative of *Friend* is told mostly from Chŏng Chin-u's perspective. Sun-hŭi's voice is marginalized and must remain entombed in the deep chambers of the patriarchal society. The criteria for revolutionary fiction are met in *Friend:* the presence of a positive hero, criticism of problematic individuals, and overcoming a conflict and finding a solution. This may be a universal narrative framework, but North Korean literature lays emphasis on the process of transforming aberrant individuals to become loyal followers of the Party. In my reading of *Friend,* Sun-hŭi's highest obligation is to herself rather than to the ubiquitous demands of the Party. The unitary language coupled with the totalizing ideology of the state attempt to enclose and homogenize Sun-hŭi's voice into the Same, where stories like hers have never had a chance to challenge the oppressive patriarchal language, perhaps until the publication of *Friend.* Sun-hŭi is ultimately a voice for which there is no language, thus wholly incompatible with the regime of the Same.

But we must not read *Friend* as a tragic or hopeless narrative. The double negation of Sun-hŭi's resistance ("I can't do that! I can't stand it anymore!") is an affirmative proclamation of women's agency against the prescriptive delimitations of the patriarchal social order. She speaks to the man, against the man, in his face, to his face, in his own language; and, even in her silence, she makes sure that he hears her. Speaking out against the patriarchal society is a method of exercising her agency.

The next chapter analyzes the expression of a mother's agency through her deliberate reconstruction of memory that alters the nation's grand narrative of history. Much as Sun-hŭi's memory diverges from the national narrative, the mother's memory in the next chapter also digresses from glorifying the nation. In her memory, the mother reprograms her son—the future of the political society—not in accordance with state standards of education but in accordance with her own desires and values.

CHAPTER FIVE

Motherhood Revisited

Disrupting National History

> His mother couldn't help but laugh at the absurdity of the portrait.
>
> *Ri Hŭi-nam, Eight Hours*

The newly redesigned Victorious Fatherland Liberation War Museum in Pyongyang is yet another display of North Korea's desire to create a collective memory of the Korean War. The space is carefully planned and the architecture magnificent. As visitors pull up to the parking lot, the first design they see is a large arch—resembling a minimalist or brutalist version of the Arch of Triumph in Pyongyang—with the beginning year and the ending year of the Korean War on either side and an open space in the middle that frames the museum sitting in the distance. Within this frame, the museum appears as if painted on a canvas with the central figure of a bronze soldier calling his comrades to war. Beneath the bronze soldier is another inscription of the beginning and ending years of the war. The arch as a frame is an important piece of architectural design not only because it predetermines the museum as a work of art but also because it informs visitors of the historical fact that the Korean War began in the year 1950 and ended in the year 1953 (although it still has not yet ended). The arch occupies a determinable space and has time inscribed into that space as the authoritative voice of history. The arch sets the narrative parameters for how the history of the DPRK is going to be framed and collectively told. The resemblance to the Arch of Triumph is also meaningful in that the Korean War, for the DPRK, was yet another victorious chapter of the nation's history.

Once past the threshold of the arch, the visitors enter the pristine museum park, decorated with neatly trimmed grass, vibrant flowers, and a large water fountain that stretches to the entrance of the museum. The park is vast, achieving a balance of classical grandeur and quiet solemnity. At the same time, the park represents the battlefield on which North Korean soldiers have fallen, with statues of charging soldiers lined up along the sides of the park, fighting to preserve the dignity of the nation. The park reminds visitors that the soldiers did not fight in vain and that the perpetrators of the Korean War (the Americans) received their due punishment. On the fringes of the park, there are small passages that lead visitors to a lower level, which is designed to look like war trenches, juxtaposing the serene surface of the park with the brutality of the war on the lower level. There, trophies of dismembered American tanks, incinerated airplanes, and other paraphernalia testify to who the real victors were in the Korean War. The Victorious Fatherland Liberation War Museum is an architectural monument that reconstructs and honors the collective memory of the DPRK.

The national narrative already begun at the arch continues inside the three-storied museum building. Upon entering the colossal doors to the museum, one encounters the image of theater curtains that are raised to welcome visitors to what will be a memorable experience. On either side of the curtains is yet another inscription of the dates of the beginning and ending of the war. Visitors are then greeted by a tall wax figure of the young Kim Il Sung, who closely resembles Kim Jong Un (or the other way around). The interior of the museum is just as magnificent as the exterior. The museum guide leads visitors through several chambers, which represent the different stages of the Korean War. (The museum also houses the history of the nation since the colonial period, featuring Kim Il Sung leading his anti-Japanese guerrilla army.) The artifacts from the old Korean War museum have been transferred to this new museum, so the content has not changed except for pockets of displays that have wax figurines and grand show-cases of artworks to make the tour a living experience of the war. That is, the national narrative is not solely based on historical artifacts but on the interactive component of the museum that makes the past relevant to the present. In this sense, the wax figure of the young Kim Il Sung in the middle of the museum was cosmetically modified to resemble the current leader in order to invoke the past as a living and continuous narrative leading to the present. The museum is the embodiment of national history, and so is the wax figure.

The Korean War, or the Victorious Fatherland Liberation War as North Korea calls it, was arguably the most traumatic moment in modern Korean history. The DPRK insists that the Americans started the war and proudly asserts its victory over the Americans at the end of the war. Despite the focus on triumph in national discourse, North Korean literature has accentuated the harrowing experience of the war, keeping the nation in, what Sonia Ryang refers to as "a constant state of emergency." Ryang argues that fiction written in the 1970s and 1980s differs from that of the 1950s in that the former portrays individuals' deep commitment to the leader, whereas the latter shows the effects of the war. She says, "This war and North Korea's self-proclaimed victory as well as its material devastation at the hands of the United States consequentially strengthened, rather than destroyed, North Koreans' fundamental commitment to the leadership of Kim Il Sung."[1] According to Ryang, the historical event itself is not the focus of fiction in the 1970s and 1980s but rather is used to signal a reiteration of the state of emergency and a redefined devotional connection with the leader. The publication of war stories in North Korea provides an ideological trajectory that creates, unites, and solidifies collective memory to persist in the present.

Whereas Sonia Ryang examines the shifts that have occurred within war stories, Kim Chae-yong argues that North Korean literature in the 1980s as a whole shifted away from writing about the war compared to literary works from previous decades.[2] Kim states that, unlike literary works in the past, fiction in the 1980s hardly mentions the war, and when it does it is not in the main trajectory of the narrative. The most common reference to the war is to characters' fathers (occasionally mothers) who have died fighting on the battlefield. Rather than the war itself, such literature highlights the effects of the war on present conditions. According to Kim Chae-yong, the reason for the change is that North Korean writers of the 1980s could not personally relate to the war, as most of them were born after it or were too young to remember the traumatic event.

Although this may sound like a reasonable explanation, it does not account for the continuing practice of writing about the war, the colonial period, and even historical events from hundreds of years ago. Lack of personal experience has never stopped North Korean writers (or other writers) from reconstructing the historical past in fiction. Kim Chae-yong's argument overlooks the lingering traumatic effects of the Korean War in fiction as a component of the national narrative revealing a constant state of emergency. That is, every literary work of fiction in North Korea (and in South Korea) is written on the premise of national division, on both the conscious and the unconscious understanding of divided national identity. North Korean literature is not its own self-identifiable body of writing but is defined by the presence of South Korea and vice versa. Political references to *Chosŏn* (Korea, according to North Korea) and *Hanguk* (Korea, according to South Korea) are an ideological semiotic elision that attempts to displace the other country from its own historical narrative, where *puk* (north) and *nam* (south) are always already implied in national discourse. That is why when North Korea publishes an anthology and calls it "Korean" literature, South Korean works are always effaced and unacknowledged, and the same ideological process occurs in South Korea. In this sense, the intentional elision of the other country is actually a testament to the other's existence and presence that deeply affects its own national history.

North Korean national narrative, then, is ontologically divided, fractured, and suspended from ever becoming totalized. The teleological trajectory of the North Korean state strives to eradicate all differences, oppositions, and deterrents that obstruct the grand narrative from actualizing as a sustainable, secure nation. Counternarratives, counterhistoriographies, or personal memories that may disrupt the teleological progression of the grand narrative of the nation-state are relegated to the fringes, if not eradicated. There is to be only one history, one narrative that bespeaks the homogeneity of the nation. Collective memory for North Koreans is supposed to sing the glorious history of Kim Il Sung's revolutionary past in unison, and literature supposedly functions as a generator of that collective memory.[3] The rationale behind this endeavor is to solidify and fortify the national boundary, to enable the nation-state to shape and stabilize its identity. However, no matter how hard the state tries to spin the Arduous March of the mid-1990s with a positive light and no matter how many more attempts there are at making a hydrogen bomb at the expense of improving the livelihood of the people, the message to North Koreans is less one of national security than of a constant state of emergency.

Literature provides a discursive gateway into the nation's past and its lasting effects on present conditions. In *Nationalism and Gender,* Chizuko Ueno reminds us that "the naïve view that history is simply an exercise in narrating the events of the past as they actually happened is no longer tenable."[4] When I say the nation's past, I am not referring simply to historiography, but, as Ban Wang says, "a culture's discursive and aesthetic institution that engage the past in the interest of the present."[5] To take it even further than Ban Wang, I would say that writing history in North Korea is an ideological reinforcement of the present political agenda. The past is the lost referential of the nation's history, and so the function of literature is not to recuperate the past as a nostalgic gesture but to create the past that fits the political ideology of the present.

A historic event is re-created, repeated, and validated (validated because it is repeated and repeated because it is validated) as an epistemological truth that formulates and constructs the grand narrative of the nation. In other words, an event is only an event because of the surrounding discourse that provides meaning to such an event. The Korean War, then, is considered an event in the DPRK not only because it was a devastating moment for Koreans but because it tested the limits and the impossibility of determining a singular national identity. For North Korea, the armistice was a failure to unify and project its political identity onto the South, and therefore it had to turn its focal point in revising the grand narrative of the DPRK to the time and place of Kim Il Sung's anti-Japanese guerrilla years. Nevertheless, the Korean War nominally persists in the present day and continues to define and shape the national identity of North and South Koreans. The injunctions of the state to remember it, to believe its voice and its history, and to honor it are for North Korean readers like the ghost of Hamlet's deceased father who beckons Hamlet to believe and remember the faceless specter as his father. Likewise, the faceless North Korean state must be remembered, and it must be given a name, a language, and a history. Thus, North Korean fiction and the institution of the Writers' Union have the ignoble task of (re)creating the past in the present through the narrative as a form of memorializing the nation.

In *History as an Art of Memory,* Patrick Hutton investigates the interplay between repetition and recollection as the foundation for any consideration of the problem of memory and history. For Hutton, repetition concerns the presence of the past, as we bear forward images of the past that continue to shape our present understanding in unreflective ways.[6] Recollection, then, concerns present efforts to evoke the past, as we consciously reconstruct images of the past in the selective way that suits the needs of our present situation.[7] Hutton argues that the balance between repetition and recollection makes historical thinking possible. In the case of North Korea, the repetitive inscriptions of the beginning and ending years of the Korean War at the museum are an ideological gesture to consolidate collective memory and reify the historiography of the nation.

This chapter examines the contention between national narrative and personal memory. Whereas most North Korean literary works fuse personal memory with collective memory, in Ri Hŭi-nam's *Yŏdŏl sigan* (Eight Hours, 1988), personal memories are *ateleological* and disjointed from the grand narrative of the nation, creating fault lines in the state's attempt to totalize the individual's experiences. Though memories often bespeak some glorious past event, the immanent logic in each memory contains its own negativity—a story that simultaneously constructs and deconstructs the semiotics of the imaginary state. *Eight Hours* shows the trauma of the Korean War and its effects on surviving family members. In the novel, it is the mother who recalls the past, and, in her memory, she expresses her agency by reconstructing the grand narrative of the nation for her son. Before we examine the mother's subversive act, it is important to understand the context of *Eight Hours* and the allegory of the state of emergency.

The State of Emergency

Eight Hours is about the lives of working-class youths at an ore mine: Ch'ŏl-u, Sun-gi, and Su-ryŏn. Sun-gi is handsome, articulate, and has leadership qualities, whereas Ch'ŏl-u is reclusive and always hesitant to speak his mind in fear of others mocking him. Su-ryŏn is sincere, strict, perhaps too square, but passionate, stubborn, serious, and truthful. Ch'ŏl-u confesses his love to Su-ryŏn, but she rejects his proposal because she does not feel that he is quite the revolutionary man that he ought to be.

One day, a large boulder caves into a new mining shaft. The workers come up with various ideas to break through the blockage, but the risk on the workers' lives is too great. The Party secretary, supervisor, and other cadres restrain the workers from entering the shaft, but Ch'ŏl-u decides to override the bureaucratic decision and throws himself into the shaft with tools and explosives. Sun-gi tries to show his leadership and courage by entering the shaft and resolving the situation, but he is overcome with fear. In contrast, the reclusive Ch'ŏl-u charges the shaft with unanticipated intrepidity. Once the debris is cleared away and there is enough space, Ch'ŏl-u takes a jackhammer and drills through the boulder. Eventually, after eight hours of strenuous labor, Ch'ŏl-u succeeds in completing his daring endeavor. Su-ryŏn realizes that Ch'ŏl-u is more of a revolutionary man than she had thought and that she is less of a revolutionary woman. In the end, Su-ryŏn accepts Ch'ŏl-u's love, and all the workers celebrate Ch'ŏl-u for his heroism.[8]

The *DPRK Almanac* considers *Eight Hours* a prime example of a heroic struggle to produce ore by the working class.[9] At the outset, the narrative follows a young miner of the working class who overrides bureaucratic officials and overcomes the obstacle before him. *Eight Hours* portrays the bureaucratic structure as a systemic problem in North Korean society that fails to meet the needs of the people. The multifarious chain of command that is not only vertical but also horizontal delays the Party's directives from reaching the people. Novels such as *Eight Hours,* then, raise these concerns to criticize middle management, local officials, cadres, and Party secretaries and stimulate change in the sociopolitical structure.

South Korean scholar Jae Jean Suh believes that criticism directed at cadres (or middle management) are a circumscriptive method of criticizing top officials of the DPRK or even the nation's leaders. Suh argues that the cult of personality of Kim Il Sung and Kim Jong Il has withstood public criticism because of the political strategy to deflect social problems away from the nation's leaders and shift the blame to middle management and lower-level units.[10] Suh also reads North Korean fiction as texts that demonstrate the correct method of criticizing oneself rather than directing blame toward the leaders. He compares North Korea with Christianity in that Christians would never blame God for mishaps in life but pray to him for deliverance.[11] Likewise, for Suh, North Koreans have looked to their leaders for assistance and deliverance, particularly when the nation struggled economically in the 1980s and 1990s.

Although it is true that works of North Korean fiction can function as a means of attacking the nation's leaders, Jae Jean Suh seems to presume that the entire country is governed by one person. Suh portrays the North Korean social and political structure as a simple top-down system that channels Kim Il Sung's or Kim Jong Il's every word directly to the people. Not only is this a reductive way of looking at North Korea, but it also shows a lack of understanding of the way in which politics operate in both communist and noncommunist societies. Political power is dispersed in vast networks of bureaucratic compartmentalization, with hierarchies within hierarchies in each department, horizontal transference of power, systemic failure of communication, and above all individuals seeking their self-interest, perversion of power, and manipulation of the political system.

Every individual in the DPRK is required to be a member of one of the many government-controlled organizations called *chipdan* or *chojik*. Much of an individual's time and energy are spent at these organizations; they thus constitute his or her lifestyle, known as *chojik saenghwal* (organizational life). The organizational life serves dual purposes of surveillance and indoctrination.[12] Each member is closely monitored by others affiliated with the organization and is trained to work and think within the tightly structured organization. The Central Committee of the Workers' Party, Chosŏn Sonyŏndan (DPRK Children's League), the League of Socialist Working Youth, Sa'roch'ŏng (another youth league that derived from the Socialist Working Youth), Chosŏn Chigŏpch'ong Tongmaeng (DPRK Work Union), the DPRK Agricultural Union, the DPRK Women's Union, the Writers' Union, the Democratic Youth League, Pulgŭn Ch'ŏngnyŏn Kunwidae (Red Youth Military League), and all the different departments and bureaus within the Party are but a few of the large and visible bureaucratic groups in North Korea that consume the lives of each citizen. Additionally, the Party and some of the leagues extend their subdepartments into concentric geographical spheres: *to* (province), *si* (city), *kun* (districts), and *ri* (communities).[13] The cadres, Party secretaries, and cell (*sep'o*) cadres are responsible for the different levels and tiers of each league in each concentric geographical sphere. In *Eight Hours*, for example, the workers answer to the on-site manager (*chibae'in*), who answers to the vice superintendent (*pubujang*), who then answers to the superintendent (*pujang*), who answers to the Party secretary (*tangbisŏ*) of that factory in that *kun* (district). In the story, the vice superintendent and his upper officers are not even present at the factory but are only contacted through a telephone call. Thus, rather than secretly undermining the authority of the nation's leaders, the bureaucratic problems raised in 1980s fiction reflect writers' responsibility to voice the nation's systemic problem concerning the political structure of compartmentalized hierarchies.

Eight Hours allegorizes the state of emergency of the DPRK at a time when domestic and international problems contributed to economic stagnation. Much as most scholars, Hazel Smith assesses North Korea's debilitating economy as the consequence of military fortification, increasing labor shortages, and dependence on foreign countries (particularly for cheap oil).[14] Similar to Jae Jean Suh, Smith says, "Kim blames slow progress in achieving improved living standards on inadequate political work by Party officials and United States sanctions which had first been imposed on the DPRK in the 1950s, despite the fact that, during the Kim Il Sungist era, North Korea was not prevented from trading with other countries, including western Europe."[15] The blame had to be directed away from the nation's leader and focused on management in order to maintain the personality cult. In addition to blaming his own people, Kim Il Sung also condemned communist states that did eventually adopt capitalist economic methods, principally Gorbachev's Soviet Union, as traitors.[16] I am not an economist, and I am not trying to trace North Korea's problems to a determinable past that would explain its present conditions. However, myriad elements in both domestic and international relations caused an insurmountable obstacle or "boulder" in North Korea's path to self-sufficiency, creating the state of emergency.

For me, *Eight Hours* is more than a story about young Party-minded workers who succeed in overcoming a problem at a local mine shaft in a remote, unknown part of North Korea. Reading the "boulder" as that which put the mine shaft in a state of emergency, *Eight Hours* portrays the agency of individuals in resolving the situation, which can perhaps be extended to a call on North Koreans to become agents of their own fates in the desperate moments of the country's imminent economic disaster. Rather than depending on the state to provide for the people's everyday needs, the story passes the responsibility over to individuals to finds means to overcome such conditions.

Although there is a stringent chain of command, workers don't always obey the orders emanating from the Party secretary. In *Eight Hours,* the orders from the top are clear: first, remove miners from the shaft to prevent any fatal accidents; second, research a new area to build a shaft; and, third, work on increasing the productivity of the new shaft. These orders sound logical and responsible. The problem in *Eight Hours* is not disregarding orders from the bureaucrats but in dealing with the bureaucrats. The Party secretary may appear to have offered rational advice on handling the dire situation, but *Eight Hours* is targeting indifferent bureaucrats who simply give orders from a distance without recognizing the needs of the people. Author Ri Hŭi-nam shows that workers are not mindless recipients of bureaucratic directives but are rather agents capable of their own decision making, as individuals in *Eight Hours* find their own means to rectify the situation in the shaft without the help from top officials.

Criticism of local cadres and bureaucratic tendencies has been a consistent theme in North Korean literature from the 1960s to the present day. Ri Chŏng-suk's *San saedŭl* (Mountain Birds, 1964), Ch'ŏn Se-bong's *Angae hŭrŭnŭn sae ŏndŏk* (Fog Creeps Over a New Hill, 1966), Ch'oe Hak-su's *Pyongyang sigan* (Pyongyang Time, 1976), Ri Hwa's *Sogŭmkkot* (Salt Deposits, 1984), Paek Nam-nyong's *60 Nyŏnhu* (After Sixty Years, 1985), Kim Sam-bok's *Hyangt'o* (Land, 1986), and Kim Mun-ch'ang's *Yŏlmang* (Desire, 1999) are but a few works that expose the discordant relationship between workers and bureaucrats. On the level of the readership, social criticism against local cadres may be more cathartic than criticism directed at the Great Leader and his son for the obvious reason that everyone confronts local cadres every day at the sites of one's organizational life, such as schools, factories, farms, and other military or social institutions, leagues, and unions.

The form and content of these antibureaucratic narratives resemble fiction that has influenced them from the Soviet Union and China. Among Stalinist novels, Gladkov's *Cement* (1925) and Lyashko's *The Blast Furnace* (1925) both articulate the protagonists' discontent and frustration with local officials and bureaucrats who deter the reconstruction and reopening of the factory/blast furnace with petty paperwork and indifference. In Maoist literature, Lo Tan's *Dawn in Wind and Rain* (1959) retraces the plot of Gladkov's *Cement,* where the protagonist is saddened by the dismal sight of the steel structures at the factory and decides to renovate them against the cadres' insistence otherwise.[17]

In both Ri Hŭi-nam's *Eight Hours* and Gladkov's *Cement,* the metaphor of the "boulder" of bureaucracy blocks and stands in the way of achieving the desired goal. Before the protagonist Gleb's arrival in *Cement,* the factory bureaucracy had been like the prerevolutionary bureaucracy—hoarding, corrupt, and interested in personal gain.[18] Gleb wants to understand "this impassable bulwark of the Economic Council and the factory administration," "this massive rock [that] stood in his path all the time."[19] Gladkov's *Cement* is a story that shows the transformation of the hero from spontaneity to consciousness. For Ch'ŏl-u in *Eight Hours,* the boulder also allegorizes the bureaucratic system that has prevented workers from carrying out their lives for themselves.

The difference in the two texts lies in the motivation for destroying the "boulder." For Gleb, the reconstruction and regeneration of the neglected factory drives him to question, contest, and retaliate against the bureaucratic officials.

Gleb, a former revolutionary soldier, won the military front, but he is now engaged in the reformation of the economic front.[20] Gleb, according to Eric Laursen, achieves political consciousness and guides the masses to a truly proletarian revolution.[21] Ch'ŏl-u, in contrast, decides to drill the boulder for a different reason, which is not predicated on leading the phantasmagorical masses to an even more illusory socialist revolution. Ch'ŏl-u is not a leader per se like Gleb. In fact, he is a taciturn worker who cannot make a clear decision on his own. Ch'ŏl-u's impetuous decision to pick up a jackhammer and begin drilling away on the boulder is out of the ordinary or out of character. For Ch'ŏl-u, the state of emergency at the mine defers the bureaucratic hierarchies and calls for immediate individual action. In many ways, *Eight Hours* has little to do with the hero's acquiring the correct Party-mindedness and more to do with individual agency in times of national crisis.

North Korean fiction is constantly memorializing the nation's history to abate the anxiety of the people. The nation's state of emergency is interconnected with national or collective memory in fiction that memorializes Kim Il Sung's glorious victory over the Japanese during the colonial period. The rationale behind such memory is that the leader has done it once, so he can do it again. Narratives that memorialize Kim Il Sung do not expect the leader to resolve all problems in the state, but rather the expectation is on individuals who are inspired by the leader. For example, in Pyŏn Hŭi-gŭn's "Ch'ŏlŭi ryŏksa" (History of Iron, 1967), the protagonist feels dejected for not knowing how to revive the old steel factory until he recalls Kim Il Sung's success over the Japanese colonialists. "History of Iron" is not only a tale about the history of a steel factory but also of Kim's anti-Japanese exploits that become the muse for individuals in the state of crisis. Rather than truly finding innovative and realistic solutions to North Korea's economic crises, collective memory of Kim Il Sung's victory over the enemies in public discourse is repeated and ritualized as a testament to the nation's teleological trajectory toward success.

Circularity of Collective Memory

For Kim Jong Il, collective memory of the Great Leader needs to be state orchestrated, a construction by the state to "educate" the masses accordingly so that the continuity of the past and present can be sustained. Memorizing or memorializing is a state-run exercise or ritual that collectivizes disparate individuals in North Korea by the reproduction of sentiments and rhetoric of what Benedict Anderson calls *nation-ness*. For instance, the primary literature for secondary school students in Pyongyang preparing for their university entrance exams is

Kim Il Sung's *Memoirs (Hoegorok).*[22] These students are required to memorize Kim Il Sung's infallible memory of his own peerless achievement of redeeming Koreans from the colonial grips of the Japanese and the imperialistic enslavement of the United States.

The Immortal History series and the Immortal Leadership series are sets of literary works of fiction that portray the revolutionary history of Kim Il Sung and Kim Jong Il. Along with these works, *Chosŏn'ŭi pyŏl* (Star of Chosŏn, 1980–1987) is a ten-part film series that recounts Kim Il Sung's revolutionary days; the lead actor supposedly underwent cosmetic surgery to resemble Kim. In addition to Kim's memoirs, novels, cinema, and visual artworks, Pyongyang itself is a commemorative ground on which memory and memorializing persists. Mosaic artworks depicting images of the leaders and specific historic moments, bronze statues of Kim Il Sung and Kim Jong Il, Juche Tower, the Arch of Triumph, Chollima statue, the Victorious Fatherland Liberation War Museum, and the Revolutionary Martyrs Cemetery are but a few examples of monuments and edifices that remind city dwellers and visitors of the illustrious history of the DPRK.

The Revolutionary Martyrs Cemetery is a particularly interesting site of the interplay between memory and national history. The cemetery has lines of bronze busts of revolutionary guerrilla and nonguerrilla martyrs who died for Kim Il Sung during the colonial period. Many of the martyrs died without leaving a photo behind to record their faces. However, the Great Leader Kim Il Sung, in his infinite wisdom, remembered each of the martyrs and fashioned their busts according to his memory of each of their faces. According to Suk-Young Kim, this episode of how Kim Il Sung personally shaped the faces of martyrs figures metonymically to illuminate a larger practice of making history in North Korea.[23] The Revolutionary Martyrs Cemetery is another example of the superimposition of signifiers on other signifiers to validate the circular reasoning of the national narrative. The cemetery precedes the actual martyrs (for their bodies do not exist) and becomes a memorial site on which North Koreans and visitors from around the world are supposed to commemorate the memory of Kim Il Sung's memory of the martyrs. Memory, in this case, was an individual effort by the nation's leader—one that must be recalled, regurgitated, recited, and repeated without altering any of the "facts."

Much of North Korean literature can be referred to as "memorial literature," where celebrating Kim Il Sung or the Party either takes center stage or streams across the narrative, determining an ethnonationalistic hegemony. Literary works become cultural artifacts that presuppose and circumscribe an imaginary social homogeneity. Memories or flashbacks in North Korean fiction typically conjoin and construct the linear grand narrative of the nation. A character's personal memory turns out to be a segment of the nation's history. For example, in Hwang Yŏng-ho's "P'adosori" (Sound of Waves, 1972), an elderly manager recounts his days of working for the Japanese colonialists at a factory and how the Japanese capitalists mistreated him. He then recalls the glorious day when Kim Il Sung drove out the capitalists and declared the workers as owners of the factory. After listening to the elderly manager's memory of Kim Il Sung, a young worker goes off to a technical institute, learns new technological skills, and returns to the factory to improve working conditions by installing a brand new ventilation system. "Sound of Waves" is just one of the many examples of literary works in North Korea that conflate one's personal memory with national history. In fact, one's personal memory is not personal at all. It was always a retelling of the establishment of the DPRK and how the past affects present conditions. Raising the consciousness of an individual requires collective effort, collective binding, and collective memory. Such collectivity disciplines, controls, and shapes individuals' behavior, consciousness, and beliefs. North Korean literature, therefore, can be read as a collective remembrance of the past that conditions performance in the present for the materialization of an ideologically determined future of the nation.

An entirely different literary genre that also relies heavily on individual memory is the defector tale. Many North Korean defectors have given accounts of their lives in the oppressive regime and their dramatic escapes. Nearly every account is action-packed, feeding into the sensationalist journalism of many Western media outlets. These defector narratives are published and marketed in a fashion that resembles the very propaganda in North Korea that these texts are attempting to devalue. Such stories have been published in recent years through the voices of Western journalists or writers. The defectors are not the storytellers but merely muses from whom these Western writers receive inspiration to construct a politically driven narrative. These defector tales do not only describe the North Korean totalitarian state, repressive culture, and starving people, but they implicitly edify the security position of the United States against the regime. By condemning the propaganda in North Korea, these tales erect a stronger propaganda of nationalism for American readers.

Defector tales "sell" because the stories are reconstructed to provoke readers and because they reconfirm and perpetuate preconceived ideas of the DPRK repeated in Western media. Titles such as *In Order to Live: A North Korean Girl's Journey to Freedom*, *Escape from Camp 14: One Man's Remarkable Odyssey from North Korea to Freedom in the West*, *Dear Leader: My Escape from North Korea*, and many more contain dramatic and political rhetoric that presupposes the narrative.[24] The defectors' personal memories become discursive "evidence" through which they are collectivized into a single narrative that constructs the "reality" of the DPRK for outside observers. As of 2015, an estimated 29,000 North Korean refugees in South Korea are subsumed in the sensationalist collective memory, as if all 29,000 individuals' personal narratives are reflected in the dominant defector narrative.[25] The appeal of the defector narrative is that the more tragic the story, the more it legitimizes the defector narrative, and thus the more the DPRK becomes a harrowing *reality* for Western observers. The defector narrative was predesigned in content and form for outside readers. It became the collective memory for all defectors whether they lived those experiences or not, instantiating the supremacy of the dynamic duo of democracy and capitalism not to themselves but to the wider readership.

In addition to defector tales, foreigners who have visited and written of their harrowing experiences in North Korea justify the imperialistic and orientalist perspective of the United States. Perhaps the most unethical and irresponsible account is Korean American Suki Kim's *Without You, There Is No Us*.[26] Kim entered the country under the guise of being a teacher at Pyongyang University of Science and Technology and lived among the students as an undercover journalist, intent on revealing the "truth" to her Western readers. Her book and TED Talks presentation are in harmony with Western propaganda against North Korea; she does not say anything particularly new but reiterates the same prescriptive portrayal of the country. The content of her story is problematic in and of itself, but the motive behind writing her narrative infringes on the trust she built with her colleagues and students at the university. Her book does not reveal the "truth" of North Korea, but it has won her fifteen minutes of fame at the expense of jeopardizing people with whom she interacted at the university.

The critical project of collectivizing individual memory is a form of nation building for South Korea and the United States. It is an ideologically dominated enterprise to bolster the existing governments. Whether it is the defector's memory or the protagonist's memory in North Korean fiction, both narratives reinforce the grand narrative of the state, which, in the case of the defectors, is the confirmation of South Korea as the safe haven for all suffering North Koreans and, in the case of North Korean fiction, is the reassurance of a strong Kimilsungist utopia. The fractured self in the past and present is made complete with memory, as the memory is no longer a personal recollection but a collective one. Personal memories in both defector tales and North Korean fiction are always cast into the political or are reconfigured to reinforce the politics of undermining the sovereignty of the other country. The individual must recognize that his or her memory must learn to speak in the same cadence as the political discourse.

The predominant use of memory in North Korean fiction is not only a literary strategy of filling in narrative gaps but also a political strategy. The North Korean literary critic Kim Ryŏ-suk explains the reason for using memory in literature: "In literary works, memories are designed to delineate the character's psyche. It is one of the most commonly used strategies. . . . Memories derive from ordinary circumstances and situations, elucidating the character's ideological background, and reveal the character's origin and direction."[27] Indeed, North Korean fiction and films are littered with flashbacks and memories revealing a character's political ideology and the glorious history of the DPRK. Such flashbacks and memories can be regarded as additions or supplements to the existing narrative to make it more ideologically sound. Or, to put it in another way, flashbacks and memories are not integral components to the narrative in its original design, but rather are added to complete and compensate for a lack in that which was already complete. The narrative does not need memory or flashbacks, but having them makes the content of the story more politically correct.

Memories, in North Korean fiction, are their own narratives, which are constructed for a purpose. Memory is often a crisis-narrative. When an individual faces a crisis or is in an insoluble difficulty, memory is an effective narrative strategy to enable him or her to overcome the situation, normally by the recognition of Kim Il Sung or the Party as the ultimate source of inspiration. Memory does not always have the intervention or deus ex machina of Kim Il Sung. Particularly in short stories written before 1967, there may be allusions to Kim Il Sung, but he is neither explicitly written into the plot nor the driving force behind a character's motivation. However, works after 1967 typically delineate Kim Il Sung as the muse that provides the contrived inspiration. Generally, Kim Il Sung does not hand out advice indiscriminately or lecture lengthily to the characters. Most of the time, all that is required is a pat on the shoulder, a smile followed by a few words of encouragement, a handshake, or some other negligible gesture that is not related to the problem. The appearance or the thought of Kim Il Sung itself is enough to motivate the character to pull himself or herself out of the crisis.

However, *Eight Hours* resists the prototypical framework of collective memories and experiences. In *Eight Hours,* Ch'ŏl-u's memories neither encourage him to overcome the boulder problem nor lift his downcast personality. Although past events explicate Ch'ŏl-u's introverted behavior, *Eight Hours* destabilizes narrative patterns by elucidating a personal memory that conditions the possibility of questioning the reconstructive processes of forging a mythical nation.

Disruptive Memories in Ri Hŭi-nam's *Eight Hours*

In *Eight Hours,* Ch'ŏl-u's personal memories and his mother's memories of Ch'ŏl-u's childhood reveal a disjunction in how the past affects present conditions. *Eight Hours* contradicts the conventional writing practice in North Korea by demonstrating that personal memory and the nation's narrative are mutually exclusive. The omniscient narrator in *Eight Hours* says, "Ch'ŏl-u began to bury himself quietly in past memories that had nothing to do with the current situation."[28] The current situation at the ore mine is a state of emergency where a boulder has blocked the mineshaft. This dire situation is momentarily suspended or disjointed by the interjection of Ch'ŏlu's personal memories, which are not even about the nation's history.

I consider moments like this to be *disruptive memories,* as they serve no purpose in perpetuating the discourse of memorializing the history of the nation. Ch'ŏl-u is not inspired by Party directives or by Kim Il Sung. Ch'ŏl-u's personal memories are ateleological, disrupting the novel's attempt at a prescriptive characterization of the hero. *Eight Hours* shows the shape of memories to be always disjointed in their very attempt at re-presenting the lost referential, always creating fault lines in the goal-oriented trajectory of the nation's history. Three significant disjointed memories appear among the recollections mentioned in the novel. I do not reorder them to make sense of the temporality of the memories, but, rather, I order them as they appear in the novel to show the disjunctions and disruptiveness of memory.

Memory 1:

> "Father." It was the one word that he really wished to call out with all his heart. Ch'ŏl-u eagerly wanted to feel his father's warm embrace and his loving hands, but there was no way for him to know this.
>
> "Mom, what did father look like?" asked Ch'ŏl-u, not being able to contain his yearnings anymore.
>
> The sight of her son yearning for his father was so touching that his mother had to hold back her tears as she proceeded to explain slowly his father's facial features.
>
> Then Ch'ŏl-u brought back a funny portrait of a man in his sketchbook, asking if this was the correct image of his father. Ch'ŏl-u was not at the age where he was able to understand the principles of drawing, and, no matter how carefully he tried to depict his father, there was no way for Ch'ŏl-u to portray him correctly.
>
> His mother couldn't help but laugh at the absurdity of the portrait.

"Ch'ŏl-u, let's have a look. If you make the eyes a bit bigger, it may resemble your father."

The fading embers in Ch'ŏl-u's eyes were relit.

The next day, Ch'ŏl-u returned to his mother with another portrait of the father.

The mother felt despair. That was because the revised portrait appeared even more absurd than the first one. However, she did not reveal her thoughts and proceeded to alter the nose and the ears. It was difficult for the mother to try to explain to her son her own vague image of his father. She wished there was a photograph of his father, but even that had been burned during the bombing.

The next day, Ch'ŏl-u returned with a picture of an ordinary People's Army soldier with a long rifle, advancing toward enemy lines.

"Mom, is this father?"

The picture did not look anything like his father. Although Ch'ŏl-u could not imagine his father's face, he was able to depict the father's final charge toward the enemy with great detail. The mother tightly embraced her son saying, "It is your father! This is exactly how your father fought!"[29]

Memory 2:

The prankster snatched away Ch'ŏl-u's picture and raised it above his head to show the rest of the classmates.

"Look at this. Ch'ŏl-u's drawing!"

The prankster did not know that this was Ch'ŏl-u's picture of his father. The prankster just wanted to show the class the peculiar picture.

Ch'ŏl-u did not like what the prankster was doing, so he grabbed his wrist and pulled him down.

They both grabbed the picture and began a tug of war. Suddenly, the picture that Ch'ŏl-u had focused on with much effort and later titled "My Father" ripped.[30]

Memory 3:

It was a late spring night with rain sprinkling outside the window.

As usual, Ch'ol-u was drawing another portrait of his father rushing toward enemy lines, and his mother was sitting on the floor staring at the troublesome drawings.

Suddenly, a voice outside the window was quietly calling for his mother.

"It's me," said the voice from the darkness.

"Ch'ŏl-u, open the door. He might get drenched in the rain," said mother with an anxious tone.

"No! Don't go out. You must not go out," Ch'ŏl-u shouted.

"Ch'ŏl-u," said mother with a feint voice. She stared into Ch'ŏl-u's eyes with resentment for a moment. She let out a deep sigh and leaned against the wall. With an enervated voice, she called to the man standing outside.

"This is not going to work."

"What?"

"It's not going to work out for us. Just . . . forget me please . . . forever."

Then, mother dragged her feet across the floor to the corner of the other room. She glared at the drawings on the floor and quietly sat still.[31]

Memory 1 and Memory 2 are recounted by Ch'ŏl-u's mother. Memory 3 is one of Ch'ŏl-u's many memories. These three memories invoke the image of the lost father who died on the battlefield during the Korean War. Whereas other North Korean novels use the Korean War as a historic context in which the DPRK is victorious over the Americans, thus reinforcing the national grand narrative, *Eight Hours* presents a completely different perspective of the effects of the war on the family. It is then crucial that Memory 1 and Memory 2 are recalled by the mother, as it is the woman who contests the nation's patriarchal/patriotic narrative. The mother tells *herstory,* which subverts the memorializing project of the nation's history.

The three memories are not in chronological order. Ch'ŏl-u's memories "take turns going to and fro [*pŏnkal'a ogo'ga*] from his childhood to his early adolescent years."[32] Chronologically, Memory 2 would come after Memory 3. However, for author Ri Hŭi-nam, memories are never (re)told in the chronological, linear structure common to North Korean narratives. *Eight Hours* demonstrates that the very nature of memories disrupts structure and resists teleology; memories are suspended from time and space and escape the appropriation of the narrative.

It is difficult to contextualize each of the three memories in the narrative as these memories emerge sporadically and without warning—they are atemporal and aspatial. When Ch'ŏl-u takes a break from drilling the boulder or when he is in a reclusive location away from others, he falls into deep thoughts that trigger memories of his childhood without any connection to the present situation. In some ways, memories in *Eight Hours* resemble Proust's involuntary memories in *Remembrance of Things Past,* in that the stream of consciousness is "in search of lost time." Ch'ŏl-u's memories and the mother's memories of Ch'ŏl-u's childhood are a journey into a past that does not conjoin with the historical continuity of the nation. *Eight Hours* is one of the few literary works in North Korea that truly question the function of memory and offer a critique of the practice of memorializing the strength, solidarity, and pride of the nation.

Economy of the Patriarchal State

There are many father metaphors in North Korean fiction, most notably Kim Il Sung, who represents both mother and father (*ŏbŏi*) of the nation. North Koreans call their own nation *choguk* 祖國, or fatherland, in which the Chinese character *cho* means ancestors or forefathers. An elderly man at a factory or collective farm is often referred to as *abai*, which is a familial way of respecting a patriarch. In *Eight Hours*, Ch'ŏl-u has always been surrounded, metaphorically speaking, by "fathers." Although he has never once used the term to address his biological father, he has come to realize the oddity of not having a father at home. Ch'ŏl-u learns from the state that the normal, ordinary family consists of a father and a mother and thus feels that his family is out of the ordinary.

At the same time, there are many absent fathers in North Korean fiction. It is not unusual for widows to rear their children to become successful citizens of the DPRK without the physical presence of a biological father. For example, in Kim Mun-ch'an's *Miners*, the daughter of the protagonist miner wants to marry a man from her father's mine, but the man, whom she loves, does not have a father. This becomes a contentious struggle between true love and the cultural stigma against children with a single parent. A more drastic example would be orphaned children in the DPRK. One of North Korea's most renowned authors, Ch'oe Hak-su, wrote a short story called "Haepit palkŭn nara" ("Radiant Country," 1972) that celebrates an orphaned boy who becomes a respected architect in Pyongyang with the personal help of Kim Il Sung. The architect's loss of his biological father is replaced with Kim Il Sung as the surrogate father. The short story proposes that one is never deprived of a family as long as one understands that true kinship is found in working for the construction of the Kimilsungist state. The reading here is obvious: Kim Il Sung is the father to all families and is a better father than biological ones because he provides eternal guidance, a hearth, and optimism to the citizens of the DPRK. The children of the DPRK are supposed to cry out to Kim Il Sung as the paternal and maternal leader, who can resolve their existential and familial crises.

However, in *Eight Hours*, Ch'ŏl-u calls for his biological father and not Kim Il Sung. "Ch'ŏl-u eagerly wanted to feel his father's warm embrace and his loving hands, but there was no way for him to know this."[33] The mother recalls, "During Ch'ŏl-u's infant days suckling on his mother's breasts, he did not know the pain of not having a father."[34] Ch'ŏl-u has never seen his father, who died on the battlefield defending the nation from the Americans, so there was no need for Ch'ŏl-u to speak of his father. The term "father" was not part of young Ch'ŏl-u's lexicon. However, after many years, Ch'ŏl-u inquires about his father or, rather, he longs for his father. Ch'ŏl-u desperately desires to utter the word "father" as in other normal families. This simple word has not been spoken at home with his mother; it has been the missing link to Ch'ol-u's identity. Ch'ŏl-u may wish to call out that word with all his heart, but what he truly desires is the exchange, the reciprocation, the economy of that language. He wants to hear his father say "son." Ch'ŏl-u's young heart is torn not because he cannot utter the word "father" but because there will be no response.

Ch'ŏl-u's mother feels estranged by her son's request. She fears that Ch'ŏl-u will soon leave her for the state, as is required of the child. According to DPRK political discourse, a mother is supposed to prepare her child to enter the public domain. Although the mother has known this, she did not think that it would happen so soon. As a woman, she has no part in male-dominated state affairs. She also has no name that identifies her individuality in *Eight Hours* (like many mothers in North Korean literature). She is simply "the mother." The mother is always removed or *replaced* in the patriarchal discourse, or, as Luce Irigaray says, "The order of this empire decrees that when a proper name (*nom*) is given to a child, it substitutes for the most irreducible mark of birth, the navel (*nombril*)."[35]

There is a deliberate play in the way Irigaray uses *nom* and *nombril*, where the center/navel (*nombril*) of one's life is replaced or subverted by the recentering of the proper name (*nom*) of the father. In other words, the child is rightfully the mother's, but the child takes on the father's name and therefore severs his or her natural ties with the mother. For Irigaray, the child ineluctably implicates herself or himself in the patriarchal society at the moment of the severance and of acquiring the father's name. There thus exists an elemental identity tag or scar for every individual: the umbilical cord or the womb of the mother. Every human being was once housed in a mother's womb before entering into the patriarchal world. The economy between mother and child is the most elemental and life-giving exchange. The economy between mother and child is exchanged through the gift of nourishment from the mother's breast to the child's dependence on the mother. But, for Irigaray, this economy becomes severed from the moment the umbilical cord is cut. The exchange is no longer between mother and child but between father and child. Irigaray says, "Her womb, sometimes her breast, gape open as a result of the gestation, the birthing, the life which have issued from them, without reciprocity."[36] The mother's identity as woman is replaced by the economy of the patriarch.

Irigaray observes a transition from the natural to the political, from essentialism to discursive construction. Her claims have also become fodder for heated debate within feminist circles. Irigaray posits herself as a poststructuralist and a Lacanian insofar as she believes that the subject is a discursive construct, making identity unstable; but, in order to rescue women from what she sees as the repressive effects of phallocentrism, she proposes an alternative feminine discourse modeled on the female genitals, essentializing the body of the woman.[37] I am not attempting to engage in this philosophical debate, but what I find admirable in reading her works is her manifesto-like energy in attempting to undermine the logocentric, phallocentric history marginalizing women in the West, which I see also at play in the linear historicity of the North Korean grand narrative.

The DPRK has been excluding, repressing, and marginalizing women from state politics and public affairs despite its ostensible legislation allowing women to participate in politics; women's sole responsibility is to support the nation through their role as mothers. Although gender equality, new marriage and divorce laws, and women's participation in the workforce, the military, and other social institutions suggest a paradigmatic shift of a progressive North Korean nation-state, women's essential function in society is to reproduce the next generation of Kimilsungist revolutionaries. Much as Friedrich Engels argues in *The Origin of the Family, Private Property, and the State,* North Korean women are socialized and incorporated into the state only insofar as they continue to generate and educate children to work for the state.

The patriarchal economy (*oikonomia,* or literally "household management") begins for Ch'ŏl-u at home (*oikos*), the very domain to which his mother has been subjected, confined, and relegated. The mother unwittingly (perhaps indicated through the tears she holds back) gives Ch'ŏl-u a medium through which he can translate his yearning for his father: the description of his father's face. The economy is initiated through the practice of drawing the father's face. Even after numerous attempts and with guidance from his mother, Ch'ŏl-u can only draw an ordinary soldier of the People's Army advancing toward enemy lines. The mother is discouraged by the fact that the picture resembles nothing of Ch'ŏl-u's father but is just another representative of the nation-state. To the mother, Ch'ŏl-u has not connected the signifier (the common soldier) to the signified (the actual father). Rather, he has developed an understanding of the language of the patriarchal nation-state through the image of a soldier. The image of the soldier substantiates the *state economy* for Ch'ŏl-u: born of the womb, raised at home, enters the political world, commits to be loyal to the state, and sacrifices one's life for the state. And the cycle begins all over again: "As usual [*yŏjŏnhi*], Ch'ol-u was drawing another portrait of his father rushing toward enemy lines, and his mother was sitting on the floor, staring at the troublesome drawings."[38]

The drawings of the father/soldier are troubling to the mother, who remains outside of the patriarchal economy. Her input on the correct way of depicting the father comprised the last words she spoke before being excluded from the male exercise. For the mother, Ch'ŏl-u's drawings are troubling, problematic, complex, and multilayered because of the exclusionary practice that marginalizes the very body from which patriarchy first derived. "The scar of the navel is forgotten" are the words of Irigaray and possibly what the mother is thinking as Ch'ŏl-u focuses on his drawings rather than engaging with his mother.[39] In fact, Ch'ŏl-u and his mother hardly converse with each other throughout the novel, which further demonstrates the exclusionary practice of the patriarchal economy. As usual, Ch'ŏl-u continues the practice of drawing his father in the presence of his mother. As usual, Ch'ŏl-u perpetuates an economy that excludes his mother. As usual, Ch'ŏl-u has forgotten about the economy that he once shared with his mother. And, as usual, the mother finds these drawings to be troublesome.

The logic of economy is predicated on the "as usual," or the circulation, and without it, the notion of economy comes to an abrupt halt. The exchange must be repeated or repeatable. The portraits of the father are troubling to the mother because she knows that there is no economy in the practice of drawing. Ch'ŏl-u will never hear his father's voice or feel his embrace through the drawings. The mother already knows that these drawings have no economic value, no value of exchange or reciprocity. Economy may begin at home, but it cannot and must not remain at home if it is to continue. In order for the patriarchal economy, the language of the father, to persist, one must enter the public space. Ch'ŏl-u takes his picture to school.

Individual versus State/School

Eight Hours exemplifies the contention between the domestic space and the state's negligence toward the nuclear family. Unlike other North Korean fiction, *Eight Hours* does not demonstrate that the state takes responsibility for dissipating the family with compensation or other forms of social welfare. The Great Leader does not visit the widow and her child and bestow promises to uplift their downtrodden spirits as he had in 1960s and 1970s narratives. This is because, as Sonia Ryang aptly puts it, "Kim Il Sung was transformed from a theroetico-ideological leader into an ethico-spiritual one."[40] Kim Il Sung no longer appears in flesh and blood; he has become an abstract "father" to the nation, where his spirit dwells within the people's memory. The state does not honor Ch'ŏl-u's father, who died on the battlefield during the Korean War. There is no recognition for his valor. The state, the Party, and the Great Leader have conveniently forgotten about Ch'ŏl-u and his mother.

The state's neglect of Ch'ŏl-u is further demonstrated in the incident at school in which a prankster finds Ch'ŏl-u's picture and shows it to the class. This may have been the optimal moment for Ch'ŏl-u to share his patriotism with his classmates—to tell his peers how his father valiantly fought to protect the nation and how they must all prepare themselves to do the same. However, the picture is too personal and private for Ch'ŏl-u. He does not feel that the representation of his father should be shared beyond the confines of his own imagination. More important, Ch'ŏl-u believes that his father did not die for the nation but only for him. As the struggle begins between Ch'ŏl-u and the prankster, an unpredictable incident happens at school: "They both grabbed the picture and began a tug of war. Suddenly, the picture that Ch'ŏl-u had focused on with much effort and later titled 'My Father' ripped."[41]

The ripped picture of the soldier is an iconoclastic detail in the mother's memory as it refers to the desecration of the representation of the state. The irony is that the picture is torn asunder at the very institution that raises and educates children to become patriotic soldiers of the state. The prankster dismembers the only remnant of Ch'ŏl-u's image of his father. The image of the People's Army soldier is ripped, literally severing or disjointing the memory from the circularity of the nation's narrative. Ch'ŏl-u retaliates by punching the prankster across the chin. The school reprimands Ch'ŏl-u's impetuous and violent behavior rather than disciplining the prankster for provoking this incident. Ch'ŏl-u feels he is a victim of the school's injustice, which is juxtaposed with the adult Ch'ŏl-u's growing agitation with the bureaucratic system at the mine. He feels marginalized by both his school and the collective state.

The linear trajectory of the glorious nation's history faced irreparable economic damage in the mid-1990s. Stephan Haggard and Marcus Noland say that by the late 1980s the North Korean economy was in a secular decline, accelerated by the breakup of the Soviet Union and the dissolution of the Eastern Bloc.[42] They continue, "With the state unable to provide food through the socialist public distribution system, small scale units—household, work units, local party organs, government offices, and even military units—initiated entrepreneurial coping behavior, much of it technically illegal, to secure food.[43] What Haggard and Noland portray in their research is a form of social unrest stemming from economic problems that were generated by poorly designed political reforms. Based on their interviews with defectors, Haggard and Noland find that a sizable number of defectors preferred to participate in market activities to defray the economic situation and the state's lack of material assistance.[44] The Juche idea of self-reliance was to be a literal one—independence from the state's control.

I am not suggesting that *Eight Hours* directly reflects the socioeconomic problems in North Korea in the late 1980s. However, the trends exposed in novels written in the 1980s illustrated shortcomings and inadequacies of the socialized state vis-à-vis the general public that would culminate in the economic problems of the 1990s. Literary works of fiction in the 1960s and 1970s also deliberated on individuals' dissatisfaction with problematic social conditions. These appraisals were not directed at the state, however, but at ideologically misguided individuals. The state and the collective body of upright citizens would resolve the imminent danger and restore peace in the community. In contrast, individuals in 1980s novels express their angst toward the state or representatives of the state rather than toward illusory villains residing in the community.

The tacit resistance of these individuals shows a change in the literary depiction of protagonists and the narrative trajectory. The nation's revolutionary history continues to decorate the pages of these novels as a reminder to the individuals in the narrative (and readers) of the unfailing commitment of the state to the people. The political discourse continues to underscore that happiness and prosperity lie within the collective. But *Eight Hours* also shows that Ch'ŏl-u will have to develop another form of economy that grants value to his identity. That is, his identity as a loyal citizen, a defender of the revolution, and a devoted follower of the Party is not predicated on the memory or history of his father (or Kim Il Sung) but rather on his personal commitment to himself. The incident at school changes Ch'ŏl-u's behavior and attitude in his social world as a young adult. He becomes a reticent, faceless worker at the mine, reluctant to participate in collective activities.

Demise of the Ritual

In the introduction to *North Korea: Beyond Charismatic Politics*, Heonik Kwon and Byung-Ho Chung state, "The puzzle of the North Korean political system is therefore not the practice of an extraordinary cult of personality but the extraordinary continuity of this practice."[45] The two authors refer to this phenomenon as "legacy politics" (*yuhun chŏngch'i*) and "politics of longing" (*kŭriumui chŏngch'i*). I discussed legacy politics to some extent in Chapter 1 in terms of the legend of revolutionary history. In this section, I will discuss the notion of longing for the absent father in *Eight Hours* as a ritual or practice of discursive (re)production that precedes the real or the actual father.

Jean Baudrillard's understanding of the postmodern as simulacra is apropos to my discussion. Baudrillard says, "The territory no longer precedes the map, nor does it survive it. It is nevertheless the map that precedes the territory—*precession of simulacra*—that engenders the territory."[46] Following Baudrillard's thinking, it is questionable whether the territory has ever existed. The constant drawing and redrawing of maps (political, physical, topographic, climate, economic, road, traffic, thematic, satellite, Google) reveals a certain fetish (loss of the referential) to the practice of depicting a territory. The map is never the real territory, and it is perhaps not even concerned about the real. The territory no longer functions as *the* referential, but, rather, each successive map functions as its own reference—the practice of referencing references.

In North Korea, the death of Kim Il Sung in 1994 propelled the nation toward heightened forms of simulacra, changing the landscape into the everlasting performance and practice of the Great National Bereavement. "Kim Il Sung is dead" did not eliminate or decrease the level of moral principle by which North Koreans ought to have lived, as Nietzsche's proclamation of "God is dead" was supposed to. Instead, the direct opposite occurred: North Korea's moral and filial responsibility increased, and the Party demanded greater loyalty than ever before. Kwon and Chung attribute the politics of longing to the fortification of the military-first policy (*sŏn'gun*):

> Military-first politics may have provided a solution to a crisis in the family state and to challenges to the partisan state. In advancing this solution, however, the new partisan state politics, called military-first politics, and the new family state politics, which created the landscape of longing, resulted in one of the most tragic events of death in modern history, in which the commemoration of one man's death contributed to the loss of innumerable human lives, the lives of people who were all categorically the deceased man's children.[47]

The nation bereaving the death of the Great Leader must not be taken for granted. The death was a serious ordeal not only for political officials attempting to maintain control over the people but also for the people themselves, who were supposed to offer their utmost devotion. The problem with North Korea's politics of longing rests in the Party's demand to the people to yearn for the discourse of *a* Kim Il Sung rather than the referential Kim Il Sung, the so-called real. Kim Il Sung the man may have physically died in 1994, but the discourse of *a* Kim Il Sung persisted throughout the man's life and still persists. The politics of collective longing demand that North Koreans long for the act of longing, a collective practice that displays unity, solidarity, and the strength of the nation. It is a perpetual self-referential cycle with no end in sight, at least for the present. The slogan "The Great Leader Is Forever with Us" is not only to be read as a religious/spiritual symbol of Kim Il Sung's omnipresence but points to the haunting reality that the rhetoric (such as this slogan) of the Great Leader is forever programmed in the lexicon of North Korea's daily discourse.

Memory 3 in *Eight Hours* may help elucidate the theoretical concept of the simulacra: "As usual [*yŏjŏnhi*], Ch'ol-u was drawing another portrait of his father rushing toward enemy lines, and his mother was sitting on the floor staring at the troublesome drawings."[48] Earlier I discussed the notion that the repeatability of a practice is necessary in order for it to have economic value. Following that thought, in this section, I will focus on the notion of repetition as the subject of the practice of ritualization. The quotation above begins with "as usual" (*yŏjŏnhi*). As usual, Ch'ŏl-u is resimulating what his father has done on the battlefield according to the previous drawing. Ch'ŏl-u is tapping into his memory of his previous drawing in order to construct a new memory in a new drawing. It is not important what his father actually did, but it is important that the discourse of a People's Army soldier rushing toward enemy lines remains static in Ch'ŏl-u's imaginative reproduction. Ch'ŏl-u reperforms, reproduces, and re-creates the discourse of longing through his repetitious drawing. The politics of longing for Ch'ŏl-u is in the very ritual of reperforming, reproducing, and re-creating the image of his father, which is a chain of references without a referent, a chain of signifiers without a signified. The drawings are caught in the cyclical pattern of simulating the previous portrait: a simulation of a simulation.

Moments before the recollection in Memory 3, the mother recalls that some war veterans had visited Ch'ŏl u's house and given them a photograph of Ch'ŏl-u's father out on the battlefield. Ch'ŏl-u then realizes that the portrait he has been drawing and the photograph of his father are not identical at all.[49] He has spent his early childhood rendering a portrait of his father as if it were his actual father. But this begs the question: Why the numerous reproductions of the same portrait? Would one not have sufficed? Or perhaps he could have produced an image of his father as some other figure than a soldier? Even more baffling is that Ch'ŏl-u is not terribly disappointed or confused by the photograph that actually portrays the image of his father. He acknowledges the photograph of his actual father yet still considers his childhood of reproducing the portrait as precious and invaluable. To put it in another way, the man who comes out of the cave in Plato's allegory is blinded by the truth and realizes that he has been fooled by mere representations on the walls of the cave, but Ch'ŏl-u dismisses the truth and returns to the cave to delight in the reflections. Ch'ŏl-u revels in the reproduction of simulacra; his identity is constructed around the ritualization of drawing and redrawing the image of his father.

Ch'ŏl-u cherishes the practice of reproducing the portrait more than the creation of a realistic or truthful depiction of his father. The practice becomes a ritual, and it is in the ritual that Ch'ŏl-u finds comfort, in perfecting each portrait and making the next one better than the previous one. Each rendition of the same portrait will always be slightly different from the previous one. This is not such a peculiar practice or ritual if we consider the thousands of paintings of Christ hanging along on walls of the Uffizi Gallery or the Louvre Museum, or the thousands of selfies people take with their phones and post on social media. The preoccupation with such practices resides in the practice itself. The photograph of Ch'ŏl-u's father does not discourage Ch'ŏl-u from drawing portraits of *a* father rushing toward enemy lines. His actual father may have physically died on the battlefield, but *a* father lives on through the reproduction of the same discursive portrait rushing toward enemy lines and with the title "My Father."

The title "My Father" confirms Ch'ŏl-u's belief that the portraits represent his father, but the title and the drawing have no association with each other—the title is not a signifier of a signified (the drawing) but rather a signifier among signifiers (the multiple drawings). The title "My Father" indicates neither the drawing (for it is not his father) nor his actual father (for he has never seen his father). At the same time, the title "My Father" indicates both the title of the drawing (whether or not the drawing is his father) and the episteme of a father. Ch'ŏl-u draws numerous portraits of a father, a soldier along with the title "My Father," to validate the meaningless signifiers with some truth value. For Ch'ŏl-u, the meaning of each portrait is derived from a title; without it there is no reason for him to draw all those pictures.

> "Ch'ŏl-u, let's have a look. If you make the eyes a bit bigger, it may resemble your father."
>
> The fading embers in Ch'ŏl-u's eyes were relit.
>
> The next day, Ch'ŏl-u returned to his mother with another portrait of the father.
>
> The mother felt despair. That was because the revised portrait appeared even more absurd than the first one. However, she did not reveal her thoughts and proceeded to alter the nose and the ears.[50]

The mother takes great pains in revising and altering the facial features of the absurd portrait. She, too, has but a faint memory of her husband. The narrator informs readers that she had been married for only a year before the husband was sent to the battlefield, and now she is given the challenge of re-creating her husband truthfully for her son. The fact is even the mother cannot reproduce her husband, whom she has actually seen. It is an impossibility for Ch'ŏl-u to imagine the father whom he has never seen. He can only rely on what he does know and has seen in public. The myriad portraits, statues, mosaics, and propaganda slogans that decorate the entire nation are more than enough to serve as a referential for Ch'ŏl-u:

> The next day, Ch'ŏl-u returned with a picture of an ordinary People's Army soldier with a long rifle, advancing toward enemy lines.
>
> "Mom, is this father?"
>
> The picture did not look anything like his father. Although Ch'ŏl-u could not imagine his father's face, he was able to depict the father's final charge toward the enemy with great detail. The mother tightly embraced her son saying, "It is your father! This is exactly how your father fought!"[51]

Surely, it is not "exactly" how his father fought but a simulation. The mother resorts to lying to her son because of the impossibility of reproducing a truthful image of the father. However, her lying ("It is your father!") becomes the discursive truth for Ch'ŏl-u. The soldier is not his father but becomes so through the utterance of "It is your father." The biological father is replaced by a universal or ordinary soldier, an image of the patriarchal state. The soldier becomes the source of the repeatable practice, the simulacrum. The discourse of the soldier rushing toward enemy lines must be told and retold, drawn and redrawn rather than excavating and researching the truth of his father's face.

This is the same method used to give "faces" and "names" to the martyrs at the Revolutionary Martyrs Cemetery. As Ch'ŏl-u's portrait of his father replaces the actual father, so do the bronze busts of the martyrs. Long before the photograph of Ch'ŏl-u's father is delivered, Ch'ŏl-u has been engaged in the practice of reproducing the portrait of his father. The absent father is made present through this simulacrum, and, in some ways, the delivery of the photograph is not necessary. As the "truth" or "truthfulness" of the father's features is unnecessary for Ch'ŏl-u, so are the actual features of the martyrs. The truth is not found in the actual but in the current reproduction and reconstruction of the bronze busts. The presence of the busts provides the truth of revolutionary history, which is aligned with the national narrative.

When will such labor-intensive efforts at reproducing revolutionary history in literature ever cease? Volumes and volumes of literary criticism recite, recall, and regurgitate the "words" of the revolutionary history in such a circular way that there does not appear to be an alternative method of breaking away from the circularity of the collective writing. The Writers' Union institutionalized the practice of writing and rewriting the same faceless and meaningless revolutionary history in a way that resembles Ch'ŏl-u's ritualized practice of drawing his father. The only viable method of disrupting the circular practice is revealed by the prankster at school, who rips Ch'ŏl-u's portrait, signaling the end and the demise of Ch'ŏl-u's ritual. The politics of longing ends for Ch'ŏl-u at the very moment when his image in torn; that is, it is not the photograph that Ch'ŏl-u later receives that concludes the politics of longing but rather the ripping of the iconic image of his father that ends his ritual. The compounding realization is that his mother has served as the accomplice to this demise.

Laughter of the Mother

Article 62 of the DPRK Constitution of 1972 states: "The state liberates women from their burdensome housework and supports all their efforts to enter into society." According to the Constitution, the state liberates women by providing them with social programs and institutions such as maternity leave (paid and extended if necessary), public nurseries, preschools and kindergartens, and other benefits.[52] In essence, mothers do not have to be concerned about their children's welfare. The purpose of the programs and institutions is for mothers to enter into the workforce and relinquish their children to the state. A child belongs to the state and must be raised, trained, and educated by the state. The patriarchal state also provides maternal care for the children of the DPRK. As discussed in Chapter 1, the role of the mother in North Korea is to provide a channel through which her children can become loyal citizens of the state. This is the legislation of state-sponsored feminism, which Chizuko Ueno calls "contemporary feminism bound within the confines of both nationality and culture."[53]

The Constitution restructures the paradigm of the domestic and public spaces in such a way that the state functions as *the* domestic space in which the child's growth—physical, ideological, and intellectual—is secured. The mother's body functions solely to bring the child into the world; responsibility for the child's general welfare is not to infringe upon her efforts for the state. The DPRK Constitution considers the assumption that mothers rear their own children to be an outdated and unfair division of labor. Therefore, mothers are just as important in the workforce as fathers, justifying the breakdown and blurring of gender roles and of domestic and public spaces.

As I have discussed in previous chapters, gender equality in socialist states did not eliminate gender differences but homogenized genders into a single masculine gender. In the name of gender equality, the nation masculinized gender—the *nom* has replaced the *nombril*. The masculine discourse of the nation-state that has conveniently eliminated gender difference and equality establishes the hegemony of males. To paraphrase Irigaray, there has always been only one sex: the male body or the male fantasy. It is from this one sex that the imagination of the female emerges. Irigaray tries to reformulate the idea of (at least) two sexes in Western philosophy and to rethink the imaginary other as the feminine. In Irigaray's essentialist viewpoint, there already exists an essential feminine body wholly independent and autonomous from the masculine body. However, I believe that, instead of starting with the essentialist notion of existing sexed bodies, it is more productive to read Irigaray's works as voiced through the masculine political order. In defense of Irigaray, Claire Colebrook succinctly writes, "one can write through the voice of the male fantasy, exposing it as a fantasy, and thereby create the feminine speaking position as that which relates to, plays with, and differs from its masculine other."[54] Likewise, the mother in *Eight Hours* is forced to articulate the patriarchal language to her son as she proceeds to describe his father, reintegrating herself as a mother and as a wife back into the patriarchal society.

In a socialized state like North Korea, the domestic or private space creates the possibility of disharmony and rupture with the Party's policies. The domestic space must be made public and controlled by the collective, whether it is by the neighborhood watch (*inmin panjang*), the local Party secretary and cadres, or neighbors and friends. However, it is impossible to control every aspect of human lives, domestic or public. Ri Hŭi-nam's *Eight Hours* reveals this impossibility through the mother's complex thoughts—her unideological and all too personal resentment toward the state expressed in the solitude of her domestic space. The mother clearly demarcates the line between public and private spaces, fortifying her domestic space as her sovereign domain. It is at home and away from public scrutiny that she does the unthinkable: she "laughs at the absurdity of the picture."

> The mother couldn't help but laugh at the absurdity of the portrait.
>
> "Ch'ŏl-u, let's have a look. If you make the eyes a bit bigger, it may resemble your father."[55]

The laughter of Ch'ŏl-u's mother must be taken seriously. Her laughter poses a serious threat to the state as it conditions the possibility of dismembering the state's harmony from within—from within the family that stands as the immanent Other to the state, from within femininity that resists the patriarchal discourse, and from within motherhood that disavows the state for reducing and excluding the woman from the state economy. The mother's laughter is supposed to be directed at Ch'ŏl-u's inability to draw. The young child's earnest attempt at representing a soldier is supposed to be adorable. But a second look at this passage also suggests the mother's laughter is directed at the notion of a soldier, a metonym for the state. It is not how Ch'ŏl-u drew the soldier but the fact that he can only think of drawing his father as a soldier. To Ch'ŏl-u, the image of his father or fatherhood conflates with his military service to the nation and consequently his death. The signified of the term "father" is the state, and it is at the state that Ch'ŏl-u's mother laughs. The mother's laughter defaces the simulacrum, the very practice of providing meaning to the term "father." Ch'ŏl-u's consignment of an arbitrary soldier to "father" is arbitrary and artificial. The mother's laughter subverts the patriarchal economy as it exposes the fallacy of the state's circular reasoning.

The state has ruined Ch'ŏl-u's family by engaging in the Korean War. The state has dragged men onto the battlefield, promising a prosperous life for everyone in the DPRK. However, the promises of the state and the armistice have not improved Ch'ŏl-u's and his mother's despondent lives. The war has created an abysmal lack in their lives by taking away the father, a lack that cannot be replaced by the glorious discourse of the national narrative and the surrogate role of political leaders.

Yet the state continues to demand that mothers produce the next generation of revolutionary soldiers—to commit their lives to the state with death as the only honorable reward. Both the men who fight on the battlefield and the mothers who produce soldiers are faceless, expendable machines. Ch'ŏl-u's image of the soldier victimizes the mother as a widow and someone who will have to "let go" of her son to the state; her only son cannot draw anything but the image of a state-produced soldier. Indeed, the son has been indoctrinated with the correct political ideology, which, as viewed by the mother, is an intrusive act of dislocating her natural connection with her child—the severance of the umbilical cord.

The mother in *Eight Hours* decidedly refuses to comply with the state's expectations. It is her turn to dismember the iconic image of the state by personalizing the father's facial features. She demonstrates to her son the importance of detailing his father's image. The memory of Ch'ŏl-u's father is not to be a faceless soldier, universal and indistinguishable from the rest. He is not to represent the "faceless" guerrillas depicted in *Sea of Blood* but rather a human father who died heartbroken, never having seen his own son because of the state's orders to fight in the war.

The mother consoles Ch'ŏl-u's yearning heart by imagining and superimposing her definition of what his father ought to look like. She reconstructs his facial features to convince Ch'ŏl-u that the image resembles his father. But Ch'ŏl-u simply returns the next day with a picture of yet another ordinary soldier. The narrator's tone and word choice are noteworthy, as they reflect the way the mother feels and reacts to the drawing:

> The next day, Ch'ŏl-u did the most ridiculous [*ŏngttunghan*] thing. He returned with a picture of yet another [*wen*] soldier of the People's Army, holding a long rifle and advancing toward enemy lines.
>
> "Mom, is this father?"[56]

The narrator, who is supposed to present the mother's thoughts, does not say that Ch'ŏl-u came to her the next day but says that he "did the most ridiculous thing." The mother's tone fortifies her disavowal of the portrait. I have taken the liberty of using the phrase "yet another" for Korean *wen* in the subsequent sentence. Normally, *wen* would be closer to "some" or "for some reason." The question *"wen il'iya?"* would mean "What's the problem?" or "What brings you here?" It generally suggests an element of surprise or unexpectedness. The sentence might be translated as "Of all things, Ch'ŏl-u drew a soldier of the People's Army." However, the mother's tone also conveys a sense of annoyance, as in "Ch'ŏl-u brings to his mother *yet another* picture of a soldier of the People's Army."

The mother's dismissal and annoyance at her son's creation must be read and accentuated; it must be taken as seriously as her laughter. It is words like *wen*, which can easily be overlooked, that set the tone for the way the mother feels and (re)acts toward the patriarchal state within the confines of her domestic space. Such words provide a way in which the mother can voice her angst through the male-dominated economic system that has long excluded the woman's voice.

The mother's annoyance at the pictures is further emphasized in Memory 3. Ch'ŏl-u, "as usual," is reproducing the image of his father while the mother looks on at her son. Suddenly, a man comes to visit the mother. Ch'ŏl-u prevents his mother from engaging with this unknown man. The mother resolutely bids the man farewell and returns to the living room where Ch'ŏl-u proceeds to redraw the image of his father:

> "It's not going to work out for us. Just . . . forget me please . . . forever."
>
> Then mother dragged her feet across the floor to the corner of the other room. She glared at the drawings on the floor and quietly sat still.

> Mother neither blinked nor seemed to breathe. With her two arms wrapped around her knees and her lips slightly awry, she stared forlornly at the drawings with a sense of resolution.[57]

The sentence that follows assures the reader that the mother has gained the strength and perseverance to overcome her sexual temptation. The mother was only married a year when the state sent her husband to the battlefield. The husband promised to return triumphantly like every confident soldier. He wrote one letter to his wife, saying he longs to see his child whom he has never seen. He never writes again, and he does not return to his family. But, much like the faithful Penelope, who waits for Odysseus to return, the mother tries to remain faithful although she knows her husband is dead. *Eight Hours* tries to celebrate the mother for her faithfulness and devotion to her son and her dead husband, as a noble-minded individual who can overcome her carnal desires.

But has she been faithful to her dead husband? She admits that she can hardly recall his face: "Her vague memory of her husband made it extremely difficult to draw his face."[58] Then who is the man in Ch'ŏl-u's portrait? The tall man who comes to visit the mother that one evening was discharged from the army after the armistice. She has been secretly meeting the tall man ever since then. He is the man who has captured the mother's heart, and his visit that evening was to propose to the mother. Is it imaginable that the portrait Ch'ŏl-u has been drawing was never his actual father but that it was the face of the mother's secret lover? When soldiers come to the house to deliver a photograph of Ch'ŏl-u's actual father, Ch'ŏl-u is not dismayed at how the photograph and the portraits he has been drawing are not similar. But would Ch'ŏl-u have been shocked to discover that the portrait actually matched the face of the tall man who came to visit the mother that one evening? After all, Ch'ŏl-u never actually sees the tall man's face but only hears his voice. These are, of course, unsettling speculations that the Party would quickly dismiss. The narrative keeps the tall man in the dark, away from sight, and away from identification. To even consider that a devoted wife commits infidelity by superimposing her lover's face onto the face of the state would be iconoclastic. At the same time, a close reading of the three memories cited above creates anything but a simplistic and prescriptive picture of Ch'ŏl-u's mother.

The three memories not only explicate the politics of longing for Ch'ŏl-u, but they also revisit gender politics in the DPRK through the (re)action of the mother. The mother offers a "new face" to nationalism by attempting to reconfigure the ordinary image of the state into something personal and individualistic. Mothers in the DPRK bear faceless, collective soldiers for the state—the economy of the patriarchal discourse—as exemplified by the mother in *Sea of Blood*, who could not distinguish the faces of her own children marching with other soldiers toward the socialist revolution. Biological fathers are to be forgotten, replacing personal memory with collective memory and the determination of defending the fatherland. But this is not the case with Ch'ŏl-u's mother in *Eight Hours*. She speaks through the voice of the masculine state; she appropriates and inscribes difference onto the nation's emblem of singularity.

Ch'ŏl-u's mother resides at home throughout the novel until the very end, when she comes out to verify the safety of her son. The relationship between Ch'ŏl-u and his mother is asymmetrical to the relationship between Kim Il Sung and his mother, Kang Pan-sŏk. Ch'ŏl-u's mother has no business in public, nor does she want any. She may have been forced to be domesticated when her husband went to the battlefield and when she gave birth to Ch'ŏl-u, but she takes comfort in knowing that she has been able to demonstrate her angst toward the state by reprogramming her son at home.

In Ri Hŭi-nam's later fiction such as "Pulgŭn nunbora" (Red Blizzard, 1999), one detects an ostensibly different type of work, which may suggest that some narratives were commissioned by the Writers' Union for specific purposes.[59] The narrative in "Red Blizzard" focuses on Kim Jong Il's visit to his father's tomb on New Year's Eve. With a series of flashbacks and the overt symbolism of the color red to suggest communism and the continuity of the body politic, Ri Hŭi-nam seems to project a rather different image of the nation-state from that in *Eight Hours*.

In "On Reading North Korean Short Stories on the Cusp of the New Millennium," Stephen Epstein closely reads the "fissures within the conscious myth-making" in the short story "Red Blizzard." Instead of presenting another optimistic conclusion to the narrative, Ri Hŭi-nam displaces the narrative away from such formulaic logic and saturates it with an upsurge of sentimental emotions that allow for the text to provide hope during North Korea's most economically trying period. Epstein considers Ri's gesture to be "authorial sleight of hand in order to sweep the reader away in its hopeful conclusion."[60]

Ri Hŭi-nam's writing patterns can be further identified by comparing *Eight Hours* with Epstein's analysis of "Red Blizzard." In both *Eight Hours* and "Red Blizzard," Ri does not withhold sentimentalism, especially in moments where characters recall past events. But the most striking moments in both texts involve what Epstein succinctly calls "the disjunction between timeless nature and human beings who age." In "Red Blizzard," Kim Jong Il looks at this deceased father and wonders why white frost settles on the hair of the Great Leader if nature is verdant, which to Epstein is the "reassurance of the Great Leader's immortality [that] needs to be given in the face of evidence of his obvious mortality."[61] Likewise, in the last sentence of *Eight Hours,* the narrator contemplates on the disjunction between static nature and changing humans: "O, the poplar tree receives abundant nutrients from this great land. It remains verdant and stands upright despite the house that has changed with time. O, how many countless memories and lives have been etched on the bark of this poplar tree."[62]

In both narratives, Ri glorifies the timelessness of nature while indicating the transient characteristics of humans. For Ri, humans change, will change, and, in some cases, must change. In that last sentence in *Eight Hours,* Ri shows that the history of the DPRK does not consist of one story but of "countless memories and lives." The beauty of the nation, for Ri, is precisely the different, plural stories that have been etched on the land. In the passage above, the house (or the nation) that shelters people changes its features, its characteristics, its structures as do the people who dwell in it.

The way I read North Korean fiction, writing conditions the possibility for such change to occur within the country. Novels such as *Eight Hours* provide insight into the changing literary stage on which writers in North Korea perform. Ch'ŏl-u's *as usual* performance of drawing his father may appear to be an identical procedure, but each portrait engenders difference—difference in the repetition, particularly as his mother enables the difference to exist. Much the same can be said about literature produced in North Korea, where it appears as though one narrative imitates the previous pieces of literary work. However, I have tried to show that the practice of writing resists singularity, that no single work of literature can ever be identical to the previous one, and that literature can never speak the Party's political discourse in unison. The literary culture is dynamic and constantly changing, adapting to a changing political system and resisting banal prescriptions set by the Party. Creativity is performed every time the writer approaches his or her work. Ri Hŭi-nam's *Eight Hours* may appear to be *yet another* literary work that criticizes the local bureaucrats at an ore mine, a love story involving Party-minded individuals, and a heroic tale of the working class augmenting the pride of the nation. Yet, within this seemingly repetitious narrative, there exists difference that creates the space for imagination and new literary frontiers.

Conclusion

Literature and Ideological Change

"Under the candle light, I slowly take off my clothes. . . . I pull down my underwear. . . . I lower my hands to reveal my breasts. . . . I undress him and lie on the bed. . . . I slowly move down on his body. . . . I quietly whisper, 'Close your eyes . . . close them. Close your eyes and enjoy the pleasure I'm about to give you.' His entire body trembles as though a volcano were about to burst, and then he groans loudly."[1] This excerpt is taken from Hong Sŏk-jung's *Hwang Chin-i,* first published in Pyongyang by Munhak Ch'ulp'ansa in 2002 and then reprinted in Seoul by Taehun Publishing Company in 2004. South Korean literary critics read the novel and awarded it the Manhae Literary Award, one the most prestigious awards in South Korea. Hong Sŏk-jung then took a trip down to Seoul from Pyongyang to accept the honor. To this day, Hong Sŏk-jung is the only North Korean novelist to receive a literary award from South Korea since national division.

That is correct: the sexually explicit excerpt is taken from a North Korean novel, written by a North Korean novelist, reprinted in South Korea, given a prestigious literary award, and the North Korean writer went into enemy territory to accept the award. Spirits were high between the two Koreas in the early 2000s when liberal president Kim Dae Jung (1998–2003) took office, followed by Roh Moo Hyun (2003–2008). Kim's Sunshine Policy called for a new approach in dealing with the DPRK rather than the previous Cold War policies of political isolation and containment. The new policy was an attempt at coexistence, cooperation, assistance, and exchange on the Korean peninsula. The timing of the publication of Hong Sŏk-jung's novel and the reprinting of the novel in South Korea could not have been better.

Part of the reason for *Hwang Chin-i*'s wide reception and success in South Korea was the ostensible absence of Party ideology and glorification of Kim Il Sung because the novel takes place in sixteenth-century Chosŏn Korea. The novel has been read as an allegorical criticism of draconian government of the DPRK. The heroine is a courtesan who encounters starving masses, corrupt officials, and a governor "completely immersed in booze and women."[2] Donald Macintyre, a journalist for *Time* magazine, quotes Brian Myers on his response after reading *Hwang Chin-i:* "I read some parts with my jaw hanging open. The parallels to the current political situation are really just too obvious even for the most obtuse, literal-minded reader to miss."[3] According to Myers, the novel's portrayal of starving masses and criticism of power-hungry government officials can be read as allusions to the current North Korea.

One issue concerning the publication of *Hwang Chin-i* is the audience for whom the explicit sexuality in the novel was intended. Whereas Brian Myers speculates that the novel was intended for South Korean readers and was, therefore, permitted by the Party to narrate graphic moments,[4] South Korean scholar Kim Chae-yong disagrees. After a visit to North Korea and a meeting with the author, Hong Sŏk-jung, Kim Chae-yong is not convinced that the novel was written solely for foreigners but believes it was originally intended to be read by North Koreans.[5] The problem with Kim Chae-yong's argument is that we will never really know the readership and reception of this novel in North Korea.

The novel was a bestseller in South Korea, popular enough for the film industry to adapt it into a film and cast highly celebrated South Korean actors.[6] To this day, no other literary work in North Korea has described sexual acts with as much ribald and pornographic detail as *Hwang Chin-i*. Unfortunately, since the release of *Hwang Chin-i* in 2004, no other North Korean literary work has received literary recognition in the South. Although Hong's novel may have altered some South Koreans' perception of North Korean literature, one novel was not going to be enough to change the prevalent assumptions about the literary culture or the everyday life in the DPRK.[7]

What sort of "change" are we expecting from North Korea? Analysts have been making predictions about the country's future for decades, assuming that circumstances would lead the country to a Soviet Union–like *perestroika*. The death of Kim Il Sung in 1994 and the subsequent Arduous March were considered clear indications that the dictatorial regime would face its demise, but they proved to be incorrect. Cultural exchanges with South Korea under the Sunshine Policy of the early 2000s were intent on inciting internal, domestic change, but these exchanges were short-lived. The death of Kim Jong Il in 2011 and the rise of a young, Westernized leader in Kim Jong Un opened up further possibilities for change, but these expectations were not met. Pessimistic analysts have given up on predicting North Korea's future and have resolved that the country will remain unchanged unless external coercion takes place.[8]

The problem with these predictions is that they are based on a future trajectory for North Korea predetermined by other countries, namely, the United States and South Korea. These two countries want North Korea to head in the direction that follows their standards, particularly with regard to issues of denuclearization and military reduction. Analysts have given North Korea two options for major reform: follow either the East German model or the Chinese model, total collapse or economic boom. These options not only limit possibilities for other kinds of changes, but they also insist that they are the only way to take North Korea off the internationally most wanted list and pull itself out of economic turmoil.

Hazel Smith, in her book *North Korea: Markets and Military Rule,* states: "What is needed from outsiders is an end to ideological grandstanding and the development of a coherent global strategy to obtain a comprehensive settlement that includes denuclearization of North Korea as a top priority."[9] Smith's position is that other countries should stop intervening and punishing North Korea with sanctions like a miscreant student at school and instead find means to cooperate with the country as in the case of Northern Ireland. Scholars such as Hazel Smith and Stephan Haggard view North Koreans themselves as the agents of change and believe that "reform from below" takes precedence over top-down political reform.[10]

North Koreans have already found markets and other entrepreneurial outlets, which have proven to be their source of survival and sustainable income. Smith says, "The self-directed activity of millions of small traders, led by women, who swapped, bartered, sold and generally engaged in the whole spectrum of non-state-directed, private economic transactions, transformed society from below and from inside; social change was not led from abroad."[11] Smith perceives private marketization in the DPRK as evidence of a changing society on its own terms rather than from outside pressure or coercive measures.

In *North Korea: Beyond Charismatic Politics,* Heonik Kwon and Byung-ho Chung aptly state, "If North Korea appears to be an unchanging, unchangeable actor on the international stage, it is probably because the changes the country is now undergoing are unfamiliar and therefore not easily perceptible to the outside world rather than because North Korea is truly defying change."[12] Indeed, the DPRK has undergone and continues to undergo significant social, political, economic, cultural, and literary change that at times escapes the international community. Such changes may appear to be minimal or nonexistent compared to the changes that have occurred in South Korea within the last two decades. South Korea's economic explosion cannot be the standard of change by which North Korea is measured.

Although Kwon and Chung say the changes in North Korea were not perceptible to the outside world, I would argue that there has been resistance to acknowledging that such changes have any significance for modernized and industrialized nations. That is, these changes have been overlooked because they do very little to promote the self-interest of the rest of the world. The only real interest that countries such as the United States and South Korea have in North Korea regards the continuing military investment to stave off an imminent threat to national security. Young South Korean men not only must serve in the military for eighteen months but are educated and trained to think that North Korea is South Korea's absolute enemy. The negative discourse propagated in the South Korean military is the consistent ideological component that has perpetuated mistrust, suspicion, and resistance toward the DPRK since the Korean War. Military indoctrination is not something we should overlook. Hundreds of thousands of South Korean soldiers undergo this training each year, which over time constitutes a large portion of the population of South Korea.

Explicit military education against North Korea is problematic, but so is the refusal to acknowledge North Korean literature as part of "Korean literature" in the academic curriculum. Only recently has Korean Federation of Proletarian Art or leftist literature been taught at South Korean universities, and they are still not a formal component of the wider education curriculum. Middle school and high school curricula implicitly insist that "pure literature" (*sunsu munhak*) is characterized by freedom of humanistic expression and that socialist literature is ideologically indoctrinated and thus worthless to study. Government institutions such as the Literature Translation Institute of Korea refuse to consider any literary work from North Korea as "Korean literature" unless it was written during the colonial period.[13] South Korea's political rhetoric of humanizing North Koreans is quickly undermined and when it comes to considering North Korean literature or any North Korean cultural products as part of the "Korean" identity. To put it more bluntly, South Korea seems only willing to reunify when all cultural products in North Korea have eradicated all remnants of socialism, Kimilsungism, or any other ideology seen as posing a threat to South Korea. The exclusion of North Korean literature is perhaps the most ideologically detrimental indoctrination that has hegemonized South Koreans since the Korean War. Thus, I believe that, before any "real" change is likely to occur in the DPRK that will satisfy the outside world, countries such as South Korea and the United States need to eliminate their fundamental and ideological resistance toward the DPRK in order for an exchange of cultures and ideas to be mutual and effective. At this point, the attitude of South Korea toward its counterpart is one of imperialism and condescendence, as reflected by the ideological statue of a South Korean soldier holding a North Korean soldier in front of the War Memorial of Korea in Seoul.

South Korean scholars have written about North Korean literature, but North Korean literature itself has not been included in the canon of what South Koreans calls "Korean Literature." The elision of North Korean literature in South Korea's educational curriculum provides another way of understanding this book's argument regarding how the North Korean state has subsumed women and sexual difference in the regime of the Same. The way women have been discursively constructed in fiction to be absorbed into the male-dominated state structure follows the same political strategy used by the South Korean government against the DPRK. That is, the portrayal of North Korea is only to be normalized in South Korea's state discourse as the absolute enemy, the absolute difference, and the absolute other in order to rationalize and define South Korea's identity.

South Korean scholars interested in North Korean literature have published essays in anthologies such as the four-volume *Pukhan munhak'ŭi ihae* (Understanding North Korean Literature, 1999, 2002, 2004, 2007), which maps the history of the literary culture and offers a diverse range of North Korean literary theory, fiction, and poetry. Although this series is rich in information and breadth, its underlying argument is that North Korean literature is dictated by political policies and that the only way to truly understand the literature is in the context of top-down infrastructure. Placing each novel in a specific historical and political context is certainly an important way of understanding the literary culture, but literature is not a transcription of Party directives. Rather, Kim Jong Il's *Juche munhak'ron* (Theory of Juche Literature, 1992) and other state policies serve merely as guiding principles for writers to use in creating their fiction.

Rewriting Revolution presents some of the notable changes that have occurred in the narrative form and content of North Korean fiction. I have chosen fiction from the 1980s as the topic for this book, but changes are not limited to this particular decade. Fiction in the 1960s showed the collective energy of the workers and their visions for a socialist utopia; works in the 1970s reconfigured the narrative strategy to focus on the growing number of intellectuals, who were delineated as the hope for the nation; narratives in the 1990s often expressed mourning and loss for the Great Leader and a tone of solidarity and national strength; and the literary works of the 2000s reflected the changing social environment by alluding to some of the global events that affected the country. An interesting addition to works of the 2000s is the honest and critical treatment of topics that writers in the past would not have dared to mention, such as doubts about socialist ideology after the fall of the Soviet Union, problems with the Arduous March, and individuals returning from prison. I will not go so far as to say that these topics are the current narrative trend; however, they are notable in showing the changes in North Korea's literary history.

In the 1980s, the most evident shift in the approach to writing fiction was in the portrayal of women, the family, and memory. I began with an analysis of the discursive construction of motherhood as the model for the characterization of women in fiction. Chapter 2 examines the instability of the state's political discourse of developing a revolutionary subject when the individual's desires are affected by sexual encounters. Although North Korean fiction is supposed to ensure the absolute enclosure of the subjectivity of individuals, it actually reveals tensions and fissures that disrupt the certainty of one's political devotion. This idea is further explored in Chapter 3, where the family faces unprecedented problems when individuals are too committed to their revolutionary duties. As women question the veracity of their husbands' political rhetoric, dissatisfaction toward the state becomes a subversive force that resists the teleological trajectory of a "happy ending." Chapter 4 makes explicit what was implicit in Chapters 2 and 3 as women voice their resistance to the state in the form of divorce. Marital problems are seen not only as strife between husband and wife but also as a metonym for the contention between women and the male-dominated state. Divorce, then, is a forceful metaphor that suspends individuals from ever becoming state-desired subjects. Finally, in Chapter 5, I discuss the reconstruction of personal memory that opposes the grand narrative of the nation's history. In most North Korean fiction, when individuals recall the past, it is to reinforce the solidarity of collective memory and the legitimacy of the nation's revolutionary history. However, personal memories provide an alternative space and time to the state-prescribed narrative form of collective memory. Such personal memories remind us that North Korean society is not a homogeneous body of individuals with identical experiences of the past but rather heterogeneous and at times conflicting. Diversity of thought and lifestyle is not something to be disciplined, controlled, and transformed but must be celebrated and encouraged in order to show the strengths of a promising country.

This book has not attempted to present a history of North Korean literature that accounts for where it began, where it is, and where it is heading. Although I have provided political context, I have avoided reducing North Korean fiction to mere recitations of Party directives and other authoritarian principles, such as Kim Jong Il's "seed theory" as the thread that connects narrative seams. To me, this thread was never the voice of literary authority, and the narrative seams were always somehow coming undone by the instability of meaning. North Korean fiction demonstrates that becoming a revolutionary hero or heroine is neither formulaic nor a given fact but always challenged, disrupted, and questioned by individual desires, decisions, doubts, and imagination. Through the agency of women in 1980s North Korean fiction, I have tried to show that the family is neither a pure locus of the private sphere nor a docile object of absolute state control. Instead, this book has focused on a nuanced understanding of the relationship between the state and individuals that conditions the possibility for a more insightful reading of North Korea's literary culture.

Notes

Introduction

1. *Literature from the "Axis of Evil": Writing from Iran, Iraq, North Korea, and Other Enemy Nations,* Words Without Borders Anthology (New York: The New Press, 2006).

2. *Samizdat* (from Russian *sam,* "self," and *izdatelstvo,* "publishing"); literature secretly written, copied, and circulated in the former Soviet Union and usually critical of practices of the Soviet government. *Encyclopedia Britannica,* http://www.britannica.com/EBchecked/topic/520512/samizdat, accessed February 1, 2012.

3. Editor's Note, in *Literature from the "Axis of Evil,"* xix.

4. Adam Johnson, "Adam Johnson Recalls North Korea: A Country With No Books," *The Daily Beast,* December 21, 2011, http://www.thedailybeast.com/articles/2011/12/21/adam-johnson-recalls-north-korea-a-country-with-no-books.html, accessed January 9, 2012.

5. Robert A. Scalapino and Chong-Sik Lee, *Communism in Korea: The Society* (University of California Press, 1973), 890.

6. Marshall R. Pihl, "Engineers of the Human Soul: North Korean Literature Today," *Korean Studies* 1 (1977): 74.

7. Tatiana Gabroussenko, *Soldiers on the Cultural Front: Developments in the Early History of North Korean Literature and Literary Policy* (University of Hawai'i Press, 2010), 1.

8. Kim Chong-hoe, "Ek'o'ui munhak" (Echo Literature), in *Pukhanmunhak'ui pyŏnhwa'wa chŏnmang* (Changes in and Outlook for North Korean Literature through Its Works), ed. Kim Chong-hoe, Ko In-hwan, and Yi Sŏng-ch'ŏn (Seoul: Tosŏch'ulp'an Yŏngnak, 2007), 148.

9. Kim Jong Il, *Art of the Cinema,* 59, cited from Alzo David-West, "The Literary Ideas of Kim Il Sung and Kim Jong Il: An Introduction to North Korean Meta-Authorial Perspectives," *Cultural Logic* 2009:18.

10. David-West, "Literary Ideas of Kim Il Sung and Kim Jong Il: An Introduction to North Korean Meta-Authorial Perspectives," 19.

11. Andrei Lankov, "Kim Takes Control: The 'Great Purge' in North Korea, 1956–1960," *Korean Studies* 26, no. 1 (2002): 91.

12. Sonia Ryang, *Reading North Korea: An Ethnological Inquiry* (Cambridge: Harvard University Asia Center, 2012), 16–17.

13. According to the South Korean scholar Sŏnu Sang-yŏl, Kim had made several speeches regarding his revolutionary activities to writers, most notably on May 7, 1946. Sŏnu Sang-yŏl, *Kwangbok hu pukhanhyŏndae munhak yŏn'gu* (Study of North Korean Modern Literature after Liberation) (Seoul: Tosŏ ch'ulp'ansa, 2002), 29.

14. Ryang, *Reading North Korea,* 25.

15. Refer to Barbara Johnson's introduction to Jacques Derrida's *Dissemination* (Chicago: University of Chicago Press, 1981), xiv.

16. Claire Colebrook, *Gender* (New York: Palgrave Macmillan, 2004), 55.

17. Jacques Derrida, "Structure, Sign, and Play in the Discourses of the Human Sciences," in *Writing and Difference*, trans. Alan Bass (Chicago: University of Chicago Press, 1978), 279.

18. David Bates, "Crisis between the Wars: Derrida and the Origins of Undecidability," *Representations* 90, no. 1 (2005): 4.

19. Kim Chae-yong, *Pukhan munhakui yŏksajŏk ihae* (Historical Understanding of North Korean Literature) (Seoul: Munhakgwa chisŏngsa, 1994), 264–271.

20. Essays by these optimistic scholars are collected in *Pukhan munhak-ui chihyŏngdo* (Topography of North Korean Literature) (Seoul: Ehwa yŏjadaehakkyo ch'ulp'anbu, 2008).

21. Hwang Sŏk-yŏng, *Sarami salgo issŏtne* (There Have Been People Living There) (Seoul: Siwa sahoesa, 1993), 199.

22. Pak Se-gil, *Tasi ssŭnŭn hangukhyŏndae'sa* (Rewriting Modern Korean History) (Seoul: Tol Pegae, 1997), 236–237.

23. Namhee Lee, *The Making of Minjung: Democracy and the Politics of Representation in South Korea* (Ithaca: Cornell University Press, 2007), 139.

24. Ibid., 127.

25. Sunyoung Park, *The Proletarian Wave: Literature and the Leftist Culture in Colonial Korea, 1910–1945* (Cambridge: Harvard East Asian Monographs, 2015), 4.

26. O Ch'ang-un, "Pukhan munhak'i pyŏnhago itda" (North Korean Literature Is Changing), in *Pukhan munhak-ui chihyŏngdo,* ed. Ehwayŏjadaehakkyo t'ongilhakyŏn'guwŏn (Seoul: Ehwa yŏjadaehakkyo ch'ulp'anbu, 2008), 13.

27. Ibid., 13.

28. "Rural fiction" is Gabroussenko's coinage rather than North Korea's categorization. It derives from Gabroussenko's observations of narratives that occur at collective farms. See Gabroussenko's "North Korean 'Rural Fiction' from the Late 1990s to the Mid 2000s: Permanence and Change," *Korean Studies* 33 (2009): 69–100.

29. Stephen Epstein, "On Reading North Korean Short Stories on the Cusp of the New Millennium," *Acta Koreana* 5, no. 1 (January 2002): 33–50.

30. Ryang, *Reading North Korea.*

31. For a more in-depth description of academic trends in studying North Korea, refer to Charles Armstrong's article "Trends in the Study of North Korea," *Journal of Asian Studies* 70 (2011): 357–371.

32. Kim Il Sung, "The Duty of Mothers in the Education of Children," speech delivered to the National Meeting of Mothers, November 16, 1961, in *On the Work of the Women's Union* (Pyongyang: Foreign Languages Publishing House, 1971), 9.

Chapter 1: Desexualizing Motherhood

1. Jean Baudrillard, *Simulacra and Simulation* (Ann Arbor: University of Michigan Press, 1994), 43.

2. Ibid., 2.

3. Yung-Hee Kim, "Creating New Paradigms of Womanhood in Modern Korean Literature: Na Nye-sŏk's 'Kyŏnhŭi,'" *Korean Studies* 26, no. 1 (2002): 2.

4. Sunyoung Park, *Proletarian Wave,* 201.

5. Suzy Kim, *Everyday Life in the North Korean Revolution, 1945–1950* (Ithaca: Cornell University Press, 2013), 181.

6. Sunyoung Park, *Proletarian Wave*, 198.

7. Ha Sang-il, "Sahoejuŭijŏk yŏsŏngjuŭiwa yŏsŏngsŏsaŭi silhyŏn" (Socialist Feminism and Women Narratives), in *Kang Kyŏng-ae: Sidaewa munhak* (Kang Kyŏng-ae: Era and Literature), ed. Kim In-hwan and Kim Chae-yong (Seoul: Random House Korea, 2006), 65.

8. Jayawardena, *Feminism and Nationalism*, cited from Sunyoung Park, *Proletarian Wave*, 199.

9. Kyŏng-ae Kang, "Chosŏnyŏsŏngŭi palbŭl kil" (The Path of the Korean Women), *Chosŏn ilbo*, November 28–29, 1930.

10. Ruth Barraclough, "Red Love and Betrayal in the Making of North Korea: Comrade Hŏ Chŏng-suk," *History Workshop Journal* 77 (2014): 89.

11. Ibid., 89.

12. Ibid., 99.

13. Suzy Kim, *Everyday Life*, 116–119.

14. Refer to Suzy Kim's chapter on "Revolutionary Motherhood" in ibid.

15. Sonia Ryang, "Gender in Oblivion: Women in the Democratic People's Republic of Korea (North Korea)," *Journal of Asian and African Studies* 35 (July 2000): 337.

16. Kim Il Sung, "Duty of Mothers," 28.

17. Hye-sŏk Na, "Toksin yŏsŏngŭi chŏngjoron," *Samch'ŏlli*, October 1935. In this essay, Na defined marriage as a transaction for sexual gratification and promoted licensed prostitution for both single men and single women to satisfy their sexual needs before their marriage.

18. Kim Il Sung, "Duty of Mothers," 28.

19. Ibid., 30.

20. Ibid., 16.

21. This is a deliberate play on Simone de Beauvoir's famous claim that "one is not born but becomes a woman."

22. Suk-Young Kim, *Illusive Utopia: Theater, Film, and Everyday Performance in North Korea* (Ann Arbor: University of Michigan Press, 2010), 243.

23. Judith Butler, *Bodies That Matter: On the Discursive Limits of "Sex"* (New York: Routledge, 1993), 1.

24. Ri Chŏng-suk, "Hyŏngmyŏngjŏk chu'ingonggwa kajŏng hyŏngmyŏnghwa'ui myosa" (The Revolutionary Protagonist and the Portrayal of the Family Revolution), *Chosŏn munhak* 1967, no. 9: 80.

25. This novella was first published serially in *Chosŏn munhak* in 1961. The narrative focuses on women textile factory workers during the Chollima era who live in factory dormitories and share their lives together. Despite the women workers' different backgrounds, they all conjoin to become one large family of the factory and of the nation.

26. I do not refer to a specific time when this phrase was first used in the DPRK. I refer here to the discursive construction of Kim Il Sung's family members who contributed to the anti-Japanese revolutionary struggle. See Chŏn Ch'ang-chŏl's "Hangil hyŏngmyŏngsigie irukdwoen kajŏnghyŏngmyŏngŭi pitnanŭn chŏnt'ong" (The Illustrious Historical Construction of Family Revolution during the Anti-Japanese Revolutionary Struggle), *Kŭlloja* 6 (1971): 37–43.

27. Baudrillard, *Simulacra and Simulation*, 1.

28. Suzy Kim, *Everyday Life*, 202–203.

29. Ibid., 196.

30. No Kwi-nam, "Kajŏng saenghwal: sosŏl sok'ŭi mosŭp chungsimuro" (Family Life: Focusing on Literature), in *Pukhanŭi sahoe munhwa* (Social Culture of North Korea), ed. Kim Tong-han (Seoul: Sejong yŏn'gusŏ pukhan yŏn'gusentŏ, 2006), 394.

31. Although Kim Chŏng-suk is Kang Pan-sŏk's daughter-in-law, Kim is also elevated to the status of the nation's Mother in the DPRK official discourse.

32. Charles Armstrong, *The North Korean Revolution 1945–1950* (Ithaca: Cornell University Press, 2003), 226.

33. *Mrs. Kang Ban Sok: Mother of the Great Leader of Korea* (Pyongyang: The Central Committee of the Korean Democratic Women's Union, 1968), 19.

34. Ibid., 43.

35. Ibid., 1.

36. Chŏng-ung Kwon, "Ch'ongsŏ Pulmyŏlui Ryŏksa chung changp'yŏnsosŏl *1932*-i naogikkaji" (Publishing the Immortal History Series, Particularly *The Year 1932*), *Chosŏn munhak* 2007, no. 6: 26.

37. *Immortal History: The Year 1932* (Pyongyang: Foreign Language Publishing House, 1977), 134.

38. Ibid., 132. In North Korean literature, Kim Il Sung was known by his sobriquet Kŭm Sŏng. In early works of the Immortal History series, Kŭm Sŏng was the preferred name for Kim Il Sung.

39. Ibid., 134.

40. *Mrs. Kang Ban Sok: Mother of the Great Leader of Korea*, 74.

41. Charles Armstrong, *North Korean Revolution*, 94.

42. *The Year 1932*, 463.

43. Ibid., 470.

44. Heonik Kwon and Byung-Ho Chung, *North Korea: Beyond Charismatic Politics* (Lanham: Rowman and Littlefield, 2012), 85.

45. *Sea of Blood* is the DPRK's pride, as Kim Jong Il allegedly directed or, at least, played a significant role in making the film. This film was produced in 1969 and was later turned into a novel in 1982.

46. *Sea of Blood* (Pyongyang: Foreign Languages Publishing House, 1982), 490.

47. Kwon and Chung, *North Korea*, 57.

48. *The Year 1932*, 129–130.

49. Sŏk Yun-gi, *Pom'ure* (Spring Thunder) (Pyongyang: Munye ch'ulp'ansa, 1985), 737.

50. Ibid.

51. Refer to Andrei Lankov, "Continuity within Change: Soviet Influence on the North Korean Education System," *Acta Koreana* 3 (July 2000): 70.

52. Tina Chanter, *Ethics of Eros: Irigaray's Rewriting of the Philosophers* (New York: Routledge, 1995), 158.

53. Suzy Kim, *Everyday Life*, 179.

54. Olga Voronina, "Soviet Patriarchy: Past and Present," *Hypatia* 8, no. 4 (1993): 100.

55. Heidi Hartmann criticizes Marxists for not addressing the issue of sexual inequality but only differences in the economic system between men and women. Heidi Hartmann, "The Unhappy Marriage of Marxism and Feminism: Toward a More Progressive Union," *Capital & Class*, 3 no. 2 (1979): 2.

56. Ri Kyŏng-hye, *Nyŏsŏng munje haegyŏl kyŏnghŏm* (Resolving the Woman Question) (Pyongyang: Sahoe kwahak ch'ulp'ansa, 1990), 24.

57. Ibid., 46.

58. Ibid., 45.

59. Refer to Kim Jong Il's treatise called *Sahoejuŭinŭn kwahakida* (Socialism Is Science) (Pyongyang: Chosŏn rodongdang ch'ulp'ansa), 1–21.

60. Voronina, "Soviet Patriarchy," 109.

61. Ri Kyŏng-hye, *Nyŏsŏng munje haegyŏl kyŏnghŏm,* 179.

Chapter 2: Kiss and Tell

1. Barbara Demick, *Nothing to Envy: Real Lives in North Korea* (London: Granta, 2010), 88–89.

2. Ibid.

3. Michel Foucault, *History of Sexuality,* vol. 1, translated by Robert Hurley (New York: Vintage Books, 1990), 34.

4. Cathy Popkin. "Kiss and Tell: Narrative Desire and Discretion," in *Sexuality and the Body in Russian Culture,* ed. Jane T. Costlow, Stephanie Sandler, and Judith Vowles (Stanford: Stanford University Press, 1993), 141.

5. Ibid., 139.

6. Ryang, *Reading North Korea,* 77.

7. Katerina Clark, *The Soviet Novel: History as Ritual* (Indianapolis: Indiana University Press, 2000), 183.

8. Ibid.

9. Ibid.

10. Ibid., 185.

11. Haiyan Lee, *Revolution of the Heart: A Genealogy of Love in China, 1900–1950* (Stanford: Stanford University Press, 2007), 256.

12. Ibid., 257.

13. Ibid., 286.

14. *Chosŏn chung'ang nyŏn'gam* (DPRK Almanac) (Pyongyang: Chosŏn chung'ang t'ongsinsa, 1988), 206.

15. Ch'oe Chŏng-hyŏn and Kim Min-ae, *Chosŏn ch'ŏngnyŏnŭi changjŏm* (The Virtue of Korean Youth) (Pyongyang: Munye ch'ulp'ansa, 1991), 2.

16. Ibid., 4.

17. Ibid., 10.

18. Ibid., 85.

19. Ibid.

20. Refer to Kim Jong Il's *Chuch'e munhakron* (Theory on Juche Literature) (Pyongyang: Chosŏn rodongdan ch'ulp'ansa, 1992), 9.

21. Mikhail Stern and August Stern, *Sex in the USSR* (New York: Times Books, 1980), 31.

22. Kwak Yŏng-ch'an, *Ch'amdwen samgwa ch'ŏngch'un* (True Life and Youth) (Pyongyang: Kŭmsŏngch'ŏngnyŏn ch'ulp'ansa, 1986), 207.

23. *Chosŏn munhak* is the oldest running journal in the DPRK. It was first published in July of 1947 through the Pukchosŏn Yesul Ch'ongyŏngmaeng (North Korean Artists Union). The journal was originally published under the title *Munhwa chŏnsŏn* (Cultural Frontline),

later became *Munhak yesul* (Literary Arts), and then *Chosŏn munhak*. It is a monthly journal that continues to this day.

24. *Chŏllima* is another monthly journal that contains short stories, articles, and cartoons. The word *ch'ŏllima* refers to a legendary winged horse, which became the state emblem for rapid production during the period of national reconstruction shortly after the Korean War in the 1950s.

25. Sŏ Chŏng-ho, "Padagach'ŏnyŏdŭl" (Young Women of the Sea), *Chosŏn munhak* 1974, no. 3: 48–58.

26. Ryang, *Reading North Korea*, 205.

27. Kim Jong Il, "Let Us Create More Revolutionary Films Based on Socialist Life," speech given on June 18, 1970, in *Kim Jong Il Selected Works*, vol. 2 (Pyongyang: Foreign Languages Publishing House, 1995), 88.

28. Julia Kristeva, *About Chinese Women*, translated by Anita Barrows (London: Marion Boyars Publishing, 1977), 76.

29. Anke Bernau, *Virgins: A Cultural History* (London: Granta Publications, 2008), 128.

30. Refer to Suk-Young Kim's *Illusive Utopia: Theater, Film, and Everyday Performance in North Korea* (Ann Arbor: University of Michigan Press, 2010), 225–227.

31. Ibid., 218.

32. Ibid., 224.

33. Kim Mun-ch'ang, *T'anbu* (Miners) (Pyongyang: Munye ch'ulp'ansa, 1986), 117.

34. Ch'oe Wan-ho, "Nyŏsŏngdŭl'ui ryejŏlitgo kŏmbakhan mal" (Women's Courteous and Plain Language), *Munhwa'ŏhaksŭp* (Study of Cultural Language), February 1981, 56.

35. Ibid., 57.

36. Sŏ Tong-ik, *Inmini sa'nŭn mosŭp* (The Life of the People), vol. 1 (Seoul: Charyowŏn, 1995), 39.

37. Foucault, *History of Sexuality*, vol. 1, 81.

38. Ibid., 61.

39. Paek Nam-nyong, *Pŏt* (Friend) (Pyongyang: Munye ch'ulp'ansa, 1988), 37.

40. Sŏ Tong-ik, *Inmini sa'nŭn mosŭp*, vol. 1, 173.

41. Paek Nam-nyong, *Pŏt*, 39.

42. Ibid., 38–39.

43. See Michael Pettid's *Unyŏng-jŏn: A Love Affair at the Royal Palace of Chosŏn Korea* (Berkeley: University of California Press, 2009), 47.

44. Sŏ Tong-ik, *Inmini sa'nŭn mosŭp*, vol. 1, 89.

45. Ch'ŏng-nam Kim's "Naega saranghanŭn saram" (The Man I Love) appeared in the September 1978 issue of *Chosŏn munhak*.

46. Jae-cheon Lim, *Kim Jong Il's Leadership of North Korea* (London: Routledge, 2009), 139.

47. Kim Ch'ŏng-nam, "Naega saranghanŭn saram," 37.

48. Ibid., 34.

49. Foucault, *History of Sexuality*, 65.

50. Kim Ch'ŏng-nam, "Naega saranghanŭn saram," 36.

51. Nancy Armstrong, *How Novels Think: The Limits of Individualism 1719–1900* (New York: Columbia University Press, 2005), 48.

52. Ibid., 51.

53. Ri Hwa, *Sogŭm kkot* (Salt Deposits) (Pyongyang: Munye ch'ulp'ansa, 1984), 82.

54. Paul de Man, *Allegories of Reading: Figural Language in Rousseau, Nietzsche, Rilke, and Proust* (New Haven: Yale University Press, 1979), 301.

55. Paul de Man, "The Concept of Irony," in *Aesthetic Ideology* (Minneapolis: University of Minnesota Press, 1996), 167.

56. Rolf Breuer, "Irony, Literature, and Schizophrenia," *New Literary History*, 12, no. 1 (1980): 108.

57. Lee R. Edwards. "Schizophrenic Narrative," *Journal of Narrative Technique*, 19, no. 1 (1989): 28.

58. Ibid., 29.

59. Ri Hwa, *Sogŭm kkot*, 82.

60. Ibid.

61. Breuer, "Irony, Literature, and Schizophrenia," 111.

62. Ri Hwa, *Sogŭm kkot*, 183.

Chapter 3: The Woman Question(s)

1. Barbara Einhorn, *Cinderella Goes to Market: Citizenship, Gender and Women's Movements in East Central Europe* (London: Verso, 1993), 216.

2. Ibid., 218.

3. G. W. F. Hegel, *The Phenomenology of Mind*, trans. J. B. Baillie (New York: Harper and Row, 1967), § 475.

4. Ibid.

5. Ibid.

6. G. W. F. Hegel, *Elements of the Philosophy of Right*, trans. H. B. Nisbet (Cambridge: Cambridge University Press, 1991), 213.

7. Simone de Beauvoir, *The Second Sex* (New York: Bantam, 1952), 249.

8. Judith Butler, *Bodies That Matter: On the Discursive Limits of "Sex"* (New York: Routledge, 1993), 12.

9. Diane Elam, *Feminism and Deconstruction: Ms. en Abyme* (London: Routledge, 1994), 28.

10. Claire Colebrook, *Gender* (New York: Palgrave Macmillan, 2004), 57.

11. *Chosŏn chung'ang nyŏn'gam*, 1977, 226.

12. Interview with North Korean defector and poet Ch'oe Chin-i on December 9, 2011.

13. "North Korean officials seemed to be setting their eyes on Western standards to catch up with the latest fashion modes, which would diversify the binary dress codes based on traditional female garments including *chosŏn'ot* (Korean traditional dress) and other clothing for domestic labor and military outfits" (Suk-Young Kim, *Illusive Utopia*, 252).

14. Janice Radway, *Reading the Romance: Women, Patriarchy, and Popular Literature* (Chapel Hill: University of North Carolina Press, 1984), 212.

15. Nancy Armstrong, *Desire and Domestic Fiction: A Political History of the Novel* (Oxford: Oxford University Press, 1987), 18.

16. Ibid., 253.

17. Radway, *Reading the Romance*, 213.

18. Ibid., 212.

19. Kim Kyo-sŏp, *Saenghwalui ŏndŏk* (Heights of Life) (Pyongyang: Munye ch'ulp'ansa: 1984), 17.

20. Ibid., 18.
21. Ibid., 6.
22. Ibid.
23. Ibid., 147.
24. Ibid., 163.
25. Ibid., 164.
26. Ibid.
27. Ibid., 238.
28. Kim Jong Il, *Art of the Cinema,* 194.
29. Kim Kyo-sŏp, *Saenghwalui ŏndŏk,* 20.
30. *Uri sidae'ui yŏng'ungdŭl* (Heroes of our Generation), vol. 1 (1988), vol. 2 (1989), vol. 3 (1990) (Pyongyang: Kŭllo tanche ch'ulp'ansa).
31. Refer to Kim Chae-yong's *Pukhan munhakui yŏksajŏk ihae* (Historical Understanding of North Korean Literature) (Seoul: Munhakgwa chisŏngsa, 1994), 85. I will discuss the hidden hero further in Chapter 4.
32. Yong-Soo Park, "The Political Economy of Economic Reform in North Korea," *Australian Journal of International Affairs* 63, no. 4 (2009): 531.
33. Jin Cheol Jo and Seymour Adler, "Planning in the Socialist Developing Country: The Case of North Korea," *Habitat International* 26 (2002): 254.
34. Hy-Sang Lee, "North Korea's Closed Economy: The Hidden Opening," *Asian Survey* 28 (1988): 1267.
35. Refer to Moon-soo Yang's "North Korea's External Debts: Trends and Characteristics," *Korea Focus,* http://www.koreafocus.or.kr/design2/layout/content_print.asp?group_id=104047, accessed August 17, 2014.
36. Refer to Yutaka Akino's "Soviet Asian Policy in a New Perspective," in *Perestroika: Soviet Domestic and Foreign Policies,* ed. Tsuyoshi Hasegawa and Alex Pravda. (London: SAGE Publications, 1990), 222–241.
37. Michel Foucault, *Discipline and Punish: The Birth of the Prison,* trans. Alan Sheridan (New York: Vintage Books, 1995), 201.
38. Ibid., 200.
39. Travis Workman, "The Partisan, the Worker, and the Hidden Hero: Popular Icons in North Korean Film," in *The Korean Popular Culture Reader,* ed. Kyung Hyun Kim and Youngmin Choe (Durham: Duke University Press, 2014), 161.
40. Ch'oe Sang-sun, *Saebyŏk pyŏl* (Morning Star) (Pyongyang: Munye ch'ulp'ansa, 1987), 214.
41. Ibid., 46.
42. Ibid., 52.
43. Ibid., 124.
44. Ibid., 141.
45. Ibid., 60–61.
46. Ibid., 2.
47. Ibid., 1.
48. Ibid., 26.
49. Ibid., 60, 62.
50. Ibid., 108.
51. Ibid., 128.

52. Ibid., 169.
53. Ibid., 178.

Chapter 4: Women, Divorce, and the State

1. Refer to Stephen Epstein, "On Reading North Korean Short Stories on the Cusp of the New Millennium," *Acta Koreana* 5, no. 1 (January 2002): 33.
2. Article 22 of the 1948 DPRK Constitution. Pak Sang-chŏl and Kim Ch'ang-kyu, *Pukhan'ui hŏnpŏp kaejŏngkwa ip'pŏptonghyang* (North Korean Constitution Revision and Legislative Trends) (Seoul: Han'gukpŏpjaeyŏn'guwon, 1994).
3. Hwang Sŏk-yŏng, *Sarami salgo issŏtne* (There Have Been People Living There) (Seoul: Siwa sahoesa, 1993), 199.
4. This quotation regarding *Friend* is found in the appendix of the South Korean republication of Paek Nam-nyong's *60 Nyŏn hu* (After Sixty Years) (Seoul: Han-ung Ch'ulp'ansa, 1992).
5. Kim Hyŏn-kyŏng, "Pukhan TV dŭrama *Kajok* 9hoe pangyŏnghu toryŏn chungdan" (North Korean Television Drama *Family* Discontinued after Nine Episodes), MBC News, October 17, 2001, http://imnews.imbc.com/20dbnews/history/2001/1882521_13453.html, accessed March 1, 2010.
6. Ri In-ch'ŏl, "Mangne ttal" (My Youngest Daughter), *Chosŏn munhak* 1980, no. 11: 57–65. The DPRK has published numerous short stories and poems from Korean *zainichi* in Japan, particularly in the 1970s and 1980s, because of its attempt at repatriating Japan's Korean residents to North Korea. The general didactic discourse in these works of fiction is that the true home of the *zainichi* is in the DPRK.
7. Sin Hyŏng-gi and O Sŏng-ho, *Pukhan munhaksa: hangilhyŏngmyŏng munhak'e-sŏ chuch'e munhakkaji* (History of North Korean Literature: From Anti-Japanese Literature to Juche Literature) (Seoul: P'yŏngminsa, 2000), 321.
8. Ko In-hwan, "Juche-ui kyunyŏlgwa yongmang: *60 nyŏn-hu* wa *Pŏt*" (Fissures and Desires in Juche: *After Sixty Years* and *Friend*), in *Pukhan munhak-ui chihyŏngdo* (The Future of North Korean Literature), ed. O Ch'ang-ŭn (Seoul: Ehwa yŏjadaehakkyo ch'ulp'anbu, 2008), 309.
9. Refer to Tatiana Gabroussenko, "North Korean 'Rural Fiction' from the Late 1990s to the Mid 2000s: Permanence and Change," *Korean Studies* 33 (2009): 79–81.
10. Paek Nam-nyong, *Pŏt,* 56.
11. Ibid., 158.
12. Ibid., 165.
13. Jacques Donzelot, *The Policing of Families* (New York: Random House, 1979), 91.
14. Ibid., xii.
15. Paek Nam-nyong, *Pŏt,* 18.
16. An Yong-duk, *Pukhanui kajokbop* (DPRK Family Law) (Seoul: Hanyangdang, 1998), 156–157.
17. Ibid., 157.
18. Kim Chae-yong, *Pundan kujowa Pukhan munhak* (The Structure of the Partition of the Korean Peninsula and the Literature of North Korea) (Seoul: So-myŏng ch'ulp'ansa, 2000), 292.
19. Kim Il Sung, "Samdae hyŏngmyŏng-ŭl himitge pŏlyŏ sahoechu-ui kŏnsŏlŭl tŏ-uk tagŏch'ija" (Let Us Put More Effort into the Construction of Socialism by Supporting the

Three Revolutions), speech delivered March 3, 1975, in *Kim Il Sung chŏjakjip* (Kim Il Sung's Collected Works), vol. 30 (Pyongyang: Chosŏn rodongdan ch'ulp'ansa, 1985), 112.

20. Ch'ae Rim presents a markedly different type of villain from the villains of the past. Refer to Alzo David-West, "The Literary Ideas of Kim Il Sung and Kim Jong Il: An Introduction to North Korean Meta-Authorial Perspectives," *Cultural Logic* 2009:1–34, and Kim Jong Il's *On the Art of the Cinema* for a description of prototypical villains in literature.

21. David-West, "Literary Ideas of Kim Il Sung and Kim Jong Il," 20.

22. Kim Chae-yong, *Pukhan munhakui yŏksajŏk ihae* (Historical Understanding of North Korean Literature) (Seoul: Munhakgwa chisŏngsa, 1994), 274.

23. Ibid., 90.

24. Paek Nam-nyong, *Pŏt,* 23.

25. Ibid., 11.

26. Refer to Barbara Wolfe Jancar's *Women under Communism* (Baltimore: Johns Hopkins University Press, 1978) for her analysis of women's second shift and the social imbalance of gender politics.

27. Paek Nam-nyong, *Pŏt,* 182.

28. In North Korea, the term "new man" is not gender specific. "Man" (*in'gan*) simply refers to a human being. What is gendered is that the "new man" or the new revolutionary must abide by the patriarchal political order. Men and women of the DPRK are called to participate in the male-dominated political system, which in turn constructs the state-desired "man."

29. Paek Nam-nyong, *Pŏt,* 195.

30. Heonik Kwon and Byung-Ho Chung, *North Korea: Beyond Charismatic Politics* (Lanham: Rowman and Littlefield, 2012), 21.

31. Ibid., 22.

32. Paek Nam-nyong, *Pŏt,* 15–16.

33. Ibid., 146.

34. Ibid.

35. DPRK Civil Procedure Acts and DPRK Constitution of 1972.

36. Paek Nam-nyong, *Pŏt,* 88.

37. Ko In-hwan, "Juche-ui kyunyŏlgwa yongmang."

38. Paek Nam-nyong, *Pŏt,* 7.

39. Ibid., 106.

40. Ibid., 9.

41. Jean-François Lyotard, *The Differend: Phrases in Dispute,* trans. Georges Van Den Abbeele (Minneapolis: University of Minnesota Press, 1988), 13.

42. Ibid., 93.

43. Paek Nam-nyong, *Pŏt,* 55.

44. In *The Origins of the Family, Private Property and the State,* Frederick Engels says, "The care and education of the children becomes a public affair; society looks after all children alike, whether they are legitimate or not" (p. 139) (New York: International Publishers, 2001).

45. Paek Nam-nyong, *Pŏt,* 17.

46. Hegel, *Elements of the Philosophy of Right,* 200.

47. Hegel, *Phenomenology of Mind,* 493.

48. Suzy Kim, "Revolutionary Mothers: Women in the North Korean Revolution, 1945–1950," *Comparative Studies in Society and History* 52, no. 4 (2010): 742–767.

49. Paek Nam-nyong, *Pŏt,* 100.

50. Ibid., 101.
51. Ibid., 134.
52. Ibid., 135.
53. Ibid.
54. Ibid., 165.
55. Ibid., 164.
56. Ibid., 92.
57. Judith Butler, *Antigone's Claim: Kinship between Life and Death* (New York: Columbia University Press, 2000), 36.
58. Ibid., 5.
59. Ibid., 2.
60. Ibid., 6.
61. Paek Nam-nyong, *Pŏt,* 192.
62. Ibid., 195.
63. Rosi Braidotti, *Metamorphoses: Towards a Materialist Theory of Becoming* (Malden: Polity Press, 2002), 11.

Chapter 5: Motherhood Revisited

1. Ryang, *Reading North Korea,* 198.
2. Chae-yong Kim, *Pundan kujowa Pukhan munhak.*
3. Kim Il Sung, "Hyŏndaemunhak'ui sidaejŏksamyŏng" (The Mission in the Era of Modern Literature), *Chosŏn munhak* 1986, no. 12.
4. Chizuko Ueno, *Nationalism and Gender,* trans. Beverley Yamamoto (Melbourne: Trans Pacific Press, 2004), 3.
5. Ban Wang, *Illuminations of the Past: Trauma, Memory, and History in Modern China* (Stanford: Stanford University Press, 2004), 18.
6. Patrick Hutton, *History as an Art of Memory* (Hanover: University of Vermont, 1993), xx.
7. Ibid., xxi.
8. Refer to Sonia Ryang's "Technologies of the Self: Reading from North Korean Novels in the 1980s," *Acta Koreana* 5, no. 1 (2002): 21–32. In this essay, Ryang discusses how individuals in fiction discipline themselves to project the state-desired revolutionary commitment.
9. This annual publication reviews and celebrates works that were published in the past year. The works that appear in this publication are ones that the Party considers to be "worthy" of helping to build an ideologically equipped North Korean people. "Munhak" (Literature), in *Chosŏn chung'ang nyŏn'gam,* 1987, 272.
10. Jae Jean Suh, *The Impact of Personality Cult in North Korea* (Seoul: Korea Institute for National Unification, 2004), 9–10.
11. Ibid., 11.
12. Andrei Lankov, "The Organizational Life: Daily Surveillance and Daily Resistance in North Korea," *Journal of East Asian Studies* 12 (2012): 194.
13. So Tong-ik's *Inmin'isanŭnmosŭp* describes the life of youths in these different leagues that they must join. Chŏng Sŏng-jang, Chŏng Sang-don, Chŏng Sŏng-im, and No Kwi-nam explain the organization and the function of each of the different leagues and unions in the

DPRK in *Chosŏn rodongdan'ui woe-gwaktan'ch'e* (Korea Workers' Subgovernment Organizations, 2004).

14. Hazel Smith, *North Korea: Markets and Military Rule* (Cambridge: Cambridge University Press, 2015), 163.

15. Ibid., 156.

16. Ibid.

17. Joe C. Huang, *Heroes and Villains in Communist China: The Contemporary Chinese Novel as a Reflection of Life* (New York: Pica Press, 1973), 220.

18. Eric Laursen, "A New Enigmatic Language: The Spontaneity-Consciousness Paradigm and the Case of Galdkov's *Cement*," *Slavic Review* 65 (Spring 2006): 74.

19. Fyodor Vasilievich Gladkov, *Cement*, trans. A. S. Arthur and C. Ashleigh (Evanston, Illinois: Northwestern University Press, 1980), 208.

20. Ibid., 64.

21. Laursen, "New Enigmatic Language," 88.

22. One North Korean defector who studied at Kim Il Sung University recalls in an interview how her university entrance exams consisted mainly of reciting episodes and quotes from Kim Il Sung's *Memoirs*.

23. Suk-Young Kim, *Illusive Utopia*, 183.

24. Yeonmi Park and Maryanne Vollers, *In Order to Live: A North Korean Girl's Journey to Freedom* (New York: Penguin Books, 2015); Blaine Harden, *Escape from Camp 14: One Man's Remarkable Odyssey from North Korea to Freedom in the West* (New York: Penguin Books, 2013); Jang Jin-sung, *Dear Leader: My Escape from North Korea*, trans. Shirley Lee (New York: Atria Paperback, 2014).

25. Chu Sŏng-ha, "Orhae kungnae'ipguk t'albukja 1088myŏng . . . changnyŏn poda 20% kamso" (Twenty Percent Decrease This Year in North Korean Defectors Entering South Korea), NambukStory.com, December 22, 2015, http://blog.donga.com/nambukstory/archives/114592, accessed September 2, 2016.

26. Suki Kim, *Without You, There Is No Us: Undercover among the Sons of North Korea's Elite* (New York: Broadway Books, 2014).

27. Kim Ryŏ-suk, *Chakp'umui simnimyosa* (Psychological Delineation in Literary Works) (Pyongyang: Munhak yesul chonghap ch'ulp'ansa, 1994), 252.

28. Ri Hŭi-nam, *Yŏdŏl sigan* (Eight Hours) (Pyongyang: Munye ch'ulp'ansa, 1986), 124.

29. Ibid., 49–52.

30. Ibid., 56.

31. Ibid., 134.

32. Ibid., 125.

33. Ibid., 49.

34. Ibid.

35. Luce Irigaray, "Body against Body: In Relation to the Mother," in her *Sexes and Genealogies*, trans. Gillian C. Gill (New York: Columbia University Press, 1993), 14.

36. Ibid., 15.

37. Maggie Berg, "Luce Irigaray's 'Contradictions': Poststructuralism and Feminism," *Signs* 17, no. 1 (1991): 50.

38. Ri Hŭi-nam, *Yŏdŏl sigan*, 132.

39. Luce Irigaray, *This Sex Which Is Not One*, trans. Catherine Porter (New York: Cornell University Press, 1985), 16.

40. Sonia Ryang, *Reading North Korea,* 25.
41. Ri Hŭi-nam, *Yŏdŏl sigan,* 56.
42. Stephan Haggard and Marcus Noland, "Reform from Below: Behavioral and Institutional Change in North Korea," *Journal of Economic Behavior and Organization* 73 (2010): 134.
43. Ibid., 134.
44. Ibid., 144.
45. Kwon and Chung, *North Korea,* 3.
46. Baudrillard, *Simulacra and Simulation,* 1.
47. Kwon and Chung, *North Korea,* 33.
48. Ri Hŭi-nam, *Yŏdŏl sigan,* 132.
49. Ibid., 130.
50. Ibid., 50.
51. Ibid., 52.
52. Yi On-juk, *Pukhan sahoe yŏngu: sahoehakjŏk chŏpgŭn* (Research on North Korean Society: An Approach to Social Factors) (Seoul: Seoul National University Press, 1989), 176–177.
53. Ueno, Nationalism and Gender, 19.
54. Colebrook, *Gender,* 205.
55. Ri Hŭi-nam, *Yŏdŏl sigan,* 49.
56. Ibid., 51.
57. Ibid., 134.
58. Ibid., 50.
59. According to two defectors who were formerly members of the Writers' Union, writers were often commissioned by the union to write stories to fit specific North Korean holidays or festivals such as Kim Il Sung's and Kim Jong Il's birthdays. Interview with Ch'oe Chin-i and Mr. Han (pseudonym) in October 2010.
60. Epstein, "On Reading North Korean Short Stories," 40.
61. Ibid.
62. Ri Hŭi-nam, *Yŏdŏl sigan,* 174.

Conclusion

1. Hong Sŏk-jung, *Hwang Chin-i,* vol. 1 (Seoul: Taehun, 2004), 276.
2. Donald Macintyre and Kim Yooseung, "A Literary Thaw in Korea," *Time,* June 21, 2004, http://www.time.com/time/magazine/article/0,9171,655483,00.html#ixzz1crBDcg1P, accessed June 27, 2009.
3. Ibid.
4. Brian Myers, *The Cleanest Race* (Brooklyn: Melville House, 2010), 89.
5. Interview with Kim Chae-yong regarding Hong Sŏk-jung's *Hwang Chin-i* in June 2010; see also Kim Chae-yong, ed., *Sara innŭn sinhwa Hwang Chin-i* (*Hwang Chin-i:* The Living Mythology) (Seoul: Taehun, 2006).
6. The film *Hwang Chin-i* was released in 2007, starring Song Hye-gyo and Yu Chi-t'ae. It was directed by Chang Yun-hyŏn.
7. See Kim Chae-yong's *Sara innŭn sinhwa Hwang Chin-i,* where he discusses the impact that the novel has had in North and South Korea.
8. Refer to Andrei Lankov's "Changing North Korea: An Information Campaign Can Beat the Regime," *Foreign Affairs* 88, no. 6 (2009): 95–105.

9. Smith, *North Korea*, 331.

10. See also Haggard and Noland, "Reform from Below."

11. Smith, *North Korea*, 327.

12. Kwon and Chung, *North Korea*, 13.

13. The Literature Translation Institute of Korea was founded in 1996 and is a government-funded organization that translates South Korean works of fiction into languages of the world. The ultimate vision of the institute is to improve the value of Korea's national brand, as stated on their website: http://www.klti.or.kr/ke_01_04_011.do?admin_top_lid=ka_06&admin_m_p_seq=94.

Bibliography

Articles in the *Rodong Sinmun* Newspaper

"Hyŏngmyŏngui yogudaero sasaekhago t'amguhago ch'angjohaja!" (Let's Contemplate, Research, and Create According to the Demands of the Revolution). November 3, 1979.

"Sum'un yŏng'ung-kwa tang'ilkun" (Hidden Heroes and Party Workers). October 31, 1979.

"Tang-kwa chogukul wihayŏ idŭlch'ŏrŏm salmyŏ ilhaja" (Let's Live and Work for the Party and Fatherland Like These Revolutionaries). November 1, 1979.

"Tang-kwa hyŏngmyŏng'e ch'ungjikhan kwahakja" (Scientist Devoted to the Party and the Revolution). October 27, 1979.

"Tang-kwa hyŏngmyŏng'e taehan hŏnsinjŏkpokmu'ui sunggohan mobŏm" (Noble Models of Loyal Service to the Party and the Revolution). October 16, 1979.

"Tang-kwa inminŭl wihanŭn hanma'ŭm" (One Heart for the Party and the People). October 13, 1979.

"Yŏryŏlhan hŏnsinsŏng'ul poyŏjun sum'un yŏng'ungdŭlŭl ttarapae'uja!" (Let's Learn from the Hidden Heroes Who Have Shown Their Passionate Devotion). November 11, 1979.

Other Works

Akino, Yutaka. "Soviet Asian Policy in a New Perspective." In *Perestroika: Soviet Domestic and Foreign Policies,* edited by Tsuyoshi Hasegawa and Alex Pravda, 222–241. London: SAGE Publications, 1990.

An Yong-duk. *Pukhanui kajokbop* (DPRK Family Law). Seoul: Hanyangdang, 1998.

Armstrong, Charles. *The North Korean Revolution 1945–1950.* Ithaca: Cornell University Press, 2003.

———. "Trends in the Study of North Korea." *Journal of Asian Studies* 70 (2011): 357–371.

———. *Tyranny of the Weak: North Korea and the World, 1950–1992.* Ithaca: Cornell University Press, 2013.

Armstrong, Nancy. *Desire and Domestic Fiction: A Political History of the Novel.* Oxford: Oxford University Press, 1987.

———. *How Novels Think: The Limits of Individualism 1719–1900.* New York: Columbia University Press, 2005.

Barraclough, Ruth. "Red Love and Betrayal in the Making of North Korea: Comrade Hŏ Chŏng-suk." *History Workshop Journal* 77 (2014): 86–102.

Bates, David. "Crisis between the Wars: Derrida and the Origins of Undecidability." *Representations* 90, no. 1 (2005): 1–27.

Baudrillard, Jean. *Simulacra and Simulation*. Translated by Sheila Faria Glaser. Ann Arbor: University of Michigan Press, 1994.

Beauvoir, Simone de. *The Second Sex*. New York: Bantam, 1952.

Berg, Maggie. "Luce Irigaray's 'Contradictions': Poststructuralism and Feminism." *Signs* 17, no. 1 (1991): 50–70.

Bernau, Anke. *Virgins: A Cultural History*. London: Granta Publications, 2008.

Braidotti, Rosi. *Metamorphoses: Towards a Materialist Theory of Becoming*. Malden: Polity Press, 2002.

Breuer, Rolf. "Irony, Literature, and Schizophrenia." *New Literary History* 12, no. 1 (1980): 107–118.

Butler, Judith. *Antigone's Claim: Kinship between Life and Death*. New York: Columbia University Press, 2000.

———. *Bodies That Matter: On the Discursive Limits of "Sex."* New York: Routledge, 1993.

———. *Gender Trouble: Feminism and the Subversion of Identity*. New York: Routledge, 1990.

Chang Hŭi-suk. *Sosŏl ch'angjakgwa kusŏng* (Creation and Structure of the Novel). Pyongyang: Munhak yesul chonghap ch'ulp'ansa, 2000.

Chanter, Tina. *Ethics of Eros: Irigaray's Rewriting of the Philosophers*. New York: Routledge, 1995.

Ch'oe Chin-i. "Chakkawa Chosŏn chakka tongmaeng" (Writers and the North Korean Writers' Union). *Imjingang* 9 (2010): 142–181.

Ch'oe Chŏng-hyŏn and Kim Min-ae. *Chosŏn ch'ŏngnyŏnŭi changjŏm* (The Virtue of Korean Youth). Pyongyang: Munye ch'ulp'ansa, 1991.

Ch'oe Hak-su. "Haepitbalkŭn nara" (Radiant Country). *Chosŏn munhak* 1972, no. 4: 51–63.

———. "P'yŏnsaengŭl ma'ŭmsok'e t'aeyang'ŭi yŏngsang'ŭl mosigo" (Cherishing the Image of the Sun in My Heart Forever). *Chosŏn munhak* 2007, no. 6: 27–28.

———. *Pyongyang sigan* (Pyongyang Time). Pyongyang: Munye ch'ulp'ansa, 1976.

Ch'oe Sang-sun. *Saebyŏk pyŏl* (Morning Star). Pyongyang: Munye ch'ulp'ansa, 1987.

Ch'oe Wan-ho. "Nyŏsŏngdŭl'ui ryejŏlitgo kŏmbakhan mal" (Women's Courteous and Plain Language). *Munhwa'ŏhaksŭp* (Study of Cultural Language), February 1981, 56–59.

Chŏn Ch'ang-chŏl. "Hangil hyŏngmyŏngsigie irukdwoen kajŏnghyŏngmyŏngŭi pitnanŭn chŏnt'ong" (The Illustrious Historical Construction of Family Revolution during the Anti-Japanese Revolutionary Struggle). *Kŭlloja* 6 (1971): 37–43.

Chŏng Ch'ang-yun. "Pompam" (Spring Evening). In *Chŏngboro kŏlŏra*, edited by Ri Myŏng-ho, 49–53. Pyongyang: Munye ch'ulp'ansa, 1985.

Chosŏn chung'ang nyŏn'gam (DPRK Almanac). Pyongyang: Chosŏn chung'ang t'ongsinsa, 1970–1989.

Chosŏn munhak yesul nyŏn'gam (DPRK Literary Arts Almanac). Pyongyang: Munhak yesul chonghap ch'ulp'ansa, 2000.

Chosŏn rodongdang'ui woe'gwak tanch'e (DPRK Workers' Subgovernment Organizations). Edited by Sejong yŏn'guso pukhan yŏn'gu'sent'ŏ. Seoul: Han'ul Academy, 2004.

Chu Sŏng-ha. "Orhae kungnae'ipguk t'albukja 1088myŏng . . . changnyŏn poda 20% kamso" (Twenty Percent Decrease This Year in North Korean Defectors Entering South Korea). NambukStory.com, December 22, 2015. http://blog.donga.com/nambukstory/archives/114592, accessed September 2, 2016.

Clark, Katerina. *The Soviet Novel: History as Ritual.* Third edition. Indianapolis: Indiana University Press, 2000.

Colebrook, Claire. *Gender.* New York: Palgrave Macmillan, 2004.

David-West, Alzo. "The Literary Ideas of Kim Il Sung and Kim Jong Il: An Introduction to North Korean Meta-Authorial Perspectives." *Cultural Logic* 2009:1–34.

de Man, Paul. *Allegories of Reading: Figural Language in Rousseau, Nietzsche, Rilke, and Proust.* New Haven: Yale University Press, 1979.

———. "The Concept of Irony." In his *Aesthetic Ideology,* 163–184. Minneapolis: University of Minnesota Press, 1996.

Demick, Barbara. *Nothing to Envy: Real Lives in North Korea.* London: Granta, 2010.

Derrida, Jacques. *Dissemination.* Translated by Barbara Johnson. Chicago: Chicago University Press, 1981.

———. "Structure, Sign, and Play in the Discourse of the Human Sciences." In his *Writing and Difference,* translated by Alan Bass, 278–294. Chicago: University of Chicago Press, 1978.

Donzelot, Jacques. *The Policing of Families.* Translated by Robert Hurley. New York: Pantheon Books, 1979.

Edwards, Lee R. "Schizophrenic Narrative." *Journal of Narrative Technique* 19, no. 1 (1989): 25–30.

Einhorn, Barbara. *Cinderella Goes to Market: Citizenship, Gender and Women's Movements in East Central Europe.* London: Verso, 1993.

Elam, Diane. *Feminism and Deconstruction: Ms. en Abyme.* London: Routledge, 1994.

Engels, Frederick. *The Origin of the Family, Private Property and the State.* New York: International Publishers, 2001.

Epstein, Stephen. "On Reading North Korean Short Stories on the Cusp of the New Millennium." *Acta Koreana* 5, no. 1 (January 2002): 33–50.

Foucault, Michel. *Discipline and Punish: The Birth of the Prison.* Translated by Alan Sheridan. New York: Vintage Books, 1995.

———. *The History of Sexuality,* vol. 1. Translated by Robert Hurley. New York: Vintage Books, 1990.

Gabroussenko, Tatiana. "North Korean 'Rural Fiction' from the Late 1990s to the Mid 2000s: Permanence and Change." *Korean Studies* 33 (2009): 69–100.

———. *Soldiers on the Cultural Front: Developments in the Early History of North Korean Literature and Literary Policy.* Honolulu: University of Hawai'i Press, 2010.

Gladkov, Fyodor Vasilievich. *Cement.* Translated by A. S. Arthur and C. Ashleigh. Evanston: Northwestern University Press, 1980.

Ha Chŏng-hi. "Chakkadŭl'ui chŏngch'ijŏk sikkyŏnkwa anmok" (Writers' Political Insight and Discernment). *Chosŏn munhak* 1975, no. 3: 76–77.

Ha Sang-il. "Sahoejuŭijŏk yŏsŏngjuŭiwa yŏsŏngsŏsaŭi silhyŏn" (Socialist Feminism and Women Narratives). In *Kang Kyŏng-ae: Sidaewa munhak* (Kang Kyŏng-ae: Era and Literature), edited by Kim In-hwan and Kim Chae-yong, 47–70. Seoul: Random House Korea, 2006.

Haggard, Stephan, and Marcus Noland. "Reform from Below: Behavioral and Institutional Changes in North Korea." *Journal of Economic Behavior and Organization* 73 (2010): 133–152.

Hartmann, Heidi. "The Unhappy Marriage of Marxism and Feminism: Toward a More Progressive Union." *Capital & Class* 3, no. 2 (1979): 1–33.

Hegel, G. W. F. *Elements of the Philosophy of Right*. Translated by H. B. Nisbet. Cambridge: Cambridge University Press, 1991.

———. *The Phenomenology of Mind*. Translated by J. B. Baillie. New York: Harper and Row, 1967.

Hong Sŏk-jung. *Hwang Chin-i* (Hwang Chin-i), vol. 1. Seoul: Taehun, 2004.

———. *Hwang Chin-i* (Hwang Chin-i), vol. 2. Seoul: Taehun, 2004.

Huang, Joe C. *Heroes and Villains in Communist China: The Contemporary Chinese Novel as a Reflection of Life*. New York: Pica Press, 1973.

Hutton, Patrick H. *History as an Art of Memory*. Hanover: University Press of New England, 1993.

Hwang Sŏk-yŏng. *Sarami salgo issŏtne* (There Have Been People Living There). Seoul: Siwa sahoesa, 1993.

Hyŏn Sŏng-il. *Pukhan'ui gukkajŏllyak-kwa p'awŏ ellit'ŭ: kanbujŏngch'aek'ŭl chungsimŭro* (North Korea's State Strategy and Power Elites: Focusing on the Politics of Cadres). Seoul: Sŏn'in, 2007.

Immortal History: The Year 1932. Pyongyang: Foreign Languages Publishing House, 1977.

Irigaray, Luce. "Body against Body: In Relation to the Mother." In her *Sexes and Genealogies*, translated by Gillian C. Gill, 7–22. New York: Columbia University Press, 1993.

———. *This Sex Which Is Not One*. Translated by Catherine Porter. New York: Cornell University Press, 1985.

Jancar, Barbara Wolfe. *Women under Communism*. Baltimore: Johns Hopkins University Press, 1978.

Jo, Jin Cheol, and Seymour Adler. "Planning in the Socialist Developing Country: The Case of North Korea." *Habitat International* 26 (2002): 251–267.

Johnson, Adam. "Adam Johnson Recalls North Korea: A Country with No Books." *The Daily Beast*, December 21, 2011. http://www.thedailybeast.com/articles/2011/12/21/adam-johnson-recalls-north-korea-a-country-with-no-books.html, accessed January 9, 2012.

Kang Chin-ho. "'Ch'ongsŏ' ranŭn kŏdesŏsa hokŭn hŏwi'uisik" (The Immortal History Series' Immense Narrative or False Consciousness). In *Pukhan munhwachŏngchŏn ch'ongsŏ Pulmyŏlui Ryŏksarul iknŭnda* (On Reading the North Korea Canon's Immortal History Series), edited by Kang Chin-ho, 17–43. Seoul: Somyŏng ch'ulp'an, 2009.

Kang Kyŏng-ae. "Chosŏnyŏsŏngŭi palbŭl kil" (The Path of Korean Women). *Chosŏn ilbo,* November 28–29, 1930.

Kim Chae-yong. *Pukhan munhakui yŏksajŏk ihae* (Historical Understanding of North Korean Literature). Seoul: Munhakgwa chisŏngsa, 1994.

———. *Pundan kujowa Pukhan munhak* (The Structure of the Partition of the Korean Peninsula and the Literature of North Korea). Seoul: So-myŏng ch'ulp'ansa, 2000.

———, ed. *Sara innŭn sinhwa Hwang Chin-i* (*Hwang Chin-i:* The Living Mythology). Seoul: Taehun, 2006.

Kim Chong-hoe. "Ek'o'ui munhak" (Echo Literature). In *Pukhanmunhak'ui pyŏnhwa'wa chŏnmang* (Changes in and Outlook for North Korean Literature through Its Works), edited by Kim Chong-hoe, Ko In-hwan, and Yi Sang-ch'ŏl, 147–154. Seoul: Tosŏch'ulp'an Yŏngnak, 2007.

Kim Chŏng-nam. "Naega saranghanŭn saram" (The Man I Love). *Chosŏn munhak* 1978, no. 9.

———. "Suryŏng hyŏngsang munhak'ui sae ryŏksaga p'yŏlch'yŏjin yŏngkwangui 40 nyŏn" (Forty glorious years of the unfolding of the new history of the Great Leader's personality literature). *Chosŏn munhak* 2007, no. 6: 21–25.

Kim Chŏng-ung and Ch'ŏn Chae-kyu. *Chosŏn munhaksa* (History of Korean Literature). Pyongyang: Sahoe kwahak ch'ulp'ansa, 1998.

Kim Hyŏn-kyŏng. "Pukhan TV dŭrama *Kajok* 9hoe pangyŏnghu toryŏn chungdan" (North Korean television drama *Family* Discontinued after Nine Episodes). MBC News, October 17, 2001. http://imnews.imbc.com/20dbnews/history/2001/1882521_13453.html, accessed March 1, 2010.

Kim Il Sung. "Chajujŏkin sae sahoe kŏnsŏl'esŏ intelli'ui yŏkhal" (The Role of the Intellectuals in Constructing a New Society of Freedom). Speech delivered on August 14, 1980. In *Kim Il Sung chŏjakjip* (Kim Il Sung's Collected Works), vol. 35, 236–247. Pyongyang: Munye rodondang ch'ulp'ansa, 1987.

———. "The Duty of Mothers in the Education of Children." Speech delivered to the National Meeting of Mothers, November 16, 1961. In *On the Work of the Women's Union,* 1–33. Pyongyang: Foreign Languages Publishing House, 1971.

———. "Hyŏndaemunhak'ui sidaejŏksamyŏng" (The Mission in the Era of Modern Literature). Speech delivered on September 29, 1986. *Chosŏn munhak* 1986, no. 12: 3–6.

———. "On Some Questions of Our Literature and Arts." Speech delivered on June 30, 1951. In *On Revolutionary Literature and Arts,* 19–26. Holland: Africa Ltd-London, 1972.

———. "Samdae hyŏngmyŏng-ŭl himitge pŏlyŏ sahoechu-ui kŏnsŏlŭl tŏ-uk tagŏch'ija" (Let Us Put More Effort into the Construction of Socialism by Supporting the Three Revolutions). Speech delivered on March 3, 1975. In *Kim Il Sung chŏjakjip* (Kim Il Sung's Collected Works), vol. 30, 96–122. Pyongyang: Chosŏn rodongdan ch'ulp'ansa, 1985.

———. "To Let Us Create Literature and Arts Worthy of the Chollima Age." Speech delivered on November 27, 1960. In *On Revolutionary Literature and Arts,* 33–48. Holland: Africa Ltd-London, 1972.

———. "Yesulyŏnghwa *Uri Ryŏlch'a p'anmaewŏn'ŭl* pogo tangchungangwihoe, chŏngmuwŏn ch'aekim ilkundŭlkwa han tamhwa" (A Talk with Government

Officials at the Party Central Meeting after Watching *Our Train Vendor*). Speech delivered on January 11, 1973. In *Kim Il Sung chŏjakjip* (Kim Il Sung's Collected Works), vol. 50, 346–351. Pyongyang: Chosŏn Workers Publishers, 2003.

Kimilsung chu'ui kibon (Basic Principles of Kimilsungism). Pyongyang: Kim Il Sung University Press, 2004.

Kim Jong Il. *Chuch'e munhakron* (Theory on Juche Literature). Pyongyang: Chosŏn rodongdan ch'ulp'ansa, 1992.

———. "Creating Realistic Typification of Human Character and Life Thoroughly." Speech given on February 10, 1967. In *Kim Jong Il Selected Works,* vol. 1, 179–186. Pyongyang: Foreign Languages Publishing House, 1992.

———. "Developing a New Type of Revolutionary Literature." Speech given on February 7, 1966. In *Kim Jong Il Selected Works,* vol. 1, 107–116. Pyongyang: Foreign Languages Publishing House, 1992.

———. "Giving Wide Publicity to the Leader's Greatness among the South Korean People." Speech given on April 27, 1965. In *Kim Jong Il Selected Works,* vol. 1, 77–85. Pyongyang: Foreign Languages Publishing House, 1992.

———. "Let Us Create More Revolutionary Films Based on Socialist Life." Speech given on June 18, 1970. In *Kim Jong Il Selected Works,* vol. 2, 69–99. Pyongyang: Foreign Languages Publishing House, 1995.

———. "On Establishing the April 15 Literary Production Unit." Speech given on June 20, 1967. In *Kim Jong Il Selected Works,* vol. 1, 232–242. Pyongyang: Foreign Languages Publishing House, 1992.

———. "Ŏnŏwa minjok munje" (Problems with Language and Ethnicity). Speech given to the students at Kim Il Sung University on February 20, 1964. In *Kim Jong Il sŏnjip* (Kim Jong Il Selected Works), vol. 2, 1–7. Pyongyang: Chosŏn rodongdang ch'ulp'ansa, 1999.

———. "On Stamping Out the Ideologically Evil Consequences of the Anti-Party, Counter-Revolutionary Elements and Establishing the Party's Monolithic Ideological System." Speech given on June 15, 1967. In *Kim Jong Il Selected Works,* vol. 1, 220–231. Pyongyang: Foreign Languages Publishing House, 1992.

———. *On the Art of the Cinema.* Pyongyang: Foreign Languages Publishing House, 1989.

———. *Sahoejuŭinŭn kwahakida* (Socialism Is Science). Pyongyang: Chosŏn rodongdang ch'ulp'ansa, 1994.

———. "To, si, kun tangwiwŏnhoedŭl ape nasŏnŭn kwaŏp" (The Task of Party Committees in Provinces, Cities, and Districts). Speech delivered on April 3, 1981. In *Kim Jong Il sŏnjip* (Kim Jong Il Selected Works), vol. 7, 55–71. Pyongyang: Chosŏn rodongdang ch'ulp'ansa, 1996.

———. "Urinara sahoejuinŭn chuch'esasang'ŭl kuhyŏnhan uri sik sahoejui'ida" (Socialism of Our Style Is the Materialization of Juche Ideology). Speech given to the officials at the Workers' Party Central Meeting on December 27, 1990. In *Kim Jong Il sŏnjip* (Kim Jong Il Selected Works), vol. 14, 1–53. Pyongyang: Chosŏn rodongdang ch'ulp'ansa, 1998.

Kim Kyo-sŏp. *Saenghwalui ŏndŏk* (Heights of Life). Pyongyang: Munye ch'ulp'ansa, 1984.

Kim Mun-ch'ang. *T'anbu* (Miners). Pyongyang: Munye ch'ulp'ansa, 1986.

Kim Sam-bok. *Sedae* (Generations). Pyongyang: Munye ch'ulp'ansa, 1985.

Kim, Suki. *Without You, There Is No Us: Undercover among the Sons of North Korea's Elite.* New York: Broadway Books, 2014.

Kim, Suk-Young. *Illusive Utopia: Theater, Film, and Everyday Performance in North Korea.* Ann Arbor: University of Michigan Press, 2010.

Kim, Suzy. *Everyday Life in the North Korean Revolution, 1945–1950.* Ithaca: Cornell University Press, 2013.

———. "Revolutionary Mothers: Women in the North Korean Revolution, 1945–1950." *Comparative Studies in Society and History* 52, no. 4 (2010): 742–767.

Kim Tong-uk. *Pyŏngsa'ui kohyang* (A Soldier's Hometown). Pyongyang: Munye ch'ulp'ansa: 1982.

Kim Yong-jik. *Pukhan munhaksa* (History of North Korean Literature). Seoul: Ilchisa, 2008.

Kim Yun-sik. *Pukhan munhaksaron* (Theory of the History of North Korean Literature). Seoul: Saemi, 1995.

Kim, Yung-Hee. "Creating New Paradigms of Womanhood in Modern Korean Literature: Na Nye-sŏk's 'Kyŏnhŭi.'" *Korean Studies* 26, no. 1 (2002): 1–60.

Ko In-hwan. "Juche-ui kyunyŏlgwa yongmang: *60 nyŏn-hu* wa *Pŏt*" (Fissures and Desires in Juche: *After Sixty Years* and *Friend*). In *Pukhan munhak-ui chihyŏngdo* (The Future of North Korean Literature), edited by O Ch'ang-ŭn, 301–321. Seoul: Ehwa yŏjadaehakkyo ch'ulp'anbu, 2008.

Kristeva, Julia. *About Chinese Women.* Translated by Anita Barrows. London: Marion Boyars Publishing, 1977.

Kwak Yŏng-ch'an. *Ch'amdwen samgwa ch'ŏngch'un* (True Life and Youth). Pyongyang: Kŭmsŏngch'ŏngnyŏn ch'ulp'ansa, 1986.

Kwon Chŏng-ung. "Ch'ongsŏ Pulmyŏlui Ryŏksa chung changp'yŏnsosŏl *1932*-i naogikkaji" (Publishing the Immortal History Series, Particularly *The Year 1932*). *Chosŏn munhak* 2007, no. 6: 26–29.

Kwon, Heonik, and Byung-Ho Chung. *North Korea: Beyond Charismatic Politics.* Lanham: Rowman and Littlefield, 2012.

Kwon Young-min. *Han'guk hyŏndae munhaksa* (History of Modern Korean Literature), vol. 2. Seoul: Min'ŭmsa, 2010.

Lachmann, Renate. *Memory and Literature: Intertextuality in Russian Modernism.* Translated by Roy Sellars and Anthony Wall. Minneapolis: University of Minnesota Press, 1997.

Lankov, Andrei N. "Continuity within Change: Soviet Influence on the North Korean Education System." *Acta Koreana* 3 (July 2000): 57–75.

———. "Kim Takes Control: The 'Great Purge' in North Korea, 1956–1960." *Korean Studies* 26, no. 1 (2002): 87–119.

———. "The Organizational Life: Daily Surveillance and Daily Resistance in North Korea." *Journal of East Asian Studies* 12 (2012): 193–214.

Laursen, Eric. "A New Enigmatic Language: The Spontaneity-Consciousness Paradigm and the Case of Galdkov's *Cement.*" *Slavic Review* 65 (Spring 2006): 66–89.

Lee, Haiyan. *Revolution of the Heart: A Genealogy of Love in China, 1900–1950*. Stanford: Stanford University Press, 2007.

Lee, Hy-Sang, "North Korea's Closed Economy: The Hidden Opening." *Asian Survey* 28 (1988): 1264–1279.

Lee, Namhee. *The Making of Minjung: Democracy and the Politics of Representation in South Korea*. Ithaca: Cornell University Press, 2007.

Lim, Jae-cheon. *Kim Jong Il's Leadership of North Korea*. London: Routledge, 2009.

Literature from the "Axis of Evil": Writing from Iran, Iraq, North Korea, and Other Enemy Nations. A Words Without Borders Anthology. New York: The New Press, 2006.

Lyotard, Jean-François. *The Differend: Phrases in Dispute*. Translated by Georges Van Den Abbeele. Minneapolis: University of Minnesota Press, 1988.

Macintyre, Donald, and Kim Yooseung. "A Literary Thaw in Korea." *Time*, June 21, 2004. http://www.time.com/time/magazine/article/0,9171,655483,00.html#ixzz1crBDcg1P, accessed June 27, 2009.

Mrs. Kang Ban Sok: Mother of the Great Leader of Korea. Pyongyang: The Central Committee of the Korean Democratic Women's Union, 1968.

Myers, Brian C. *The Cleanest Race*. Brooklyn: Melville House, 2010.

———. *Han Sorya and North Korean Literature: The Failure of Socialist Realism in the DPRK*. Ithaca: Cornell East Asian Series, 1994.

No Kwi-nam. "Kajŏng saenghwal: sosŏl sok'ŭi mosŭp chungsimuro" (Family Life: Focusing on Literature). In *Pukhanŭi sahoe munhwa* (Social Culture of North Korea), edited by Kim Tong-han, 377–436. Seoul: Sejong yŏn'gusŏ pukhan yŏn'gusentŏ, 2006.

———. "Pukhanmunhak'ui hyŏngmyŏng chŏnt'ong-kwa chŏnhyŏng'ui pyŏnhwa" (Changes in the North Korean Revolutionary Tradition and Model). In *Pukhanmunhak'ui ihae* (Understanding North Korean Literature), vol. 1, edited by Kim Chong-hoe, 177–209. Seoul: Ch'ŏndtongkŏ'ul, 1999.

O Ch'ang-un. "Pukhan munhak'i pyŏnhago itda" (North Korean Literature Is Changing). In *Pukhan munhak-ui chihyŏngdo* (The Future of North Korean Literature), edited by O Ch'ang-ŭn, 13–18. Seoul: Ehwa yŏjadaehakkyo ch'ulp'anbu, 2008.

O T'ae-ho. "Choe Hak-su'ui changpyŏn sosŏl'e nat'anan suryŏng hyŏngsang'ui uimi koch'al" (Contemplation on the Meaning of the Great Leader's Personality Cult That Appears in Choe Hak-su's Novels) In *Pukhanui munhwachŏngchŏn ch'ongsŏ Pulmyŏlui Ryŏksarul iknŭnda* (On Reading the North Korea Canon's Immortal History Series), edited by Kang Chin-ho, 258–279. Seoul: Somyŏng ch'ulp'ansa, 2009.

Paek Nam-nyong. *Pŏt* (Friend). Pyongyang: Munye ch'ulp'ansa, 1988.

———. *60 Nyŏn hu* (After Sixty Years). Seoul: Han-ung ch'ulp'ansa, 1992.

Pak Sang-ch'ŏl and Kim Ch'ang-gyu. *Pukhan'ui hŏnpŏp kaejŏngkwa ip'pŏptonghyang* (North Korean Constitutional Revision and Legislative Trends). Seoul: Han'guk pŏpjaeyŏn'guwon, 1994.

Pak Sang-ik. *Pukhan'ui kwallyomunhwa* (North Korea's Bureaucratic Culture). Seoul: Hanguk haksuljŏngboju), 2008.

Pak Se-gil. *Tasi ssŭnŭn hangukhyŏndae'sa* (Rewriting Modern Korean History). Seoul: Tol Pegae, 1997.

Pak Yŏng-t'ae. "Pan-mi, Pan-kwere t'ujaeng'ŭl chujero han sosŏl chakpumdŭlŭl dŏ mani ch'angjakhaja" (Let us Create More Novels on the Theme of Anti-Americanism and Anti-Puppet Government). *Chosŏn munhak* 1986, no. 3: 75–76.

Park, Sunyoung. *The Proletarian Wave: Literature and Leftist Culture in Colonial Korea, 1910–1945.* Cambridge: Harvard East Asian Monographs, 2015.

Park, Yong-Soo. "The Political Economy of Economic Reform in North Korea." *Australian Journal of International Affairs* 63, no. 4 (2009): 529–549.

Pettid, Michael. *Unyŏng-jŏn: A Love Affair at the Royal Palace of Chosŏn Korea.* Berkeley: University of California Press, 2009.

Pihl, Marshall R. "Engineers of the Human Soul: North Korean Literature Today." *Korean Studies* 1 (1977): 63–92.

Popkin, Cathy. "Kiss and Tell: Narrative Desire and Discretion." In *Sexuality and the Body in Russian Culture,* edited by Jane T. Costlow, Stephanie Sandler, and Judith Vowles, 139–155. Stanford: Stanford University Press, 1993.

Radway, Janice A. *Reading the Romance: Women, Patriarchy, and Popular Literature.* Chapel Hill: University of North Carolina Press, 1984.

Ri Chŏng-suk. "Hyŏngmyŏngjŏk chu'ingonggwa kajŏng hyŏngmyŏnghwa'ui myosa" (The Revolutionary Protagonist and the Portrayal of the Family Revolution). *Chosŏn munhak* 1967, no. 9: 80.

———. "Tanp'yŏn sosŏl'e taehan saenggak" (Thoughts on Short Stories). In "Chakkadŭl'ui mal" (Writers Speak). *Chosŏn munhak* 1966, no. 10: 95–97.

Ri Hŭi-nam. *Yŏdŏl sigan* (Eight Hours). Pyongyang: Munye ch'ulp'ansa, 1986.

Ri Hwa. *Sogŭm kkot* (Salt Deposits). Pyongyang: Munye ch'ulpansa, 1984.

Ri In-ch'ŏl. "Mangne ttal" (My Youngest Daughter). *Chosŏn munhak* 1980, no. 11: 57–65.

Ri Ki-ch'ang. "Pitna'nŭn sedae" (Radiant Generation). *Chosŏn munhak* 1974, no. 8: 62–67.

Ri Kyŏng-hye. *Nyŏsŏng munje haegyŏl kyŏnghŏm* (Resolving the Woman Question). Pyongyang: Sahoe kwahak ch'ulp'ansa, 1990.

Ri Tong-gu. "Pyŏngsa'ui kajŏng" (A Soldier's Family). *Chosŏn munhak* 1980, no. 7: 63–70.

Ri Tong-wŏn. *Chakp'umui chu'inkong* (Protagonists in Literary Works). Pyongyang: Munye ch'ulp'ansa, 1990.

Ryang, Sonia. "Gender in Oblivion: Women in the Democratic People's Republic of Korea (North Korea)." *Journal of Asian and African Studies* 35 (July 2000): 323–349.

———. *Reading North Korea: An Enthological Inquiry.* Cambridge: Harvard University Asia Center, 2012.

———. "Technologies of the Self: Reading from North Korean Novels in the 1980s." *Acta Koreana* 5, no. 1 (2002): 21–32.

Scalapino, Robert A., and Chong-Sik Lee. *Communism in Korea: The Society.* Berkeley: University of California Press, 1973.

Sea of Blood. Pyongyang: Foreign Languages Publishing House, 1982.

Sin Hyŏng-gi and O Sŏng-ho. *Pukhan munhaksa: hangilhyŏngmyŏng munhak'e-sŏ chuch'e munhakkaji* (History of North Korean Literature: From Anti-Japanese Literature to Juche Literature). Seoul: P'yŏngminsa, 2000.

Smith, Hazel. *North Korea: Markets and Military Rule.* Cambridge: Cambridge University Press, 2015.

Sŏ Chŏng-ho. "Padagach'ŏnyŏdŭl" (Young Women of the Sea). *Chosŏn munhak* 1974, no. 3: 48–58.

Sŏ Tong-ik. *Inmini sa'nŭn mosŭp* (The Life of the People), vol. 1. Seoul: Charyowŏn, 1995.

———. *Inmini sa'nŭn mosŭp* (The Life of the People), vol. 2. Seoul: Charyowŏn, 1995.

Sŏk Yun-gi. *Pom'uroe* (Spring Thunder). Pyongyang: Munye ch'ulp'ansa, 1985.

Sŏng Hye-rang. *Tŭngnamujip* (House of Wisteria). Seoul: Chisik nara, 2000.

Sŏnu Sang-yŏl. *Kwangbok hu pukhanhyŏndae munhak yŏn'gu* (Study of Modern North Korean Literature after Liberation). Seoul: Tosŏ ch'ulp'ansa, 2002.

Suh, Jae Jean. *The Impact of Personality Cult in North Korea.* Seoul: Korea Institute for National Unification, 2004.

Stern, Mikhail, and August Stern. *Sex in the USSR.* New York: Times Books, 1980.

Ueno, Chizuko. *Nationalism and Gender.* Translated by Beverley Yamamoto. Melbourne: Trans Pacific Press, 2004.

Uri ryŏlch'a p'anmaewŏn (Our Train Vendor). Sin Chŏng-pŏm, 1972. DVD.

Uri sidae'ui yŏng'ungdŭl (Heroes of our Age), vol. 1. Pyongyang: Kŭllo tanche ch'ulp'ansa, 1988.

Uri sidae'ui yŏng'ungdŭl (Heroes of our Age), vol. 2. Pyongyang: Kŭllo tanche ch'ulp'ansa, 1989.

Uri sidae'ui yŏng'ungdŭl (Heroes of our Age), vol. 3. Pyongyang: Kŭllo tanche ch'ulp'ansa, 1990.

Voronina, Olga. "Soviet Patriarchy: Past and Present." *Hypatia* 8, no. 4 (1993): 97–112.

Wada Haruki. *Kimuiruson to Manshū kōnichi sensō* (Kim Il Sung and the Anti-Japanese War in Manchuria). Tokyo: Heibonsha, 1992.

Wang, Ban. *Illuminations from the Past: Trauma, Memory, and History in Modern China.* Stanford: Stanford University Press, 2004.

Workman, Travis. "The Partisan, the Worker, and the Hidden Hero: Popular Icons in North Korean Film." In *The Korean Popular Culture Reader,* edited by Kyung Hyun Kim and Youngmin Choe, 145–167. Durham: Duke University Press, 2014.

Yang, Moon-soo. "North Korea's External Debts: Trends and Characteristics." *Korea Focus.* http://www.koreafocus.or.kr/design2/layout/content_print.asp?group_id=104047, accessed August 17, 2014.

Yi On-juk. *Pukhan sahoe yŏngu: sahoehakjŏk chŏpgŭn* (Research on North Korean Society: An Approach to Social Factors). Seoul: Seoul National University Press, 1989.

Yi Sang-suk. "Hong Sŏk-jung'ui yŏksa sosŏlkwa nampuk kyoryu'ui uimi" (The Significance of Hong Sŏk-jung's Historical Novel and Exchange between North and South Korea). In *Pukhan munhak-ui chihyŏngdo,* edited by Ehwayŏjadaehakkyo t'ongilhakyŏn'guwŏn, 168–187. Seoul: Ehwa yŏjadaehakkyo ch'ulp'anbu, 2008.

Yu Im-ha. "Ch'ongsŏ Pulmyŏlui Ryŏksa'ui kihoek uidowa tokpŏp" (The Planning and the Way of Reading the Immortal History Series). In *Pukhan munhwachŏngchŏn ch'ongsŏ Pulmyŏlui Ryŏksarul iknŭnda* (On Reading the North Korea Canon's Immortal History Series), edited by Kang Chin-ho, 99–118. Seoul: Somyŏng ch'ulp'an, 2009.

Yun Ki-dŏk. *Suryong hyŏngsang munhak* (Literature on the Depiction of the Great Leader). Pyongyang: Munye ch'ulp'ansa, 1991.

Index

About the Author

Immanuel Kim is assistant professor of Asian and Asian American Studies at Binghamton University of the State University of New York.